Renewal of Life

Renewal of Life

Healing from the Holocaust

Henri Parens

Schreiber Publishing
Baltimore - Washington

Renewal of Life
Henri Parens

Published by:
Schreiber Publishing
Post Office Box 858
Savage, MD 20763 U.S.A.
800-953-9929

Third printing, 2014

Library of Congress Cataloging-in-Publication Data

Parens, Henri, 1928-
Renewal of life : healing from the Holocaust / Henri Parens
p. cm.
ISBN 978-1-887563-89-5
1. Parens, Henri, 1928- 2. Holocaust survivors--Mental health.
3. Holocaust survivors—Biography. 4. Aggressiveness in children. I. Title.
RC451.4.H62P37 2004
155.4'1247--dc22

2004007085

Printed in the United States of America

With profound gratitude, for so many things,
to my mother, Rosa Pruszinowska,
to my wife, Rachel, and
to my sons, Erik, Karl, and Joshua,
and their young families.

Because of them,
By them,
I am who I am.

Contents

Part One

What Happened to My World?

You who live safe
In your warm houses,
You who find, returning in the evening,
Hot food and friendly faces:
    Consider if this is a man
    Who works in the mud
    Who does not know peace
    Who fights for a scrap of bread
    Who dies because of a yes or a no.
    Consider if this is a woman,
    Without hair and without name
    With no more strength to remember,
    Her eyes empty and her womb cold
    Like a frog in winter.
Meditate that this came about:
I commend these words to you.
Carve them in your hearts
At home, in the street,
Going to bed, rising;
Repeat them to your children,
    Or may your house fall apart,
    May illness impede you,
    May your children turn their faces from you.

Primo Levi

(From Se Questo e un Uomo [If this is a man]; Translated 1958)

Chapter 1

"*Incominciamo*"*

The Holocaust happened.

It has been said many times, "6 million Jews were murdered"—we have added up the numbers again and again. But records are missing. Many lost by the Germans' efforts as they retreated to wipe away the evidence of the horror they reaped. Primo Levi tells that Simon Wiesenthal recorded that incredulous bragging of an SS militiaman, that ". . . even if someone were to survive, the world will not believe him. . . . People will say that the events you describe are too monstrous to be believed."

The "final solution." It's stated purpose: to create a clean, purified, master race. All "undesirables" slated for extermination. Jews, political prisoners, criminals, mentally retarded, others, all pestilence, sickness-bearing cockroaches and rats.

The Third Reich's hierarchy of megalomanic paranoiacs—I am not being clinical—paranoiacs with a broad black sociopathic streak, whipped a nation of obedience-trained nationals into enthusiastic Nazi-dogma frothing followers.

"Give me some men . . .
who will fight for the [evil] they adore.
Start me with ten . . .
and I'll soon give you ten thousand more"
(with apologies to Victor Herbert).

Not all, by any means. Others, though only passively obedient, accepted the megalomanic dogma. Those the paranoiac fervor did not seduce, it whip-lashed into wretched compliance. Some, many of whom were swept up by the tidal wave of National Socialism denied, diminished and even dismissed the incredible dogma. It can't happen, not in civilized Germany. Historian Peter Gay, who lived it as a schoolboy, tells

---

* In tribute to Primo Levi, "Let us start."

how his family just did not believe it could happen—until November 9 1938, Kristallnacht. Many fled Germany to the Middle and Far East, to the Americas, and elsewhere. Many others who abhored and in their homes decried the dogma feared the widely exhibited consequences of protest. Some, morally more vigorous, did protest even in the face of widely demonstrated danger. In Germany, democracy was dead.

Six million is only our raging, mournful accounting. We forgot to add the gypsies, homosexuals, retarded, crippled, and other "contaminants of the race;" and the Communists. The Nazis of the 1933-1945 era slaughtered about 50 million people. Six million Jews out of 50 million human beings, is "just" 12 percent of those slaughtered. But it is well known that the Jews were the Reich's preferred contaminants, the most maligned and reviled. They even bested the anti-Semitism of Poles and Russians, the National Socialists' arch political enemies. It is especially in this regard that the crime the Nazis committed against humanity stands as unique in the history of mass slaughters. Wars bring slaughter. So do revolutions. But these slaughtered 6 million were non-combatant, non-revolutionary human beings, murdered by government sanction, by vile plan, by barbaric methods carried out by a civilized people debased by fear and megalomanic fanaticism—murdered just because they were Jews.

Hitler's Nazi regime, baptized "The Thousand-Year Reich"; lived intoxicated for 9 years, and in growing despair and agony for 3 more. It died in bombs, in near-destruction of its home, in cyanide and petrol-flames, and in judgment. But what is Nazi did not die with them; it goes on even today.

The Nazis. When I say "the Nazis," I don't mean "the Germans"; nor do I mean persons of the National Socialist political persuasion. By "Nazism" I mean a type of anti-Semitism, or it might be anti-Islamism, or racism, that compounds its malignant prejudice with crime, with murder. A "Nazi" is one whose malignant prejudice is consummated by lethal crime, whatever the motivating conditions. Here, I mean those Germans, Austrians, French, Poles, Russians, Belgians, Hollanders, Hungarians, and others of Europe who were overtly, outspoken Nazis and those who covertly were Nazis. My mother and I were among those directly victimized by the French Nazis and indirectly—protests to the contrary by the Vichy-French notwithstanding—by the German

Nazis. Once the work of the French Nazis was done, my mother was transported to join my brother and my father, along with many of my extended family who were, from what I know to this moment, exterminated by the German and other Nazis in Poland.

But the figure, 50 million human beings too is only a start. Many more Jews and others who were victims of the Holocaust survived the slaughter. For them, surviving the Holocaust was not the end of the Holocaust. They carried and will carry—we now know—for the rest of their lives the brutal reverberations of what happened to us. They brought these into their new worlds, to their new families, their wives, their children, their grandchildren, and beyond.

The Holocaust reached far. It even engulfed the perpetrators, their world, their families, their children. And to this day, reverberations of it continue, leaving a steady stream of pain, humiliation, shame, guilt, misery.

Survivors who were victims have told what happened, and their universe has learned about it, and continues to learn about it, to know history—and to perhaps not repeat it. Have we learned?

Now 60 years later, what have we learned? What have we done? Some have learned. Some have done good things. Some have not learned, or have learned a pathway for gratifying their social and emotional sickness, and they have done it again, not as doggedly as the Third Reich, but just as wretchedly. Some are looking to do it again.

From my Holocaust start, what have I learned? What have I done?

Looking back 60 years, I see that my Holocaust experience has determined and guided my life's work—to

Help children (and adults) tolerate and cope with the pains inflicted on them by neurosis and by all kinds of past and present traumas, and to develop constructive ways of coping;

To teach young clinicians to do just this, to help troubled children and adults; and,

To find ways to prevent man-made traumas—mostly produced by abuses, violence, and malignant prejudice—and to disseminate such prevention strategies, everywhere.

But first, what happened to my world?

Getting Into What Happened

I have long struggled with wanting to and avoiding publicly bearing witness that the Holocaust happened, that it happened to me, to my family. Since it happened, for me it has lasted a lifetime; for my wife, it has since we met; for my sons, since their birth; and from some early evidence, it may for my grandchildren. What happened to me happened in one form or another to more than 6 million of us. It is so much a part of what made me be who I became, who I am. I have for years heard that "we must bear witness," and yet, I have not been able to get to this until now. At the start of this writing I am 73. What happened, started when I was 11.

The Nazis robbed me of "my life that would have been." Mournfully, I do not mean that I wish I had lived it out. The life I do have, the life I have lived is and has been rewarding and gratifying beyond expectation, beyond measure. "My life that would have been" is the life of which the Nazis robbed me, the one I started to live, as my memory permits, in Bruxelles, Belgium, the life I lived until I was 11 years old. Resulting from the atrocities perpetrated by Nazis, of those I loved as a child, I lost all but three cousins. I lost my mother, my father and my brother; I lost innumerable family members. My mother was murdered in Auschwitz. So was my Aunt Esther; her son, my "little" cousin Joseph (I had an older cousin Joseph who fought among the British and survived) survived Auschwitz but died in Buchenwald. So far I have not found out the exact fate of the others, except for those who I do know did survive, my three Bruxelles cousins. I lost grandparents, aunts, uncles and cousins, a number of whom I knew and loved, whose faces I see (remembered by photos) but whose names I can't remember now. I lost living in the city that I love to this day, Bruxelles. I lost speaking Yiddish and French daily, both of which I love. I also lost what I might have become. I doubt that it would have been better than who I am. But I have thought: "What might I have done in that first life?"

I think at least one of the problems is that even though I don't need to have lived that first life—I doubt I would have been any more gratified and grateful than I am today—there is still somewhere in me, this experience of feeling violated, injured, robbed, and insulted to extreme. Maybe it's that I did not decide which life I would live; that I had to live the one I have lived, I could not live the one given me at birth. There is more to this feeling violated, injured, robbed, insulted to extreme than I have said. Maybe it will get clearer as I go on in this search, in this effort to further understand and record the impact of the Holocaust on me, and on those dearest to me, my wife and my sons. In a technical document I reported on some ways in which the Holocaust impacted on my psychic development (1999). This telling, now, is not technical, it's personal.

For a psychiatrist who can express feelings with much facility, feelings of love and feelings of anger and of quiet rage, with ease, I am troubled by how inarticulate I am about all this. I can only half-competently explain what made it all so bad. Maybe, as I go along, feelings and thoughts may leak out that will make clearer what, for one human being, perhaps for so many of us, made what happened so hurtful. It is not enough to say it was the insults, the losses of so much, the incarcerations, the slave labor, the murder. There is not just a word, or a phrase or a chapter that will say it. Searching here for the answer may well help me even more than I feel helped already from years of working it all through in personal psychoanalysis and in on-going self-analysis.

I started to write my witness report on August 14, 2002. The date stands out.

Nous sommes à Wellfleet, MA. Rachel, Erik, Karl, Joshua, leurs femmes et leurs enfants sont allés dans les environs, pour les explorer et jouer au bord d'un lac. Ils me laissent ici pour reflechir, pour contempler. C'est le plus pénible de tout les événements de ce passé torturé et torturant, insouvenable et inoubliable. C'est, aujourd'hui le 14 du Mois d'Aôut.

C'est aujourd'hui, il y a exactement soixante ans, que ma mère a étée convoyée à Auschwitz du camp de Drancy, camp de déportation, situé à moins de dix kilomètres nord de Paris. Le convoi numero 19 a emporte neuf cent nonante et un Juifs choisis et enlevés de Rivesaltes, par ordre et la bonne volonté du gouvernement de Vichy-France. D'après Serge Klarsfeld, les convois avais commencés a rouler en Mars ou Avril 1942.

(August 14, 2002. We are in Wellfleet, MA. Rachel, Erik, Karl, Joshua, their wives and children have gone out, to explore the environs and play at a nearby a lake. They have left me here to think, to contemplate. This is the most painful of the events of this tortured and torturing past, unrememberable and unforgettable.

Today is the 14th of August. It is today, exactly 60 years ago, that my mother was sent to Auschwitz from Drancy, a deportation camp situated about 10 kilometers north of Paris. Convoy number 19 transported nine hundred and ninety one Jews selected and plucked from

Rivesaltes, by order and the good will of the government of Vichy-France. According to Serge Klarsfeld, the convoys started to roll in March or April 1942.)

At about that time, March 1942, I was being prepared to leave OSE's life-saving Home in St.Raphael, in Southern France, to be sent to America with 49 other refugee children. My own resistance to knowing just exactly what happened, has prevented me from remembering this exact date of August 14, 1942, even though I had learned of it many years earlier, had more than once recorded it in a special place but have not been able to remember where I did so, and was therefore unable to hold on to this terrible date until this past July when the letter from Serge Klarsfeld's group informed me of the exact details here recorded.

Now I have it inscribed in several obvious rather than special places that my mother was sent to Auschwitz in Convoy No. 19, August 14, 1942. But I have painfully realized that it does not tell me the exact day or even if she was sent to the gas-chamber. She might have even been sent to a labor camp; she was in good health though starving, as we all were. I still have to further pull myself together and find out the absolute day. No doubt it is recorded somewhere; both the Germans and the Poles seem to have kept records. Though I would have guessed it was August 16; those who were there, Primo Levi, Elie Wiesel, Abraham Biderman, tell us that those not selected for labor then and there were sent to the gas chambers upon arrival. More about this later. I learned only many years later that when my mother was sent to Auschwitz, on August 14, 1942, I had been in America for about 4 months.

Ten days before this writing, outside of Paris, at the *Camp de Drancy, Les Fils et Filles des Déportés Juifs de France* (the organization, The Sons and Daughters of Jews Deported from France) commemorated on its 60th anniversary the departure from Drancy of convoy No. 19 for Auschwitz. At noontime, the names of the deportees were read by those attending the commemoration who survived or by their children. I wanted to be there; I wanted to read my mother's name aloud. I learned about this commemoration in June! We were informed so late that to plan such a trip at this time, Rachel and I would have had to turn our established summer plans upside down. These plans require much collaboration among our 4 families due to variable constraints imposed by schedules of very busy people, in order to make possible our highly prized ritual week in Cape Cod vacationing all together, Rachel and I with our 3 sons and their young families. Rachel and I agreed we would go to participate in a commemoration next year. That requires planning and inquiry. I have not kept up with my French sufficiently to understand with certainty Klarsfeld's rather formal language. Regrettable that the document was written for the well-spoken, elegant French. Don't they realize over there that those of us who left France many years ago may have difficulty reading formal letter-writing French!

Is that what is really troubling me? Klarsfeld clearly writes that the commemorations will continue for the next two years. There will be commemorations until July 31, 2004, the date when the last convoy, No. 77, 60 years ago took 300 children to Auschwitz, a convoy referred to by Klarsfeld and others on many occasions.

I feel my lack of involvement in the group processes that abound, in Philadelphia, in New York, Washington, in the U. S., and in France. In part I have not wanted to burden my family with such involvement. But I have not been very pressed to do so myself. Now and then, I feel that I would like to be involved in some ongoing proceedings, reunions, professional symposia, symposia at the Holocaust Memorial Museum in Washington or at Yad Vashem. But I don't act on that wish. I turn instead to my prevention work, to that part of my work committed to push for the prevention of other holocausts, to what mental health professionals think is pertinent to it and especially to what individual psychological traumas and stresses come before it, that set the stage for it and motivate humans toward it. So, even as I write this, again, I will turn to my prevention work, and will later talk with Rachel about going to France in 2003 to participate in such a commemoration, perhaps in May when I had agreed to present a lecture at the University of Padova in Italy.

Je suis Henri Parens, à présent j'ai l'âge de 73 ans. Mon nom de famille avant l'âge de 25 ans était Henri Pruszinowski. Voici, brèvement mon histoire concèrnant la partie de ma vie que les Nazis mon volés. Mais, je vous prie de comprendre: la partie de ma vie qu'on m'as vole n'est pas seulement une question de temps, d'annees entre 1940 et 1942.

(I am Henri Parens, presently I am 73 years old. My name before I was 25 was Henri Pruszinowski. Here briefly, is my story pertaining to that part of my life the Nazis stole from me. But, please understand: the part of my life they stole is not simply a question of time, of the years between 1940 and 1942.)

Yes, those two years were robbed of what they would have been, in Bruxelles, my mother and I, my mother working 12 hours a day if not more, I, in school, committed to learning from way back. The part of my life of which they robbed me, has continued to this day, sixty years later. With the help of many good people I filled my life with very fortunate details, rich details, details that make life—my wife, my sons and all they bring with them now—my education, my work, and the lesser details that enrich the more vital details. But the continuation of my early life, of what would have followed the first 10 years of it has been cut off; a large part of my beginnings have not continued. My life with my mother, with my family, my life in Bruxelles has been cut off—except for what I have continued of it inside myself.

It is strange. What I have lived since 1942 has been rich, rewarding, I would not be without it. But there's a hole, an empty something. As I try to grasp that empty something, it is a confluence of all that I lost, all that was in that life the Nazis destroyed—it is my loved ones, foremost my mother, my father, and so sadly, my brother, Emanuel. Nothing can take their place, even with however incredibly I have filled my life with my beloved Rachel and our three sons. One cannot undo an empty something. One can only hold it inside, live with it, and live one's renewed life. These holes remain even when there is the renewal of life. And, every now and then, on anniversaries, on occasions, on receiving mailings, on seeing a film (old or new) or looking again at some television program that details that time or that situation, the pain of that empty something grabs me. I want to share it with Rachel and with my sons; but I don't want to burden them more with it. I feel that each of them has lived it enough already, carries it in mind too much of the time. Enough is enough.

For me, it's never enough. I need to continue to work it through, continue to try to metabolize what caused that emptiness, to heal that hole. What I know so far tells me I'll never get to the end of it; it's endless. I just continue to live with it, and heal as best I can. Self-analyzing helps, enjoying what I have helps—and that is enormous, enormously good—and so does doing my work in helping patients make better lives for themselves and in pushing for the prevention of traumatization of children, and of personal and social violence and malignant prejudice.

My mother's name is Rosa Pruszinowska. She was born in Lodz, Poland. She died when she was about 41 years of age. I was then 13, and very far away from her.

My father's name is Isaach Biederman. He was born in Lodz, Poland, and still lived there when the Germans invaded Poland in September 1939. My estimation is that he was then probably 40 or so years of age. I am now, belatedly searching for what happened to him. To date I do not know. But my presumption has been that he fell victim to the Nazis. My uncertainty comes from the fact, as Abraham Biderman (sadly, not a relative) has recorded in his The World of My Past, not all Jews in the Lodz Ghetto were exterminated. Some, like Abraham Biderman, survived the Lodz Ghetto, Auschwitz-Birkenau, Dora—the missile-developing cave—and Bergen-Belsen.

My only brother, Emanuel Biederman, probably 3 or 4 years older than I, lived with my father. His fate was probably, but again, not certainly, linked to that of my father.

Both my mother and father had a number of siblings; when I returned in Bruxelles in 1953, of a large family, three cousins were left. None of us has found, to date, anyone other than us, my three cousins and me. I recently learned that two more distant Bruxelles cousins did not perish in the Holocaust. The search goes on.

All I can say to explain the differences in my mother and my father's names is that my parents were divorced before my mother migrated to Bruxelles when I was very young. Why she resumed her maiden name, and why my family name was hers and not my father's, and why she did not also bring my brother Emanuel with us, to these questions I have no answer.

Here I am, a psychiatrist-psychoanalyst, age 73, still deeply pained by what happened to so many of us, so many years ago. I am not surprised; this is how it works; you get traumatized when you're young, it's for life, for some more, for some less. But, the Holocaust is ever-present, it is for life, however short or long life may be. So much so that I have not . . . done so many things I could have done, about what happened. Foremost, why did I not search for the whereabouts of my brother and my father until recent years? I search to know the answer. I do know that my answer has a bearing on why it took survivors so long to speak out about their Holocaust experience.

Here I am, committed to understand my patients, and always at hand is understanding myself, and I don't understand so much of my behavior in this regard. Well, maybe that's too strong. I understand a good deal of it. I will take that up later.

What happened to us is unimaginable—even though it has been shown in film, talked and written about many times. It was more horrible for many than for me. It makes one weep, ache, to think of the many people, who even

today, are subjected to the searing wounds left by persecution, family destruction, incarceration, violation—sexual and other—the list of psyche wounding injuries is long. Ethnic cleansing, death to Jews, Non-Arians, Niggers, Infidels, Communists, Nationalists, "Anythings" other than what we are! The curse of conflicts between ethnic neighbors, religious neighbors, land neighbors, commonly facilitated by sick or/and injury-driven group dynamics, is found in too many parts of the world. Miserable disease in so many neighboring species that passes for the survival of the fittest. Yet, the Holocaust stands out by the way it was not just governmentally sanctioned, but ordered, legalized, planned, carried out at the end of a rifle in the hands of the law, in a land long known to be a center of highest learning, academic, scientific, literary, artistic, a center of advancing civilization. The progressive advancing of laws stripping away rights to work, to walk in the streets, permitting harassment, beatings, burning of synagogues, destruction of property, one after another eventually leading to individual and group violations, incarceration in concentration camps, degradation, and for so many eventually programmed chemical death, then pits of dead bodies and ashes. From healthy thriving human beings, to dehumanization, robotization, giving up, as happened to so many among us. Too much to bear. The pain of abuse in extremis has its own nature. Though in many of us it did not destroy self-esteem, self-regard, self-value, the leaden pain it leaves stays for life. It aches, it saddens, it mourns, it quietly rages. It depresses. But it did not and does not obliterate "me," "us," nor those I love more than myself.

We lived through it, many of us. Too many did not. For those of us who did, life went on; strange, how in all that misery life went on.

Life went on, throughout

Why weep?
Because it hurts.
Why rage?
Because it hurts too much.

Why write?
In hope of being heard say

It still hurts too much.
And not weep all the time.
To bear witness.
"I swear to tell the truth . . ."

To not let it happen again. No.
To not make it happen again.

Chapter 2

The Germans attack Belgium . . . Our Exodus

10 May, 1940

It was a lovely bright morning when we were wakened. They probably used a mild-toned bell and of course added their voices to waken those who didn't waken as easily as some of us did. It must have been my turn to empty the night pot we used to avoid going the long distance to the toilet during the night. I really did not mind; we took turns at it. It was sunny. It was after all May and like here in the States, in Belgium May is bright and sunny.

After a few minutes of being awake I noted the sound of thuds, muffled, in clusters. Unusual sounds. Like some dead weights, big things, falling without subsequent resonance. "Thud!" The sound seemed to come from far away though I couldn't guess from how far nor just from where. Other than that, things seemed really quite usual. The morning waking routine was usual; some milling around like you can expect with some forty kids moving about in one large dorm as they get going. We were in summer camp already for a few days, though it was only the beginning of May, actually as I have learned from the history books, it was 10 May 1940. I had been at this camp before and had no objection to being there, though I would have preferred to stay in Bruxelles (Brussels). The city schools were already out for the summer vacation.

It's while we were eating our petit déjeuner (breakfast) that we were suddenly told to hurry up, finish our petit déjeuner, that we all had to quickly go back to Bruxelles. The rush set in, the tone urging us to hurry was unusual; I don't recall any protest by the kids. Back in the dormitory we each packed our things, the younger kids expectably being helped by the camp staff, milling around pulling things together, we were actually ready fairly quickly. Asking what was going on didn't get us much information, it's as though the staff were not to tell us, we'd find out when we got home. Nonetheless, the tone was urgent and our exodus from the "summer camp" went fairly expeditiously taking into consideration that we were a bunch of kids, some younger than I.

It was 10 May 1940. For me, a profoundly memorable day. It would be the first of this for-always unique series of memorable days in my life, days that for the most part coincided with the sequel of memorable days that trace the progress of World War II. I tag 10 May 1940 as the first of those memorable days that trace the trailing off of the life I had been born into. When we got back to Bruxelles, we were received by near-frenzy parents, people milling again, palpably more driven than usual. My mother seemed unusually stressed out. I was 11, I asked my mother, in Yiddish, our family way of talking to each other, "Ma, wus passiert?" ("Ma, what's going on?"). "Les Boches ont attaques la Belgique. Ar'n, mir mussen awek gein" ("The Germans have attacked Belgium. Aron—my Yiddish name—we have to leave").

The next few days were troubling. For me, the tenor of the time was disquieting, verging on bewildering. The grown-ups seemed bewildered, even alarmed. Without knowing what was going on; I felt it too; it was contagious. My mother and I went from one family cluster of our extended family in Bruxelles to another. The reason, my mother told me, was to find out what they were going to do, as if, what they were going to do would decide what we would do with any of them or by ourselves. Most troubling for me, and I guess for her, was that she seemed to walk away from each encounter increasingly downcast, disappointed and, though she did pretty well in trying to hide it from me, I knew she was frightened. My mother, I know now, was not one to get frenzied; she kept a leash on her fear. But we were all frightened; the grownups were frightened; I felt the fear but not as if it were mine, it surrounded us. I'm not sure that I was afraid, yet. I didn't know the consequences that lay ahead for us. I came to sort out that in addition to her deciding what she and I would do, she had also been trying to get anyone of them to lend her some money. My impression is that she did not succeed. But why did she do this now, try to borrow money? For what? I soon found out. To get out of Belgium.

I should say here, that I speak of "my mother and I" because by this time in our family history, my mother and father had for some years been divorced and lived in different lands. I was born in Lodz, Poland in

December 1928. When I was about 3 to 5 years of age, my mother and I came to Bruxelles. I cannot be certain when we came to Bruxelles. Not having adults who have lived the history, or learned what came before them from reliable sources, leaves one with no certainty of one's family history, or even one's earliest years—one of the sobering miseries of losing one's family. No choice but to resign oneself to not knowing.

My parents, as I said, were then already divorced. I can only speculate on why my mother left my older brother Emanuel with our family in Lodz and why she left Poland at all. It has long been painful for me that my childhood family of four split this way, and especially that my mother left my brother in Lodz. I can only assume that she believed it would be impossible for her to take care of two young children in a new country—she did not yet speak French—and that our large family in Lodz would most likely provide Emanuel with better care than she could while she was coping with migration. I don't know what factors entered into her making this decision. Perhaps it was a compromise made by people naïve in what affects children detrimentally. As a Child Psychiatrist-Psychoanalyst, I doubt that the decision was a good one.

Left: the author, age 4 or 5, with his mother Rosa ("Look how my mother dents my thigh," the author notes. "She held me well) *Above*: the author's father, Isaac, with brother Emanuel, age 8 or 9; *Below*: Emanuel, age 12 or 13.

This was around 1932. A number of members of our Polish family, from both my mother's and my father's side, had already migrated to Bruxelles during the early 1900s, for the usual reasons that Jews left Russia and Poland then—the harsher maltreatment of Jews in Eastern Europe with their reputed pogroms, as compared to pre-1933 Western Europe. Antisemitism, quite more malignant in Europe that in America, was harsher in Eastern than in Western Europe. In Bruxelles, I lived through no pogrom. I was well acquainted though with that common phrase, "Sales Juifs," Dirty Jews, that besmirched an occasional wall. Still fortunately, Belgian antisemitism was no match for the Polish-Russian brand. In addition, there were better life opportunities and living circumstances in Western Europe. One of the problems I have resulting form what followed from 10 May 1940 is, as I said, that I have no one left to fill in some of the details of my family history; I am obliged to speculate. I just don't know why my parents divorced—one complaint I overheard from my mother was that my father had become a compulsive gambler, card-player, a Jewish plague among some then. Nor do I really know why my mother decided to migrate to Bruxelles when I was probably closer to 3 than 5. I do know, because my memory does go back to that time: that my mother was a seamstress who worked with Aunt Esther in a joint business they had of mass-producing, that is of making boys' clothing out of rolls of cloth—I can see them cutting cloth stretched out on a table and ingeniously sewing pieces of cloth into clothing. I gather from their productions that these were sold to a merchant who then distributed them to stores. My mother did so to near the time when the Germans invaded Belgium. Anyway, this is why I speak of "My mother and I" and not, sadly, "My parents, my brother Emanuel and I."

In Chaos We Leave Bruxelles for France

Within two weeks, my mother had decided; we packed what we could carry. We were leaving Bruxelles; we left much behind. We walked to La Gare du Midi (South Station) to get away. That train station was just about eight blocks from where we lived. Over the years I have wondered if we simply did not have the financial means to get to England, or that it was just easier to go to France since they speak French as we did in Bruxelles, or for whatever reason. I also learned later that the Belgians, the French and who knows who else, believed that France had an army that could withstand the advancing Germans. So it made sense to go to France. I never got a chance to ask my mother why we did some of the things we did. I am not sure whether I didn't know enough to ask then, or that I knew when to not ask questions; not that my mother was one to reject or be disinterested in my asking. It's that I trusted my mother to know what we should do and she knew that she could trust me to behave like a responsible, responsive kid.

La Gare due Midi was bewildering. I had seen the station before; but never like this. People were pouring in; there was a steady flow of them, some child-carrying or dragging, most baggage-harrassed, all rushing into the station. Nothing stood still. Even the steaming locomotives seemed to mark time to get going. The milling that I had been seeing of late now was frenzied. Unheard of, no tickets were needed to board the train; no destinations were indicated; by word of mouth, this train was going to France. The station's activity, trains' steaming, conductors' gesticulating and barking, the flow of people, all urged getting into wagons. People were squeezing in, grabbing seats. My mother and I settled in two, our meager baggage somewhere. The seat-searchers looked about, frightened, bags, suitcases in tow, children latched onto or carried. I watched them; I watched, observed even when I was a child. I was troubled by the distress all around. Once inside the train, things calmed some, the milling people slowed. Soon we all seemed to settle in; I don't recall anyone standing in our wagon. It was not long before the train left. I was riveted to the window. Just like that, we left my family, my home, my school, my hometown. I had no thought of goodbye or of not seeing them soon again; we just left.

We were running. Why? I had never been called "Sale Juif," Dirty Jew. But graffiti, especially malignant graffiti, was not invented in America. A wall near the house in which we lived had added to my education about antisemitism. Even in Bruxelles, my hometown, one of the commonly seen graffiti themes was "Sales Juifs" with a few additional nasty words. But I didn't know then, in early May 1940 that this really was the reason my mother decided that we had to leave immediately. I can only guess that while I had not seen a pogrom in Bruxelles, my mother probably had in Poland. She never talked to me about that. I had no idea then whether my aunts and uncles and cousins left Bruxelles or stayed. Something made us run from Bruxelles. I now have no doubt that my mother had heard, as all Jews had—except us kids—of Kristallnacht, of Hitler's ravings and threats to European Jewry.

The train stopped at Tournai—it may have been Courtray—in either case, just a step from the Belgian-French border, for longer than one would have thought given that we were in such a hurry to get out of Belgium. To check passports? No passports we needed. Tickets were not needed. This was war. It seemed more as if those in charge of the train had to orient and determine which avenue we should take into France. Once across the border into France we turned east toward Lille; further on was Dunkerque. Somewhere near Lille or Dunkerque we began to hear those "thud-clusters" again but they were much closer this time than the first time I had heard them. Sensing danger this time, I asked my mother what that sound was. Protectively, over-protectively—I was 11!—she told me not to worry, that it was only thunder. "Drôle de tonnerre" (funny thunder), I thought. I sensed that she was trying to protect me from fear. Soon though we heard the loud air-splitting humming-roar of airplanes, sounding threateningly near. The train screeching, slowed with urgency. We were told to immediately get off the train. The train stopped in the middle of nowhere; we hurriedly got off, and following instructions, we took cover—uncertain cover—some hundred yards from the train. As we crouched behind a mound of ground I did not again ask my mother what the "thuds" were; I accepted her earlier prevarication sensing she was doing so hoping I would not realize our hazardous predicament; of course she would have been troubled by my talking about it now. Sure she looked out for me; but I also looked out for her. I knew they were bombs. None came anywhere near where we were. As the sound of the planes passed beyond us, we were urged to re-embark and hurried to do so.

In minutes we were again on the way. I had no idea where we were going; but so long as I was with my mother and we were not alone, that was OK with me; not that I had any choice. I too was of the mind, "Allons, foutons l'camp!" (Let's get out of here), fast! We traveled south. By late afternoon we seemed to be moving increasingly more slowly, with a number of in the middle of nowhere stops. We seemed to just be going through countryside, no large cities. It was May. It was beautiful here too, the French campagne, fields and villages. At times we were crawling. As I think of it now, I would assume that those driving the train were in communication with their headquarters deciding what to do with this trainload of refugees from Bruxelles who were seeking asylum, just about anywhere in France, anywhere away from the advancing Germans. From the train crawlings and stops I can imagine now that they just did not expect us and did not altogether know where to send us, where to put us up. I can see, and have many times before realized that the French were not prepared—why should they have been—for this sudden in-pouring of its northern neighbors. No one expected the German invasion to proceed with such rapidity. Blitzkrieg, all right; or as William Shirer noted Sitzkrieg—sitting war—on the part of the French and their European allies. By the time our elders had come to see the lightning-speed with which the Germans disposed of Poland, I assume that it was too late to get ready for handling massive combined Luftwaffe and Panzer lightning-speed attacks. It is amply clear to me that not only were we a burdensome challenge for the French, but that we gave them quite a headache. What to do with all these foreigners at a time when France now was under threat of siege by the blitzing Germans. No one had anticipated our arrival. The Maginot Line, the French wall of invincibility was easily over-run and rendered impotent within weeks by the German war monster.

At this time, the French who came to greet our train were sympathetically disposed toward us; they were in fact generous. At those times when the crawling train stopped, people from the environs were there, some running to greet us, bringing us food. I guess our arrival had been transmitted by radio, the most common means then for being au courant of the unfolding war. The French concern for refugees from the advancing Germans felt genuine; we were all in this together. These gifts of food were most welcome since we had not eaten since we left Bruxelles, mid-morning. As the afternoon wore on, and darkness was obviously not far away, the train came to a stop, seemingly again, in the middle of nowhere, but I soon noticed that we were near a village. We were told to disembark from the train and follow those in front of us. We were led, a slow moving mass of family clusters toward a sizable village, larger than I had thought, like a very small town. We knew we would spend the night here, in barns and anywhere where people could be made comfortable enough; we slept the night on straw in a barn, I remember. I heard no complaints, though no doubt some sedatives would have helped a great deal. They did feed us; no one that I know, paid. Again I say, much generosity was extended us by totally unknown sympathetic French villagers, and I now guess probably set up by some social service type organization mobilized and intent on doing this sort of service for humanity.

The next day, my guess is that following plans evidently drawn up by some night-working French government people, social agencies, volunteers, and who knows who, we were destined for a village that I construe was in the environs south of Perigeux, somewhat north of Toulouse. I see no way that I would succeed were I to try to find that village now. Although I did have a sense that this was a temporary asylum, other than for some of the strains that come with being refugees in a time of war, our stay at this village was actually quite good.

Summer 1940 – In a French Village

I cannot access in memory how we got to the Village—I am capitalizing Village as though it were its name. I do remember the Village, not its name or specific geographic location. The Village consisted really of one "street" or road along which, on both sides there were houses. Some were simply village-houses; others were actual farms. I recall that midway but closer to the other end of the Village from where we stayed, there was a water pump that served the whole village. We all got the water we needed there. And I do remember fetching water, hand pumping it into our bucket and walking back to our ground-floor set of rooms with a feeling of being useful. My mother and I lived in a good, well-functioning "entente cordiale" (in cordial agreement); besides the fact that she and I were easily affectionate, I had already long agreed, without any verbal or written pact, to do what my mother asked me or told me to do without fuss. She was very reasonable in what she expected me to do and when she expected me to do it; and I recall that I only once objected to what she wanted of me. The noteworthy thing is that my not doing what she expected of me was so rare that I remember well the one time it occurred. I just did not want to do a chore that would serve my spoiled and frequently annoying cousin Joseph—my brat younger cousin Joseph, not my older cousin Joseph whom I still love well after his death, and who I loved being with—and much to my mother's befuddlement, highly unusual for us, I held to my refusal even with her repeated request. She was quite angry with me on that occasion; but her anger evaporated within hours. I want to emphasize that my doing what my mother expected of me was not out of fear. I don't recall ever being afraid of her, or of anything she did. We just really got along well;

we loved and respected each other; and we each knew we could count on the other. I could say more about our relationship but this is not the place for it.

I remember somewhat, the house we stayed in, in Village; it was not a farm house but rather simply a stone village house. I can see the ground-level set of rooms we were it, especially the main center of our activity, the kitchen and eating-place; the ground floor (a simple cement floor), a substantial wood burning stove, a table and several chairs. Several other families had also been quartered in the Village, one of which we seemed to occasionally spend some time with. Their daughter was the only other foreign child about my age.

At first, given the modest monetary resources my mother had made it possible for us to eat quite simply but amply. One of the activities we undertook together, my mother of course being in charge, was to make butter. I was fascinated by the fact that by treating whole milk in a prescribed manner, namely by shaking it gently but steadfastly for quite some time in a container one could easily enough reach into, the milk would separate out into a fairly dense layer of cream and a fat-thinned coalescing mass of milk residue. The cream having migrated to the top was easily separated off, then shaken or stirred further, patiently, at times tediously, got more and more dense and eventually butter-like. The latter fat-free part was poured into a cloth sack, the liquid-coalescing mass would get squeezed out, the liquid was discarded but the remains in the sack, after one or two days of just sitting there would become "du frommage blanc," white cheese curds. It was not the first time that I was impressed with my mother's clever resourcefulness. Nor was it the first nor the last time that I wondered where in the world my mother got to know these things. I saw no evidence of her acquiring the information; I just saw that she knew it.

The house in which we stayed, and for which I believe we paid no rent—whether out of sheer French peasants' generosity or perhaps paid for minimally by the French government—was occupied by one woman older than my mother. I did not see much of her; nor evidently was she particularly interested in having anything to do with an 11 year-old. But across the road from where we stayed there was a farm with an animal barn fairly close to the road, and a farming family that seemed to welcome my curiosity and occasional wandering there. I found it pleasant to be there, in the courtyard and in that barn; the odor, the chickens pecking the ground, the sound of hens and roosters, the couple horses and the cows; I liked that. After a couple months of being in Village and visiting the farm I learned a then most fascinating fact of nature. Well, I knew that all animals have sex to make babies; but I had not yet, by that time thought or envisioned how cows and bulls might do it. Wow! How did that bull lift himself to get his massive body onto and behind her back? And what a member! I remember being concerned that the poor cow was going to get crushed by that enormous bull mounted on her rear end. She survived it fine.

My wanderings on the farm paid off in yet another way. I can't remember who really ran or managed the farm. This was wartime, and it is very likely that the young men who belonged to that farm, assuming there were some, were in the military. I am inclined to believe that one or two older men and several women ran the farm and did all it needed to keep going. But when it came time to harvest the strawberries they planted, they needed some additional work-hands. Since I was a capable-enough looking boy, they offered me a few "sous" (French pennies) to help them pick their strawberries, and some strawberries to take home as well. When I checked with her, my mother had no objection, and so I was hired. The harvest was not large and the few of us who did it, sufficed to finish the job in a few days.

But our strawberries did not last long enough. A new dimension of change was progressively making itself felt. Food was beginning to get increasingly scarce. Where the food was going, whether it was not being produced at the rate sufficient to feed the villagers—and probably elsewhere in France too—or whether most of it was requisitioned for those actively engaged in the war, whatever the cause or causes, it became more and more difficult to get the supply of food we needed. This applied both to what and to how much was accessible to us. It became necessary to do some scavenging. I never had needed to go about scavenging for food before, and certainly was not exercised in taking what belonged to someone else. Nor, to the best of my knowledge, was my mother. But we were getting hungry. What to do? Whatever, how? How it came to be decided, I don't know. But I do know that I was enlisted to pick up some edibles that could be found in the farmed fields and fruit trees surrounding the Village. Children grabbing fruit from trees is probably one of those nasty things farmers everywhere struggle with. Especially in increasingly lean days as these. Still, hunger was beginning to preoccupy our free time and drive us to what I hope humankind would forgive as minor thievery in increasingly dire times. I am speaking of that part of humankind I consider deserving of this designation, though I know that, that other part of it, the part I would like to disclaim, is part of "humankind" too. But in times as these, I guess the principle that "All's fair in love and war" could be stretched to accommodate our dilemma. I did not feel good about filching food from the villagers who seemed really generously to offer us asylum in Village. Furthermore, they were feeling the gnawing of insufficient food as much as we were. No, I didn't like doing this. But it made sense that we kids—the girl about my age whose family was displaced into Village like we were and I—would be asked, not commanded, by our elders to do this illicit stuff for the good of all of us. Isn't it so that on ships in time of war, stealing food can be fatal? But maybe the rules would not be as violently applied to kids. Also, we were of an age that we were no doubt more agile than our elders and could more easily evade getting caught; smart kids can outsmart grown ups in bushes most anytime.

Though looking for ripe-enough and even not-so-ripe apples, pears, berries, cherries and some leguminous vegetables was our prime effort, stealing potatoes—since it was a brilliant idea, it must have been my mother's—was one of the things that presented itself as the most desirable of possibilities. Of course, potatoes are also regarded as more basic food staple and were therefore more hazardous to steal. Interestingly, even to this day, I find potatoes among the most gratifying of foods; I am probably one among many. I tended to go on these food hunts with this girl whose name I can't remember. So potatoes is what we would go for today. We knew exactly where to go because we had, nonchalantly you might say, in days before surveyed our possibilities. In this enterprise we faced two problems in addition to the usual ones of stealing farmers' produce. First, was that stealing fruit from low-lying tree branches or bushes, or quickly scooping some vegetable lying on the ground could be done in the blink of an eye; but snitching potatoes takes some doing. Potatoes don't grow on trees, one can't just pluck them; time is needed to get them in hand. We were not intent on destroying the plants, just to lift them aside sufficiently to be able to take a few of their bellied tubers, and drop the plants back in their bed so that they might regenerate what we had snitched. I guess that even in expert hands this task takes a bit of time. And second, which was rendered more important by the first, is that generally potato fields are wide open; and this one was especially so and being right next to one of the main roads to Village made us visible even from some distance. In this instance, the beautiful countryside was not on our side.

Whether these difficulties were what made the event so memorable that I can see it today or what happened in the process, I am not sure. Probably all of it. I recall that our venturing out on this expedition made me more frightened than the ones we had undertaken before. With the earlier ones I think we were more scared by the fact that we were "good kids" doing "bad things," stealing food when everyone was increasingly coming to know hunger; we were not dummies, we knew others were hungry too. You get to know these things by the time you're 11, especially in times like these, some things you learn fast. But this time we were additionally afraid because our chances of being found out were much greater than before, we had no idea of what the consequences of our being caught might be. Nonetheless, probably bolstering each other—our parents did not push us to it—we proceeded, armed with as ample pockets as we could muster to carry our snitch home with as little obvious visibility as possible. We did not want to move directly into the field from the main road; we would be most visible from there. We selected a spot on a small dirt path that ran from the main road along the right side of the field. As we approached out site we scouted it for any sign of human presence. As if just admiring Mother Nature's work, we selected and agreed on our spot within feet of the path, and seeing no sign of human life whatsoever, we quickly rushed to a cluster of potato plants. Gently enough, one after another, I tilted a couple plants to their side with one hand, our fingers searching for and pulling out some substantially sized potatoes, rushed them into our pockets, afraid all the while that somehow we would be seen.

We were not mistaken. Suddenly, from within a tool hut we assumed to be empty, ambled out a somewhat older man, armed with a tool in each hand, arms raised, waving these and calling out curses and threats and rushing at us as best he could. We did not consider his agility, his age, or anything else for that matter; we just ran like hell, encumbered only by the bounty bulging our pockets. Now our running was really sped up by fear, not so much by the chance of the man catching us, since our thieving spot was on the right side of the field, the side adjacent to where the tool hut was located, and we were sure that we ran faster than he could; we ran scared because we had been seen stealing potatoes from the fields in this time of growing hunger, because it would not be difficult to know that we were not Village kids but those foreigners, and we anticipated dire humiliation and troubles this would bring to our families. As predicted, we escaped and ran like hell, home. As we unloaded our pockets, with anxious excitement we told our parents how we nearly got caught, with admiration-seeking details kids thrive on. Even though our loot was not large we were well received at home. This probably mitigated some the fear and soft shame I felt at having stolen food from these Villagers, who were sheltering us in their own homes! I liked the villagers; none had been unwelcoming, until this morning, when that reasonably angry farmer probably wished we had never come to his village. Fortunately, though the robbed farmer probably circulated the story of our thievery, no repercussions came to our families from it. Maybe we were not the only ones who were scavenging for food. Maybe he felt sorry for these homeless war refugees.

The grown-up villagers accepted us; perhaps at some point they may have experienced us as a nuisance, as no doubt did that hapless farmer. But the kids welcomed us; at least I felt so. I recall two young teenagers with whom I formed some kind of friendship. Nice kids. I remember best our going to their favorite swim hole. Each had bicycles; I of course did not. But never mind, the older of the two, probably 14, just arranged some way for me to ride on the bike with him, usually side saddle on the bike frame in front of him. It was really a breath-taking ride down the large hill on a macadamized road that crossed the other end of the village—near where the strawberry field was located. The ride was glorious down that long hill through two rows of tall majestic poplar trees—they grow tall in Village—then as the ground leveled, the road curved to the right opening to view lush bushes and fields. Yet perhaps more memorable than the majestic poplar trees were the songs these guys sang as we flew down this hill, "Vas-y Léon, tappe sur le bouchon. Une partie impétante, ça fait plaisir, tu l'as vus c'est une amande, change ta tire. . ." ("Go to it Leon, hit on the cork. A rash party, that brings pleasure; you've seen it's an almond, change your aim. . .") Although even to this day I never completely understood the lyrics, I definitely had the sense that here we were riding down this beautiful hill, singing some age-appropriate salacious song about drinking and screwing. After all, I was 11; it was duly topical and correct language for our biologically-programmed adolescent interests.

Speaking about sex and my 11 year-old mind, sometime during these three summer months, another event stands out in my mind. As I was walking back to Village from one of my occasional meanderings who did I see on the road walking toward me but my mother and some French sailor I'd never seen before. Wow, where did he come from? And how was it that my mother seemed on rather chummy terms with him? We greeted each other, my mother introducing us, and we each went our way, I toward the village, my mother and her sailor-friend the other way. For some reason, I didn't ask my mother who this man was, how they met, or what they were up to. Frankly, I just imagined innocence, no doubt pushing aside many indiscreet thoughts. Mh. My mother was after all long unmarried. But I guess it's those indiscreet repressed thoughts that make this memory quite vivid for me.

I was not aware then that our stay in Village would soon be over. Sometime in September 1940, we were informed that the foreigners housed in the village were going to be transferred to, who knows where. We found out that we were to go to a specified destination in Toulouse and that we would be transported there, courtesy of the Vichy-France government. The war was well over by then, Petain having called for an armistice with the bulldozing German army on June 17, 1940.

It did not take long for things to change. Later, looking back on it I wondered, was this change compelled by Hitler's government beginning to demand of the defeated French that they round up and incarcerate Jews in France, even in the unoccupied zone, in Vichy France? Were Jews rounded up by Vichy France for economic reasons; the cost of maintaining foreign Jews in concentration camps would be less than to maintain them in villages?

Later still, I learned from Marrus and Paxton* that the Vichy government began "a legislative assault" on Jews living in France during the summer and fall of 1940. On 3 October 1940, the "Status des Juifs" ("Statute of the Jews") was enacted, assigning inferior status to the French Jews and to Foreigners. Marrus and Paxton hold that already on 27 August 1940, Vichy repealed the 1939 amendment to the 1881 "Marchandeaux Law," the amendment that "prohibited any press

---

* *Vichy France and the Jews* by Michael R. Marrus and Robert O. Paxton, published by Schocken Books, New York, 1983, page 3.

attack 'toward a group of persons who belong by origin to a particular race or religions when it is intended to arouse hatred among citizens'. . . After 27 August 1940, . . . antisemitism was free to spread itself in French newspapers." The Vichy-France government, "the new French State," bettered the newspapers in their unleashing of antisemitism in the unoccupied zone. That is why we were rounded up and transported to Toulouse.

Chapter 3

The Camps

The Round-Up

I cannot remember just when in mid-September—I believe it was even before 3 October when the Status des Juifs became law—we were rounded up, nor how many of us in Village, were in that round up. Even having an answer now, my experience of it was, "Why are they rounding us up? Because we were foreigners?" We were; no one had invited us here. We just barged in from Belgium, running as fast as we could from the Germans. Were they relocating us to a situation where my mother and the other parents could get work and we kids could go to school? I had seen no sign of school in Village. But where? My mother did not know.

When we left Bruxelles, we decided to leave. We did not decide to leave Village. They decided; whoever "they" were. I can't recall how we were transported to Toulouse. I do know that from Village, with no train station nearby, my mother and I had no means of getting ourselves to Toulouse. Besides, where is Toulouse and where in Toulouse? Hell, we didn't know where we were to go. Although, with my mother, you couldn't tell; she knew all kinds of things. "They" took us there. I do know that we did not get there by train. Most likely it was an autobus. Somehow, even though leaving Village was not of our choosing, I was curious and worried, but I did not feel threatened or frightened. What was most important and valuable to me came with me. I was with my mother, no matter where we were going, my mother was there. Still, the worried faces of the grown-ups, the anxiety floating around us, were troubling. I did not know that we were on the threshold to hell. Looking back, thank heaven, I was not alone; I was not ready to be alone.

I remember what the passage into hell looked like. In Toulouse, our first camp was a Detention Camp. Inside the barracks was gray, all gray. The gray made us all look even more haggard than we felt; what a dismal looking bunch of people around me. Maybe it was not just the light; yes, it was gray in there; but those around me looked gray. They looked so haggard, and worried, and afraid. These worried faces informed me that we were heading for difficult times. Grown ups are a headache sometimes, but I knew they are not dumb. I had my mother and a number of uncles and aunts who informed me of that, especially my mother. My mother, as always, tried to protect me from the gray around us. She was quite a woman, this woman, my mother. I won't say all I feel about her.

The gray barracks in the middle of Toulouse were dark, double bunked beds made of, I guess the universal 2 by 4s, coarse army blanketed, and of course, no sheets. They were probably straw filled "mattresses," a preview of what we would get later. It was grim. I don't remember how or what they fed us those two or three days we were there. Nor do I remember how we were transported to our next stop, Recebedou.

Récébédou – Our First Concentration Camp

Récébédou was situated some 10 kilometers from Toulouse. By its construction, no doubt, Recebedou was a permanent camp; probably a military post. The barracks were of brick; they had been there for some time, though not ages, because they looked of fairly recent vintage; they were built to be there for some time to come. Funny relief on entry here; the place wasn't so scary or distressing; though we were incarcerated, foreigners imprisoned, it was not depressing dirty-gray like the barracks in Toulouse.

We got there in late September or, possibly, in early October. The barrack to which we were assigned was partitioned into two sections, one on the right of the entry, the other on the left. Straight ahead of the entrance way, an area of perhaps 8 feet by 8 feet, was the lavatory and toilets. Only the lavatory and toilets had full walls, floor to ceiling; the other partitions were partial only, like over-sized cubicles. We were in the section on the right of the entrance. This section in turn was subdivided into about 6 cubicular areas, 3 on each side of an aisle shared by all. There were 4 to 6 of us in each cubicle. We each had a cot, a normal army type mattress, and a blanket. These Vichy-French did not believe in bed sheets. There were small windows near the ceiling that gave the cubicles light. Much better than in Toulouse. In the unisex lavatory-toilets complex we had both cold and warm water, to which of course we were all heretofore accustomed. The toilets, the civilized type you can sit on, with partial doors that allowed for some privacy. We were told that we would stay here. We settled in.

The rather large eating hall, as best as I recall filled with long tables and benches, was in a separate building, some distance away. The hall was large and the tables were long, but the food portions were small and the menu very limited, in fact unimpressive. But we had a preview of food limitations in Village where our diet already had begun to shrink, and selection increasingly became more and more limited. As time passed, these trends in our alimentation continued in palpable increments downward.

I must have been conditioned to be in school at this time of the year, the cooling season with its effects on the environs and all that; it was odd not to be in school. I do not remember befriending anyone in Récébédou ; there were no kids my age in my barrack or nearby. Idleness was beginning to set in. I liked school; I felt good in school. But there was no school. Obviously, I was not the only one to take note of that. Not too surprising, the grown-ups took note of it too. What were kids doing out of school at this time of year? And giving them due credit, they, our "they" this time, probably thought, "We don't want our kids not studying and learning." I can't explain it, but many parents are like that; some more, some less. With Jews, everybody knows that studying, Torah or anything, well maybe not just anything, anyway, studying, learning, is very, very important. Whatever the thinking, I would guess within a month, we began to have some form of school; we had some classes. The classes were few, a couple hours at a time, the one-classroom-school type, and we did not meet everyday.

Whoever started it, we were trying to build a community. Not only was school started—however meager—our "they" also began to organize yet other activities for us. Whether my mother's doing or my own, I joined "The Israelite Boy Scouts." I don't remember what we did. But I feel that it was salutary for us. I know, I felt my machismo—at 11 years of age, it's really OK for boys to feel they're tough and stuff—enhanced by being a Boy Scout. In fact, I felt so into being a strong guy that I recall going to a meeting, and juiced up by my enthusiasm for the venture—after all, we were Boy Scouts!—as I bounded along, I came across the small stream that ran through the Récébédou camp, a stream about 5 to 6 feet across at a spot that drew my interest; I was bounding along. When I came to the stream, of course, I felt, I could just leap from one side of it to the other. So there I went, flying in the air, falling square on the very muddy other side of the little stream, missing my mark by about two feet. Embarrassed at my shortfall, I quickly got myself upright, stepped out of the mud, to find that I came up one shoe missing. Good heavens, I almost lost my shoe. It was the only pair I had. We had traveled light. I retrieved it out of the muck, really only mud but it did feel like muck, cleaned it off as well as I could, and crestfallen or brought back to where we really were, I proceeded at a much slowed pace to the troop meeting. I cannot remember one thing that transpired there. The weight of my humiliation at not having cleared that little stream brought me back to "Récébédou." That's where we were; that's all I was, a detainee or an internee or a "whatever" in this unwished-for place.

Idleness was not sufficiently remedied by the few occasional classes we had—I can't remember what the classes were in, no doubt Language and Math—or by the Boy Scouts. I don't know why or how it came about that I had or made no friends in Récébédou; this was unusual for me; I always had two or several quite good friends, even in Village where I stayed only a bit more than two months. In Bruxelles and beyond, I always had a couple close friends and several more peripheral ones, if I can put it that way. The idleness,

no doubt, was intensified by my having no close peers with whom to get into some diversionary time-occupying activity. Amazing how even to an 11-year-old approaching 12, idleness can be a problem. Both adults and kids were, I guess, trying to dissolve the idleness. I should emphasize that the adults were idle too, not just us kids; this was not a labor camp; slavery might be better than idleness. Well, I would not go that far. It was a just-holding-us-out-of-the-world-camp, gathered for some further purpose, who knows what. Whoever they were, they did manage to make me, I guess all of us feel useless, aimless and what-the-hell are we waiting for, plus we were getting increasingly hungrier. At Village we had been able to add to our insufficient food supply by scavenging for fruit and vegetables. No free roaming beyond specified limits here; no chance for food hunting.

The powers-that-be, I mean of the social-service types like the Red Cross and such—not governmental ones—tried to lessen the misery of the refugee-inmate population, by somehow managing to bring some "entertainment" into the camp. I was 11; I guess I could be made to believe we were really being entertained. I remember distinctly, I can see him, the "strong man" who could with his bare hands, bend a substantial band of steel. He got volunteers to try it, in front of our eyes; they couldn't. And he, by whatever genius or trickery, just grabbed the thing and bent it with surprising facility. No doubt some trickery. I do remember a crowd of us showed up, eager for some distraction from where we really were, and we participated sluggishly in the chicanery. I admit, it did distract us and momentarily dulled our progressively growing misery.

And besides our dislocation from home, which by now felt like quite some time ago and was making itself seriously felt, and idleness, hunger continued to intensify and become increasingly preoccupying. It is really impressive how, to an 11 year-old, hunger can really be a miserable condition. I know now that it's not just so for 11-year-olds. So it was quite an event when, some two or three months into our stay at Récébédou we were informed that the Red Cross was going to bring us milk. We had not seen milk since we had left Village. The Red Cross brought it. I remember the canned milk taste of that era. In Europe even today, in some quite nice smaller hotels they still use this rotten-tasting stuff. Hungry as we were, it was good to have. Distasteful as it was, I gulped it down trying not to taste, but just drank it to quiet my need for food. I was unwisely food-sensitive then still, even in the face of hunger. But I was hungry; so I swallowed the un-milk tasting Red Cross canned-milk. Meals were prescribed for unfailing weight-loss. However, I have absolutely no memory of what we ate—some apportioned piece of bread, probably some beans, other vegetables, potatoes, maybe a rare small piece of some meat—food was sparse. I note that Récébédou left fewer prints in my brain of our life there than what followed. The early part of our stay in Récébédou for the most part was dull. We were incarcerated, space was restricted, hardly any school, no books, no special friend, idleness, not a recipe for me nor for those around me.

Time just went right on totally ignoring what "they" were doing to us. Cold weather was setting in. To this day I am a naïve geographer and climatologist, but the fact is, the weather was getting colder than I wished for. Again looking at a world map today, I am still amazed to see that Southern France where all that great Bordeaux comes from is actually at the latitude of Northern California, where the California great wines now come from. The problem is that unlike California, the weather in the environs of Toulouse, after grape-harvesting time I guess, became increasinly, strikingly chilled, more like the climates in Chicago and Boston. Actually Toulouse is at higher latitude than these glorious so well-known cold-in-the-winter cities in America. As a Boy Scout climatologist, I would guess that the air masses and cross winds given life by the interacting Pyrénées Mountains cold winds, the Méditérranée Mistral and whatever Atlantic Ocean turbulence added to the mix combined to generate this additional unanticipated miserable challenge.

The on-coming of cold weather. One of our increasing problems is that when we left Bruxelles in such a hurry, we did not anticipate needing colder climate clothing. Not that it would have been feasible to bring much of it along. The fact is that we did not have clothes to match the changing weather. In addition, there was no central heating in the Barracks; at least not that I remember. I do remember a small wood-burning furnace centrally located in the 60 or so feet long barrack. I must be mistaken because the state of permanence in the construction of these brick barracks, I would guess built for year-round occupation, must have had some kind of heating system; it would not make sense that there would not be. The French were overpopulated with Nazis, but they were not stupid.

In any case, we were getting cold. As time passed and the cold intensified—a very egalitarian thing, cold, even our Vichy-French hosts got their fair share—we needed more heat. A chore made for idle kids my age, I was among those sent out to gather whatever dry wood lay loose on the ground, to provide whatever heat we could generate in our small barrack-stove. As with other chores, I usually did pretty well. I had long learned to be industrious and do things competently—foremost I did well in school. I liked school, I liked learning; I guess it suited me. But, sans me vanter (without bragging), I did a pretty good job gathering dry wood too. How long my success would continue? No idea. Eventually, I would not be given the chance to test it out.

The cold was setting in and hunger continued to gnaw. A number of misery-causing conditions had crept in on us. Between the gnawing hunger, incarceration, idleness, and now the increasing cold, Recebedou progressively transformed into purgatory. Our ability to stand up to the increasingly miserable conditions was limited. Like we had attempted to undo idleness with school and Boy Scouts, we set out to fight the cold by gathering fire wood. Hunger was the ever-present and increasingly pre-occupying challenge; as Primo Levi said of it, among oppressed Europeans, it was a popular companion. We should study how human beings accommodate to being hungry. There's always been so much of it around. You would think by now that we would have made some genetic accomodation to hunger! Well first, you just give in to it. It'll beat you everytime. Then you try to lessen what it makes you feel by psychically defending against it, such as by some serious distraction—which was not forthcoming in this chilling purgatory—or by some serious denial of and numbing of its own brand of pain. Of course if at all possible, you make some ingenious effort to get around it. My mother tried to do something about the hunger. I admit, she did not truly succeed but I saw that she tried. She decided to become a food merchant.

One of the remaining decencies the Vichy-France government extended to its unwelcome now encamped foreign asylum seekers was, given a good enough excuse, one could get a pass for several hours out of Récébédou to do whatever one could impress on the authorities one needed to do in Toulouse. Toulouse I would soon discover could actually be accessed by tram (streetcar). Actually Récébédou is a few kilometers from one of the Toulouse tram system end-stations. I don't know where my mother got the idea, but she decided to fabricate some excuses to have to get into Toulouse where, with some of her remaining funds, she would buy some packaged dried fruit, figs and dates, I remember—the Vichy French still had goods available to them which they did not share with their Récébédou guests—and bring them back to Récébédou where people not as clever or entrepreneurial as she would buy them at some profit to us.

I can understand, I think, why we were then still allowed to leave campsite for a few hours. Recebedou, though built for the duration, was not equipped with the medical staff needed to take care of a herd like us, not even of some minor animal challenge like say treating an 11-year-old Jew who, somehow got an in-grown toe-nail. And to their feeble credit, the Vichy gatekeepers recognized the need for treatment of such a condition, even though minor. While now on the way there, Vichy France had not yet degraded to its most shameful level.

An ingrown toe-nail! Amazing how painful such a stupid little thing can be. But in fairness to myself, as a doctor I know that even grown-ups have trouble putting up with an infected in-grown toe-nail. I think I was on the verge not only of being done in by the pain but also by some mysterious fear of some major harm coming to my toe, obviously a vital body part—psychoanalysts think such things. It hurt. I needed help. I truly did not welcome the idea of visiting Toulouse under these conditions. Nor at this time. The weather was really getting bad. By now the South-Western French winter was here. The date for our pass to the Toulouse Dispensary, in some Toulouse hospital, came on a day that introduced me to the degree to which a snowstorm in Toulouse could proudly compete with one in Philadelphia, perhaps even with one in Chicago or Boston. In the morning, I would guess there already was more than two inches of snow on the ground. Not remarkable for its snow, unless your shoes, as were ours, were approaching the too-well-worn stage. What the storm did not have in snow, it had in wind; it was a serious wind-blowing snowstorm. Amazing how stiffly cutting, how bitterly painful, cold wind makes a few inches of snow. Unlike Shelley's "winter wind," this wind was as "unkind as man's ingratitude." Seeing the cold wind and snow's magnitude, given our lack of winter clothes, my common-sense mother decided that we would walk from the camp to the Toulouse-destined tram each wrapped in our bed blanket. Walking into the wind, the blowing snow was cutting into us so damned indifferently. How do the homeless do it? On top of the wind-lashing storm, I remember the agony my throbbing foot added to the mix; I was trying like hell to be brave on our way to the tram. Though it probably was no more than two or three kilometers (1½ to 2 miles), it felt like an unending day getting to that tram. Remarkable relief came with our getting inside the tram. We all know how some everyday simple things, like in Europe of that day, getting onto a tram, can under certain conditions be so major an event.

I cannot even guess how long that tram ride was. I do remember that by the time we reached Toulouse, the nasty overnight storm was dying out. Mother Nature forgive me, but it deserved to die. No more snow was falling and perhaps sheltered by the Toulouse buildings or truly by the storm's ending, the walk to the hospital was predominantly painful now due to my aching foot. All I remember of the dispensary visit are the typical hospital muck-colored corridors, some pain in the treatment of my toe, and the relief, even though my toe ached aplenty, that something had been done to eventually cure my ailing foot. It worked. Even though my toe infection was most probably lanced—this was the end of 1940; I doubt they would have even had any sulfa antibiotic available for miserable unwanted guests—and I had an aching foot, the walk back to the tram was quite less hectic. And, walking back from the end of the tram line to Récébédou was far easier than that morning's painful cutting through the storm

In terms of time, I have reconstructed that we were into the cold of late November 1940. We were informed that we were leaving récébédou. Within a few days the Jews in Récébédou were to pack their belongings, only one piece of luggage. This one-piece of luggage policy had already been in play when we came to Récébédou . Not that my mother and I traveled from Bruxelles overly encumbered with for-all-seasons precious baggage. I say the Jews because not all the récébédou inmates, even among those in our barrack, were de-camping to who knows where. My mother and a fairly attractive manly Spaniard had befriended one another during our stay, and he, unlike us, was not being separated from Récébédou. In trying to be fair to the miserable Vichy Government, many refugees from the countries North, East, and South of France looked to France for asylum in those war years. Not just those fleeing the advancing Germans from Belgium, Holland and Germany—mostly Jews—but also those Spaniards who were fleeing Franco's Nazi-sympathetic monster machine, squeezing north into France through the Pyrenees Mountains. The camps in Southern France were well situated to house the Spaniards as well as those of us who had gotten this far south. I later came to recognize that a premeditated selection had been made in this choosing the Jews over the Spaniards for separation from these climate-sympathetic brick barracks of Récébédou. Jews and Spaniards had been together. Now, we Jews were chosen to go.

In preparation for our upcoming journey, my mother succeeded in getting a last pass into Toulouse, and came back with some packaged figs and, of all things, she had gotten some bananas. How? From where? They still grew fruit somewhere. I had not seen fruit since we left Village. I guess hunger was really getting to me because these bananas caused quite a philosophic dilemma and conflict between my mother and me. I doubt there were more bananas than 4 or 5. Of course my mother gave me one to eat soon after she arrived with them. Some hours later I wanted another one. My mother had the wisdom to think of tomorrow, to want to save some for a rainy day. I was a hungry soon-to-be 12 year-old kid. My argument got a bit heated; she was really quite calm though distressed about my plight, which she knew I was not fabricating. But she held her ground; and I yielded. I was never afraid of my mother; she got angry with me at times—what mother doesn't—but she was never nasty or mean; my guess is, I yielded because I knew that what she said made sense. That was one of my problems; she usually did make sense. We did not have a battle-royal, just an overheated debate-type argument. My mother was the no-nonsense-firm type; she was smart, totally non school-educated smart. When she was growing up in Poland, in the early 1900s, most girls from our Jewish community just did not go to school. She was affectionate, responded to touch very comfortably, touched and held me comfortingly whether it came from me or from her. In one of those old studio photos of my mother seated and I, probably 4 years-old, standing on some stool next to her, the striking features of the photo are that we did not look like the happiest mother-child pair I have seen—this was soon after we had migrated from Poland and arrived in Bruxelles—and the pressure of her holding me close to her was such that her hand makes an indentation in my then-chubby thigh. So, as she wished, we packed the bananas with the rest of our things with the promise that I would get some when we got to our destination.

We boarded the train outside of Toulouse. Again, special courtesy of our host government, we did not need to make the trek to the Toulouse train station, they came to us, near our own doorstep to take us in and transported us all the way to our destination. Nor did we have to carry our packing case. These would be transported for us to our destination too. We left Récébédou about midday. History compels me to say that we traveled in passenger wagons, not the wagons that soon got put to use for purposes as these; in Vichy-French eyes we were not yet cattle.

Rivesaltes: The Shame of Vichy-France Deepens

We traveled through the night. I don't know why it took us this long to get to our destination. The distance from Récébédou, just outside Toulouse, to Rivesaltes, which is situated about 15 kilometers north of Perpignan, is just not that far as to required an overnight train ride on the basis of distance. I do remember that we crawled. Perhaps, come to think of it, our hosts thought it would be advantageous to them, of course, for us to arrive in the morning rather than late at night. Anyway, they had us neatly enough packed in the train.

We were a fairly subdued troupe of people, even though we were mostly parents with children. Looking at it now, this many children should not make for so subdued a trainload of people. Even in the night, under normal expectable conditions, a wagon-full of parents with kids, for so many hours, would not be so quiet, so waiting with bated breath. Where are we going? Perhaps the strains of these months of migration away from our homes, the now familiar hunger, the constancy of this state of deprivation, dislocation, ineffectuality in disallowing or changing what was happening to us, the unspoken sense of feelings that we are becoming lesser beings, all combined to subdue adults and children alike. In time, kids get to know when their parents are helpless to make things better.

We arrived on a bleak winter-wind-blowing day to a gray-soil plain, some 20 kilometers from foothills of the Pyrénées Orientales Mountains, spread with barracks that immediately struck me as cheaply-built, desolate, depressing; some for all appearances in need of repair. Round and round we had been brought down to this next circle of hell; maybe that's why the train trip took so long. I remember our arrival there, now 60 years later: it was a bleak part of France, at a bleak time, on this bleak day. This piece of country did not promise good days. Nor did it give the impression of permanence.

The Récébédou barracks were brick. The Rivesaltes barracks' outside walls were near-beige, plaster-covered; the inside walls were white-gray-plaster-covered. Récébédou barracks were partitioned in two then again in three sections on each side, and there was some provision for heat by means of a small wood-burning stove, the wood gathered from the surrounds within the camp. Rivesaltes barracks were one large open box: dormitory, eating place, dwelling place, all packed in one's own bed area, our bed serving all furniture purposes, chair, table, etc. The barracks were lined along their length with beds on each of the long sides. I do not remember any stove in the barrack. I guess that in addition to whatever we could put on ourselves, clothes and blankets when it got very cold, our own bodies provided whatever heat there was. We did gather wood in Rivesaltes, possibly to make small fires outdoors—or my mother and I would not have thought of my gathering wood to deceive those who might be interested in my eventual illicit activity. The bed frames were made of 2 x 4 wood beams—like the ones in the first Toulouse camp where the Vichy Government first detained us, except that the Rivesaltes beds were single beds, not double-bunks—across which stretched single, straightforward wires, north to south and east to west. A coarse-cloth mattress sack filled with straw, one coarse-wool gray blanket. Sheets? Not included. Now, my emphasis on the coarseness of both the straw-filled mattress and the blanket just made itself clear to me about one hour before this writing. I feel compelled to explain.

Soon after I decided the time had come for me to write about my witnessing and living a piece of the Holocaust, during a stretch of time from the end of July to August 14, 2002, it seemed I had managed to make contact with some poison-ivy and soon started to develop a typical, very itchy rash. Those who react allergically to poison-ivy know what I'm talking about. The problem is that having been the victim of this miserable allergic reaction before, I had become well acquainted with the various structural features and color-bound manifestations through which poison-ivy evolves during its season. But my diagnosis brought with it a dilemma: there is and there was no poison ivy on our property. As the course of my nasty and very itchy skin ailment dragged on, my Dermatologist and my Internist agreed to eliminate from my average-expectable aging-optimizing medications those medicines that might possibly cause some skin rash. My reactive skin rash had by now turned from an acute condition (a sudden, short-lasting condition) to a somewhat chronic one (a long-continuing state of symptoms or disease). My astute Dermatologist was puzzled by what I was harboring. It came to him by both a process of elimination and years of clinical know-how about diagnostic manifestations of skin disorders, to pursue in good doctorly fashion a line of thought that caused him some unease. Gently, hesitatingly probing of his psychiatrist-patient, if he was having some emotional problems, he asked, "Henri, excuse my wondering but, is something especially troubling you these days? This really looks like 'Nummular Eczema' (a specific form of the widely known skin disorder that tortures children and adults) which has strong emotional determinants (especially stress and rage) acting on a skin diathesis (specific inborn vulnerability due to some organ or system sensitivity)." I smiled, I think, and barely shaking my head in thought I told him, "Bernie, I think you just hit it on the head." And I went on to explain that I noted with some constancy, that during those times when I was writing this story, my Holocaust story, I was almost continually itching, at times squirming, and then I would feel compelled to apply the topical agent (skin medication) he had prescribed for me and/or take an antihistamine. Both stress and rage come with this writing, quiet but not so quiet rage, as in this writing, as Rachel (my wife) has wisely said, "It's a self-analysis; it may even help you more [than an analysis]." Rachel means "a psychoanalysis."

Writers, artists, psychoanalysts and many others live like that. We look for explanations and for hidden meanings. Children do this too; they have to know how things work; that's why kids take toys apart, not to break them—at least not much of the time—but to find out what makes them tick. That's why many kids annoy impatient parents with seemingly unending "Why" questions. Well, there's a lot to learn when you've just come into this unknown world. Kids have to have explanations like why glass breaks when it hits the floor, or why a bird flies away. Scientists always have to look for causes, effects, forces, hidden activity, etc. But it was just this morning, fourth month into this writing and into my reactive skin disorder (I now know that it is reactive; I have never had eczema before although I have long been wool-next-to-my-skin-intolerant) that this insight opened up. In Rivesaltes we slept on coarse sack-cloth mattresses. They could even have been olden days potato-sack cloth; at the very least they were coarse flour-sack type cloth. Just the thought of it makes my skin crawl. And we covered ourselves with that army-type coarse wool blanket. This specific insight—which probably has merit given the epiphany reaction I had to my friend Bernie's inquiry—will not immediately clear my skin. It will not clear it today because skin reactions of this nasty kind don't just wash away; they have to be, we might say, detoxified and metabolized by the psyche and by the body. For me, these torturous sleeping accommodations—so torturous in fact that I totally repressed this part of my Rivesaltes experience until this writing—, plain and simple, reflected the misery that was Rivesaltes. And, at this moment, I feel this specifically in my skin.

The toileting facilities were in another barrack. One would assume that the toileting accommodations would match the grade level of the "living place" barracks. But this was Rivesaltes. They were not; they managed to be yet a further notch of degradation. Located about 100 yards from the barrack in which we "lived," the toileting facilities we frequented, there were two as will become clear, were semi-unroofed wooden structures superimposed on a skeleton cement base or floor that was elevated from the ground by about three feet. We climbed up several steps to get to this gray slab cement level. With entrances on each side of this rectangular ugly cement-wood model of supreme, what? "military," economy-driven simplicity? aimed-to-always-offend odoriferous place? from where I walked in, the toilet cubicles were on the right, and the latrine in this unisex facility and several crude cement sinks with one cold-water-only "robinet," were on the left. (When I turn to French as I just did and have done before, it is because that is the language at hand in my brain and at times I can think of the French word but not the English, the language I chose to write in—yes, "faucet" ["robinet"] is the word I'm looking for.) In winter, somehow I believe we had no snow in the plain at the foothills of the Pyrénées Mountains, yet there was the miserable November snow storm in slightly more northern, but more landscaped Récébédou. I am not a weatherman. But my point is that while the wind was nasty, as I remember it, thought I may not have been aware of it, the temperature did not drop to the level of freezing our outdoor source of wash-water. I don't believe the water froze in the faucets even though, like in the barracks, there absolutely was no man-made heating in these ungradable—as they do for hotels these days—bathroom facilities.

The wall-latrine, typical in lesser elegant Western Europe spots, was of the grayish-green variety. Of course, smelly as all men know—in this case the women did too—; but not intolerable even to a smell-sensitive 11-turning-12-year-old, since one had no choice but to just accommodate to it. The camp was bad enough without our just smelling up the whole area rather than just focus it all in one spot with an odorous surround of about 20 feet in radius. But it's the cubicles that got the disgust prize. All I need say is that the cubicled toilets consisted of a hole in the cement slab-floor, that they had no doors, and that there was neither toilet paper nor newspapers to help us not bring some residuum of what we were trying to leave behind, back into our "living" quarters with us. I cannot remember what we used to clean ourselves. Now, this kind of toilet structure may surprise some among us, but the fact is that this kind of toilet facility was not that far from the out-house or public facility models one could find in 1940s Western Europe—and still finds in some places today. Just degrade it a few notches.

As I said, as I remember it, our wash-water faucets did not freeze. In fact a bit of freezing might have made living conditions a bit better, although, like so many people living in colder latitudes, I had really tasted freezing and it has its own texture of misery. In January-February 1941, going from our barrack to the toilet required a strategy of finding your way from one less muddy footstep to another. A little freezing, a little more solid ground would have helped, and the smells might not have traveled as far too. Somehow the toileting facilities seemed to always have a number of people there; maybe, that is not so surprising. I think I may be dwelling on this part of "camp-life" because of a very meaningful association, as we psychoanalysts say, I have to it. It touches on one of the most painful after-effects of all this—what my miserable Holocaust experience has gifted my family with. I will say more about this later. But these toileting facilities seemed to really have troubled one of my grandsons when we "visited" the remains of Rivesaltes in 1997. When my grandsons Eli (Elliot) and Arthur, their father Karl, our son, their mother Sabina, Rachel and I spent a few hours revisiting the ruin-remains of Rivesaltes—the monument it is now, somewhat like the Gedaechtsnichkierche in Berlin, the majestic partly destroyed enormous church remaining unrepaired as a memorial to the destruction of war—Eli had gone into the toileting structure to see it's remains. The cement structures were still there. It was days later when we were in Bruxelles that Eli, in his uniquely sympathetic, intimate manner, forewarning that he was going to say something to me for which he needed to prepare me for the pain we were about to share, said to me, "Zaida, is that where you went to the bathroom?" Following that with a pause and, "You know . . ." ["what I mean" didn't have to be said]. I put my hand on the back of his shoulder, "Yes, Eli, that's where we went to the bathroom." My beloved grandchildren. Eli's inquiry reminded me of what a microcosm of misery those toileting facilities were. Understand, I want my family, everyone of them, to feel, say, ask, whatever they may about what happened, whatever it may be, so that they may lessen the burden it has, I have, and what happened to me has, and continues to cause them.

But coming back to my pre-occupation here with toileting, one of the things that lightened Vichy's burden of Foreigners was attached to these toilets—dysentery. It did a number of the camp inmates in. Vivette Samuel—who wrote a book on Rivesaltes of that time, years after her voluntary stay in Rivesaltes as a member of the OSE (I'll say more about Samuel and the OSE later)—evaluating the toileting facilities and all that pertained to them, said of them, "La situation sanitaire est désastreuse" (sanitary conditions are disastrous). Most of the deaths in Rivesaltes were due to illness, including foremost those brought on by starvation and by seriously poor sanitation, both of which were disastrous to those who came to Rivesaltes with "pre-existing medical conditions" as insurance companies choose to speak of them in America. Conditions prevailing in Rivesaltes dramatically facilitated and accelerated the evolution of these "pre-existing conditions" and brought their hosts to a premature end. Rivesaltes was an unsanitary place to be; but that was only part of Rivesaltes' brutality.

I know that whatever we were going to face, my mother and I were of a disposition to do the best we could with it; at this point I could do so, as long as I was with my mother. Of course, in early 1941 we were not at the peak of European Jews' misery. That would come later. Our circumstances were not, by a long shot, as dire as many Jews would and did face later. But for now, what I learned from Primo Levi and colleagues like Henry Krystal, we were not "Mussulman," the fate of too many among us in the Death Camps, mortified, robotized humans with no fight or hope; a disastrous way of reacting to terror. January-February 1941 was early in our Holocaust history for "Mussulman" adaptation; my mother and I were nowhere near that point.

In Rivesaltes, Life Went On

Families were separated. Men and women stayed in separate quarters. Men and women could and did visit at certain times of the day; the best of my recollection is seeing Savic's father—I'll get to Savic shortly—in the late afternoon and early evening hours. Very much my good fortune, children under 14—it may have been 15—stayed with their mothers. I was just about to turn 12 when we got to Rivesaltes; so I stayed with my mother. Pas d'question (no doubt), I don't know where I would have ended up were I a couple years older.

What they fed us was just as bleak as the time in history we were going through, as bleak as the plain at the foothills of the distantly visible Pyrénées, the barracks; the whole package. Food was brought to us in man-carried drums. In the mornings we got one piece of darkish bread, at times with one spoon of watery brown syrup, probably an attempt to make the bread more palatable. It really wasn't necessary to try to make it palatable; starvation convinced us it was. I know I prized my morning and evening piece of bread, as did everyone else. Though I never participated in such activity, I would not be surprised if some bread-for-things trading went on—somewhat like Primo Levi described. Midday we were treated to watery soup with some kind of vegetation in it; I am not a gardener and did not ask, but I doubt many of us knew what vegetable it was. No bread at this meal. In the evening, we again got a piece of bread and some cut-up, I heard said, turnips or rutabagas. It is well known that hunger will make us, even most kids, overcome our distaste and even disgust with certain foods. Just as I self-protectively then did not allow myself to feel intolerant of my sack-cloth and wool bedding, so too, I swallowed turnip and rutabaga without puking. It wasn't just the environs, the barracks, the sanitation, the climate that were a significant downgrade from Recebedou; so was the food, in quality and quantity. I assume that we were also supplied with drinking water. Whether or not some coffee or tea was made available to grown ups, I can't recall. I do know that in 1940-1941, we got no milk. According to Samuel, by 1942 children were given some "legal quantity" of milk. Fortunately, I escaped that pleasure.

Hunger intensified. I recall one incident with yesterday clarity, when I was hung in the balance of disgust and yet real sympathy for some poor bastard. Progressively getting skinnier, all of us, some did whatever they could to get just a bit more food. Our food was usually brought into our barrack in metal containers and distributed by two men, the same two men for a time. One morning during the bread and syrup distribution, one of the two men dropped the container of syrup; it was not glass, it was a metal can type of thing. Nonetheless a substantial amount of the contents spilled onto the floor. By reflex, without thought or hesitancy, one of the men just dropped to the floor and with accelerating pace as if fearing someone else would compete with him for it, started to slurp up as much of the brown sugary muck from the floor as he could. After some hesistancy his distribution mate joined him on the floor, at a slower pace, I now guess, more conflicted than the other about notching down to that level to attenuate his miserable hunger, in whatever way possible. The floor was not filthy, some routine broom sweeping did occur. But this was cement; not a clean floor. It did not enter the equation for this man; "food" was lying on the floor and he was grabbing it as best he could. I must admit that in spite of my hunger, I had no push to join him on the floor. Nor did my mother. Nor anyone else. That poor man did. Yes, I was troubled with what these conditions had brought this man to; but I could sympathize with him. I was young; it was 1940-1941; I didn't know some of us would do worse things as time passed.

My preoccupation with food took me on a different path. We were waiting with increasing submissive impatience for our luggage which for weeks now had not yet arrived. Just the one piece we now owned. Yes, my interest lay more in those bananas—which would have rotted by now—than whatever else we had in the luggage. I was hungry, like everyone else; but I had a vested interest in what was ours that we had shipped along in absolute anticipation that what belonged to us would get to us. Yes, it took much longer than either my mother or I, nor anyone else for that matter, had imagined. When we were informed that our luggage had arrived, everyone, it seemed to me, experienced it as most welcoming news. Well, the news was not so good. When we got our luggage, like that of the others, we found that our meager belongings had been pillaged, luggage broken open and virtually trashed. What!? "Well, [I guess], these were Jews' belongings, so why not take what we needed?" I can understand the decrepit reasoning, what I have called "malignant distortion": "Les sales Juifs are trash; they rob good people, . . ." We all know the rationalizing: "What I do is just and right; absolutely sanctified by the gods."

To be sure, I knew my mother was not the one who caused the pillaging. But I was right, so silly and little boy, really: she should have let me have another banana. It was more annoyance with her than anger; she was as insulted, miserable and outraged as I was. I really wanted only one more; I was not a greedy kid. Who am I trying to convince? One of those I least need to convince about such matters? My mother? She never blamed me for anything that happened; she never accused me of being greedy. Nor of anything else for that matter. She never expressed or conveyed the feeling in my presence nor to me, that I was a burden to her. This theft of our meager belongings I remember as a moment where I probably silently went into expletives, like merde (shit), salauds! (bastards) and all that. Mild compared to what I would say today.

Even in the face of these miseries, life went on in Rivesaltes; it would in all but the most dire of circumstances. Children, biologically promised the right to a long life ahead, feel the need to go on. This does at times require denial of existing circumstances and conditions, just as patients with cancer or prisoners on death row often deny they are at death's threshold and plan for the future. We, several kids about my age, 2 other boys and 2 girls, at times organized ourselves into activity. It seemed to fall into place naturally. In 1940-41, in Rivesaltes, we did not have any schooling, that is the expectable schooling kids get in Western Europe. Experience was our schooling now. Nor were there boy scout type activities as we got in Récébédou. Idleness, idleness—gets boring. Other than our individual meanderings not far from our barrack and the uniquely programmed activity of wood gathering for our small outdoor fires that succeeded at briefly warming our thinning selves, we kids spontaneously fell into two memorable activities. In order of frequency they were, for the boys, playing The Three Musketeers, and on several occasions, the boys and girls spent a couple of evening hours dancing. Yes, dancing in Rivesaltes. Only kids could be that, what? Nuts? Unaware that we were increasingly at risk, targeted for further abuse, and denigration, we played, we danced. Sometimes kids are smarter than grown-ups. We had our priorities right: Live while you can; there are no absolute signs that tomorrow will be worse! I know—often we can't let ourselves know. The fact is, we did that; we played Les Trois Mousquetaires and we danced. We still could, I guess, because we could not imagine what lay ahead.

Since we were three, and all smart enough French-speaking kids 11-12 years of age have read Les Trois Mousquetaires, it is perfectly plausible that needing to fight our victimization, needing to feel heroic, that's where our fantasies would take us. We played The Three Musketeers outside, during the day, running up and down some mounds of earth and building-construction-waste remains, pretending we were the heroes encountering and, of course always, winning over the evil Cardinal Richelieu and his henchmen. That this was early in the winter of 1940-1941, before the worst to happen reached us directly, that it was early in the Holocaust denouement probably was the factor that both allowed us to still play, and accounts for our not converting in our play, the nasty Richelieu into Adolph Hitler—just typing that name into this manuscript makes me sick!

I need a break here.

What a despicable name . . .

. . .

Playing The Three Musketeers really engaged my friends and me. We would at times just fall into a brief Three Musketeers interaction as on crossing paths going to the toilet for instance. I guess we were trying to facilitate our tolerating what had and was happening to us; I guess it helped us feel we were not completely victims. I assume that Savic and our third musketeer—whose name I can't remember—might have been doing the same. We could fight evil, even if only in play, that medium which children use naturally to cope with fear, with anxiety and stress. We played it, we played it, and we played it. It must have worked fairly effectively for us, otherwise, we would have soon abandoned the game.

The other way we tried to go on living was by dancing. We did this a few times only, early during our stay in Rivesaltes. The first barrack in which we were housed had a small entry area partitioned from the rest of the dormitory-like barrack. It was probably 10 by 6 feet. Whose idea it was, what made us think we could dance—that is actually not step on each other's toes—how we would in fact do so, I can't recall. I guess it was a community-of-5 effort. The fact is that here we were two girls and three boys about 11 years old, give a year on either side, dancing to quietly provided music. I provided the music. During my earliest elementary school years in Bruxelles, I found that singing put me in a special state of feeling. It feels oddly good to sing; a unique and special good, to sing. It probably is not so surprising; my mother occasionally would sing; I liked it when she sang. I recall singing in the choir in school in Bruxelles, as I would do again later, in the U. S. Those times in Rivesaltes my singing was subdued; whether to not disturb the others on the other side of the partition, whether out of embarrassment, or out of a feeling that to sing and dance at this time, in this place, was a paradoxical thing to be doing. I don't know. Whatever mixed feelings we experienced as we tried to go on living, we danced to my quietly singing tunes popular during that time. J'attendrai—which was no doubt derived from the intermezzo in Puccini's Madama Butterfly where Cho Cho San, Suzuki, and Trouble, the young child, asleep, are waiting the return of Pinkerton; a sad, beautiful musical line—was one of my favorites. Just as Cho Cho San does, the lyrics in J'attendrai—not provided by Puccini or his librettist—speak to waiting for the soldier's return from war, "Day and night, I'll await your return. . . forever."

We were kids 11-12 years old. Until you are at death's door, life goes on.

The Move to Rivesaltes' Jewish Ghetto

Some time in March 1941, we were translocated yet a further circle downward into hell. I think, under the pretext of the soon to come Passover Holidays, and the wishes of our host government to duly respect our religious rituals and food requirements, we were told that the Jews in Rivesaltes would be relocated to an area in the Camp apart from the others. I wonder if one of those miserable Nazis in Vichy—ahead of the German Nazis "final solution"—had the clever thought that this was a Jew-given occasion to create yet a further ghetto within this already bleak ghetto, further separating out the Jews from the rest of this abominable universe. This translocation, it came down to us, would accommodate our pessachdicker (Passover-worthy) needs. Matzoh would not be distributed to the wrong people. Consider, what if matzoh was given to Spanish refugees? Not that there were any in our barracks. But with this act I found out that there were other than Jews imprisoned here in Rivesaltes; the Vichy Nazis had also imprisoned Spanish asylum-seekers. Were there yet other Vichy France undesirables in Rivesaltes?

So we were chosen again. This time it was in an effort by our hosts to see to it that our pessachdicker meals not be contaminated with their abundant non-pessachdicker products! I heard no expressions of appreciation by any among us. On the contrary, the reactions in the air transmitted that this announcement was not good news. Most likely, it was Vichy-France-government mandated, not just an improvised way some thoughtful camp administrators had of respecting and protecting the Jews' Passover.

The move to the "Jewish Quarter" further degraded our living conditions. Our new barracks were grayer and in a worse state of deterioration then the ones we just left. In these, for reasons not clear to me we seemed more chilled by that ever-present southern French wind. The French respect their winds; in fact they have identified several and given them names, like Le Mistral or La Tramontane. Here we were afflicted by La Tramontane. The walls at least protected us against its outright cold chill. Our emaciating bodies and sparse clothing were just not up to its cutting cold. I am not certain whether it is the same wind that so flagellated us in that Toulouse snowstorm. More than Le Mistral, La Tramontane is an established Southern France wind that in winter has a cutting chill, which I am certain is what earned it its not so pleasant reputation and what deemed it deserving of a name. One does not say, simply, "C'est du tramontane" as if one said "It's just wind," one says "C'est La Tramontane," "It's The Tramontane," like "It's the Grand Inquisitor." Maybe, in fact, La Tramontane's northern source was further cold-tempered by air-flows coming from the Pyrénées Mountains, that high-reaching frontier that separates and binds France and Spain.

We had no choice; we settled in. The weather these past months, apart from the Toulouse storm, was the worst we had yet experienced since we left Bruxelles; it was now getting to the end of our first homeless winter. It was a serious matter because not having winter clothing had compelled improvisation of warming garments. Our blankets served as coats. I know that I was not alone in finding that my shoes were now no longer protective of my feet. They must have reached a sufficient point of uselessness that my mother—don't ask me where she got it—made me a pair of shoes out of blanket material. Whose blanket? All I know is that my seamstress mother had made me a new pair of shoes. They worked.

Until Pessach (Passover) came, our diet was not much different than before. Maybe it all seemed just a little more gray. Rutabagas, turnips, very watery soup—really it was barely more than water with some effort at seasoning. And our two daily pieces of grayish-brown bread. To the best of my recollection, the brown syrup ran out, or at least was no longer part of our diet. Then came Pessach. Actually the diet did not change from that just described except that now, instead of bread, we got Matzoh! I am certain it was made of straw, if not entirely, at least in part! It tasted like straw; I can't be sure since though I have put straw in my mouth, I have never eaten any. It was like straw. Of course, Pessach lasted only 8 days. We returned to gray bread. I love matzoh. This was not Matzoh. But this was not Bruxelles.

Kids, at least kids like me of which there are zillions, actually find idleness a really boring and "this isn't right" kind of thing. I had not opened a book for some months now. But even though in Recebedou we had no books, at least we had some kind of learning-instruction going on. I am certain that all the teaching was by word of mouth; no books. Even so, we had some teaching! Now we had no teaching except, given our prevailing condition, how to deal with insufficient food, how to best protect ourselves when attending to our toileting needs, how to cope with the cold, how to try to stay alive in an all-but-hollow life in this second circle of Inferno. This problem did not escape the grown-ups evidently, as Vivette Samuel notes of 1942 in Rivesaltes, that to help the internees 'get out of idleness' ("sortir de l'oisivité") was just as important as augmenting their food rations. My sense is that, what made things bearable for me in this ideleness was that I had my mother, and she had me, and I had my imagination. I never contemplated that this was the end for us. But then, this was still early 1941.

Testing my imagination, how to cope with the cold gave me an assignment and responsibility that I welcomed. It must have made me feel useful; I was doing something for us. Since I can remember, I have always liked being a "Boy Scout." To do my duty, I would go out by myself usually, potato sac in hand—I have no idea where my mother got a small potato sac—, and search among the low-lying bushes in the camp, mostly briar, for any piece of burnable wood. Actually, I think most of the wood came from the briar itself, dead briar. Finding dead wood in briar bushes is not without risk. Briar protects itself with seriously prickly spines against those who would uproot it or do it whatever harm. These are not rose-thorns; these are sewing-needle size spines, big ones. Of course, none of us gathered enough dead wood on our own to accommodate our needs; but I did feel that I helped. The cold was serious. In Bruxelles, which is quite colder than the foothills of the Pyrénées, we had the clothes we needed to cope with it and of course, our home was warm and comfortable. In fact, I remember with deeply felt well-being, the warmth of approaching evening and dinner in our premier étage home, 6 Rue de l'Economie. Somehow in winter it was always cozier, warmer than at other times. In Riversaltes, we were not sartorially equipped to handle La Tramontane in winter and the gray cold of this bleak universe.

Dealing with Nature's elements got significantly worse when it rained. The mix of Southern France winter temperature and wind did not reach freezing levels—which could at least have provided us with firmer ground. Had we had freezing weather, freezing according to the laws of Physics, I might have thought otherwise. In any case, the freezing mix of wind and rain made staying indoors compelling. But of course, we did need to occasionally go out there. As I noted earlier, the challenge of avoiding inches-deep mud puddles in a mud path, knowing that we would have to relieve ourselves in the abysmal toileting accommodations to which we were restricted, made going to the toilet a very unpleasant undertaking. The only saving factors in the exercise were to get rid of waste products our bodies just could not contain and, in that space between our barrack and the odoriferous toileting island, to get some fresh air, even when it was wet and cold.

My knowledge of European history about this era, 1940 to 1945, repeated readings notwithstanding, seems to never sink into my brain. I know pieces; I have trouble putting them together. Interesting, how for one who graduated from every school I attended with High Honors—except for Music School where I only managed Honors because of my downfall, Solfeggio—, I can't put these pieces of information together in proper sequence. My brain doesn't want to cooperate in my effort. That's now. But then, having just finished 5th Grade in Bruxelles, I was not into History or Current Events, except for those that directly affected us. But no doubt, the adults knew some things that were going on then about which I had no idea whatsoever. It was not by accident, nor that my mother was getting tired of the life we traded in to get out of Belgium ahead of the advancing Germans. Information not available to me had gotten to her, is my guess, that the Jews were in serious trouble, even in Vichy-France, supposedly free from the Germans.

As I think of it now, my mother knew something very bad about our fate. I was not looking ahead; she was. The question seemed to me to come out of the blue, except that I had grasped something she and Savic's mother had been talking about. When we were alone, she presented the issue, the big question, I guess one of the biggest questions in my life. She told me that she wanted me to escape from Rivesaltes! She made it a statement of her wish, but she did pose it as a question. She conveyed its seriousness and risk. She was telling me and she was asking me if I would escape without her; she really did want to know my response. Without her, that was the big part. I saw her wish on her face. "Yoh, Ma, ch'vet teen vus du zugst" ("Yes, Ma, I'll do what you say"), is most likely what I would have said to her in Bruxellois Yiddish.

Our life together had made me fairly self-reliant, within limits of my age. She knew I could do things on my own, some things. I trusted her; and she could count on me to do what she wanted me to do. That was our history, my mother and me.

The Question of Escaping from Rivesaltes

Evidently by the time my mother told me she wanted me to escape from Rivesaltes, it was evident that she and Savic's parents had been talking about us, Savic and me, escaping from Rivesaltes together. There was wisdom in this, in that Savic and I were frequently together at this time. We were two of the Three Musketeers. Why the third boy was not included in this scheme, I don't know. It could account for my not remembering his name. I do know this though, that I had come to like Savic's mother; his father too, though he seemed less aware of "the kids"; his parents were nice people. Savic's father looked like a well-educated but not easily approachable man; his mother was a bright and warm woman. So our parents had been scheming, and Savic and I, the musketeers, had been totally unaware of it.

Why did this question of escape come up at this time, or at all? It was clear that the idea defied existing law, the law of Vichy-France, Unoccupied, Free-France. Vive la France-Libre! Yes, we had chosen to come to France. But we had not chosen to come to Rivesaltes, nor Recebedou or any of this. By 12 you have a pretty good idea about law and breaking law. Where did my mother and Savic's parents learn that this should even be contemplated? Did they get news about the murder of Jews in Eastern Europe? I guess it is not surprising that I did not hear any radio in our barrack. None of us had one. If there was one, it was hidden and probably only a few people would have been privy to it. I do remember at times hearing vague talk among the grown-ups, sotto voce, about ravages against the Jews in Poland, the kind of you're-not-supposed-to-hear-thing kids all over the world are annoyed with by grown-ups. Grown-ups always seem to have things to say that must be said with the kids around but they don't want the kids to hear. And kids always get dribs and drabs of it and are left to their own devices to sort these out—designed imagination-stirring.

But we were living in that surround; there was always a worry-weighted cloud of audible phrases and bits of talk between grown-ups about the hurts and threats against us Jews. Actually that was there even before we left Bruxelles, it was part of the ambiance of anti-Semitism in Europe. But as one might expect, since our compelled rush out of Belgium, except for the three months in Village, this cloud of threats was with us at a much more real level. This threat-surround progressively increased in intensity, as we were moved to récébédou, then to Rivesaltes, and then to the Jewish ghetto within Rivesaltes. I think the audible and emotion-weighted surround was heating up. I don't know which made me much more aware of the worry-surround: an actual increase in its intensity or my mother's telling me that she wanted me to escape from Rivesaltes. I'm not sure it matters which came first.

According to Nora Levin, at just about this time, in March 1941, following Hitler's "demand," Nazi troops started to mass-murder the Jews of Eastern Europe. "The Final Solution" was not yet declared. It was just a much more virulent advance from Kristallnacht, November 9, 1938, to mass murders in Eastern Europe, before the Wannsee Conference and the legalization of "The Final Solution." This culmination of Nazi barbarism would be activated a year from this time, in April or May 1942. BabiYar, outside of Kiev, would happen later too, on September 19, 1941. We were now in April 1941. My repeated readings of Marrus and Paxton, William Shirer, Nora Levin* and other sources over the years informed me that the mass massacre of Jews in Poland and Russia by the German Nazi troops was now beginning. I knew nothing of that then. But I would guess that our adults somehow knew. Knowing my mother, she knew. I assume that Savic's mother and father, and other grown ups knew. Sometimes grown ups just know; they find out things kids never can.

I did not weigh the pros and cons of my mother's wish, that I escape without her. I don't know if it was too difficult for me to think about, whether I was just too young to really know how to compute this question, or what. Looking back, I had no way of measuring the consequences of such a venture. It was not even a question of that. To me the question was, if my mother thought this is what I should do, this is what I would do. I was growing up. I was now 12. I would do what she said. To a degree I knew, and evidently she knew, that once out, I would figure out what I needed to do. But the question of escape from Riversaltes, that, I didn't even contemplate; it was all her idea.

At the start, plans were that Savic and I would escape together. My mother and I talked together; I don't know what Savic and his parents did. We, the two families, kids included, did not all talk together. The grown ups talked together. My mother told me what to do in broad strokes: from the barrack, to the road to Perpignan, to the train station in Perpignan and the purchase of a train ticket to Marseille, to my destination there, a specific address, that of the OSE, Oeuvre de Secours aux Enfants (Work [or Action] of Rescue [or Help] of Children). How

---

* The Holocaust: The Destruction of European Jewry, 1933-1945 by Nora Levin. New York: Thomas Y. Crowell Company, 1968.

Vichy France and the Jews by Michael R. Marrus and Robert O. Paxton, published by Schocken Books, NY,1983.

The Rise and Fall of The Third Reich by William Shirer, published by Simon and Schuster, NY, 1960.

she got that address is not clear to me. According to Vivette Samuel, the OSE would get one and then two Social Workers volunteer to serve us, encamped in Rivesaltes. Samuel, who wrote a memoires of her work with the OSE—which while a Jewish Social Service type organization was protected from incarceration—, Sauver Les Enfants (Save the Children) arrived in Rivesaltes in December 1941. So she got there after my escape. At this moment my best guess is that my mother got the OSE's address, rue de L'Italie in Marseille, from one of the workers who was already in Rivesaltes before young Vivette Samuel came in late 1941.

In any case, my mother got the OSE address. She would give me money for the train ticket. She no doubt learned from that OSE worker what it would cost for a train ticket from Perpignan to Marseille. Of course, I had to travel inconspicuously, so I would not carry a bag of any kind with my clothes in it. Being clothes-minded I guess, as a seamstress, she told me that I would wear double layers of everything, including pants. Thank goodness she didn't expect me to wear two pairs of cloth shoes; that would have been un peu drôle (a bit funny). The day selected was May 1. The reasoning was that this being Labor Day in Europe, there would be fewer guards on sentinel duty around the periphery's barbed wire fence. That barbed wire—not electified as some would be in the East—was only about three to four feet high, and besides, I knew that there were spots where there wasn't any. The French are not as efficient as the Germans; the whole world knows that.

Our planning was pretty well done. What about Savic? I am not sure how I felt about it, but several days before May 1, Savic's parents let us know that they had changed their minds; Savic is not going. Whether this came from his mother? His father? Or Savic himself, I do not know. So, I was to go alone. My mother was set; she must have felt certain that things were going to get worse soon. I got the impression that she did not want to take a chance in delaying. Interestingly, I have later read that two months after my May 1 escape, in July 1941, the Vichy government instituted yet still greater restrictions on the French Jews who then were not yet interned in camps as were the asylum-seeking Foreign Jews.

My mother was determined, and I was set. Where did she get the courage to let me go? I know that it was not easy for her to do this. She had already lost her first-born when she left Poland eight or so years earlier. My mother and father had separated while we all were still in Lodz, Poland. How long they had been separated before my mother and I left Poland for Belgium, I do not know. But the fact is that when my mother and I left Poland, my mother left my brother, her first-born with our father, my maternal and paternal grandparents and their large families. Knowing my mother as I did, as I do, she most likely felt two things. First, that my brother was in safe hands with our father and our large families in Lodz, that he would be well cared for, and perhaps even that he would be more secure there than in the unknown universe into which she was going and was taking me. Second, she probably felt that she could not manage by herself with two very young children. In fact, for a period of time, I don't know how long before she settled into work (a seamstress) in Bruxelles, she placed me in a Catholic orphanage, of which I have memories to this day: some really nice Nun-teachers in Kindergarten, one I found especially pretty; a big bully I tried to get off my back by giving him the few coins my mother gave me when she came to visit, and a state of low-keyedness especially reflected in my reaction of wonder when I saw the first snowdrops breaking out of the ground to announce better times ahead. These few notes of background may explain sufficiently why I ask, how could my mother make the determination that she wanted me to escape, that she wanted us to separate.

I think she could do it because, she told me at the time that she would very soon follow me. Years later Savic's mother would tell me that, she in fact did escape from Rivesaltes, but she was somehow found, probably reported by some loyal Vichy French antisemite, and she was returned to Rivesaltes. And when I have considered the question, Why was she among those chosen from Rivesaltes to be sent to Auschwitz the following year, I wonder if her having escaped (and been recaptured) had been a factor in her being selected for extermination. As Primo Levi noted, a simple Yes or a No could do it. Nearly two hundred years before, Franz Schubert had put Wilhelm Mueller's poems into song, one of which spoke to the "zwei kleine Woertchen . . . die beiden Woertchen schliessen die ganze Welt hinein" (the two little words contain the whole world for me).

Escape from Rivesaltes

1 May, 1941. I think I slept well-enough, the night into May 1. We were up fairly early. We waited till after we were regaled with our morning piece of bread. I absolutely do not remember our good-byes.

I probably could not bear it. I probably rejected its imprinting in my memory. Knowing my mother and me, we no doubt hugged and held one another somewhat longer than usual. I was to be inconspicuous from beginning to end. I felt odd and somewhat uncomfortable, with double layers of underclothes, socks, shirts and pants. I was already very skinny by then, so I probably did not look over-bloated. I don't know if I even said good-by to Savic or his mother. I left, armed with the small potato sac I had used for prior expeditions in our limited environs, on duty to collect wood for our still occasionally needed source of heat.

I walked to the specified outer area of the camp, in the direction that would head me toward the highway to Perpignan, as close as possible to the camp-adjacent elevated twin railroad tracks. I played the part well, I think, of taking seriously the task of bending down to pick up dead bits of wood among the briar. Casually I looked around to see where the guards were located. I was in luck; I didn't see any guards at all—maybe they were all in the latrine at once; who knows. I bent down, and still seeing no one, I dropped to the ground. With that, I could feel my whole body racing, no doubt my heart bounding. I know how I react when I get a sudden scare. Dropping to the ground frightened me. I now guess that I felt my escape set in motion just by this act. I had not felt any fear before that moment.

Determined now, I started to crawl toward the mound-elevated train track. I soon found that what I knew before of the briar was so, the live bushes had big spines that hurt when, not in my plans, I hit them head on. I used the potato sac to shield my hands and forearms as I crawled, more carefully but just as quickly as I could. Within some 20 or 30 feet from the train-track-mound I stopped, raised my head slowly as little as I needed to again see if there were any sentinels, and saw none. The mound rose about 5 feet high. Bracing myself for it, I quickly bounded up and started to run. I cleared the mound, the tracks and landed on the other side of it. Shielded now from direct view from camp-side, I had not stopped; semi-crouched I continued to run, more scared now than before. I ran like hell. I was running scared shitless through a still barren vineyard, the ground was sandy, I tripped on something, crashed harmlessly into the ground, immediately got myself back up and continued to run as if I hadn't stopped. Beyond the vineyard I continued my course through more vision-protective shrubs and trees. Once in those, feeling less visible, I slowed my pace some; I didn't stop. Unexpectedly, I had reached the highway. Good fortune had it that the highway was sided by three or so feet ditches that ran along each side, all the way from where I met the highway to Perpignan. This, I guess my mother didn't know, that there was a protective ditch I could use for as long as it went and as I needed. Also fortunate, there was no water in the long ditch, nearly a trench, along the road.

The macadam paved road, a two-lane, unmarked affair—of course this is 1941—ran to Perpignan, some 10 kilometers into the city. I marched as best and as fast as I could in the ditch. 1 May; no farmers in the fields; I doubt anyone saw me during those kilometers into Perpignan. My guess is that I got there at about 2 or 3 in the afternoon. Once into the small city—Perpignan was still small when we revisited in 1997—I had no difficulty finding the railroad station. I made a point of not looking into anyone's face, as we do when we hope no one will see us. I can't tell if I looked unusual. Skinny kids I guess were not a novelty then, anywhere. I worried most about my cloth shoes, that they might give me away as a penniless, homeless waif and who knows where he might've come from. Perpignan was not a war devastated zone; to the best of my knowledge, the Germans had not dropped bombs on Vichy-France. There were no signs of bombs anywhere; its not as though I could have been taken for some poor orphaned kid whose parents got killed when their house was blown to bits by some bomb. To be as invisible as possible was one of my prime tasks. But I had to buy a train ticket.

I got to the train station, had no difficulty seeing the ticket counter; as casually as I could I asked for a ticket for the next train to Marseilles and its cost. The next train was at about 11 p.m. that evening. I had the money needed, handed it over; I think the clerk didn't even look at me. To my relief, the clerk just handed me the ticket and some change.

Once I got my ticket, I realized to my distress that I had hours to wait. It was about mid-afternoon and the train left late that night. I could not stay in the station. I needed a secluded place where I could hide until nightfall at least. What in the world led me to decide on one of those everywhere-in-France enclosed public toilets as a hiding place? Not difficult to figure out: find a toilet with cubicles with doors and I had it made. Not a savory place, but it would keep me hidden.

Hiding from early afternoon until an 11 p.m. train departure time in a toilet stall I can see to this day, is not one of my favorite memories. I don't see the inside of the stall, I see the view of the stalls one gets on entering the toilet. I was not bored in that stall. I was out of Rivesaltes even if only for a few hours, with the promise of more. But I hated being where I was. To this day I feel rage at having been forced to hide in a toilet stall. And on top of it, I was scared. No wonder I fell flat on my face, when we came out of the train station in Perpignan many, many years later. Well, not exactly on my face; I gashed my knee falling when it hit the edge of a curb; I just did not see the sidewalk elevation from the street when we were searching for the car rental we had engaged from the U.S. This is when Rachel, our son Karl, his wife Sabina, and their children, Eli and Arthur, and I got to Perpignan in 1997. We were traveling from Barcelona into France with an itinerary first to see Rivesaltes, then go to Bésseige to search out any sign of Rachel's mother's past and origins, then to the *Côte D'Azur* to visit St. Raphaël, then Marseille, and by train then to Bruxelles, to see my remaining two cousins and theirs, as well as the city. For Karl it was a return to a city he discovered when he was sixteen, where he went to study cello for the summer with Edmond Baert, a then-renown Belgian cellist, but really foremost, in search and rediscovery of the cousins of my past.

Night finally came. I came out of hiding and went directly to the train station. There were more people in the train station than I had anticipated, not a crowd, but at least there were not just a few of us which might have subjected me to closer scrutiny by some people looking for trouble. I may have waited half an hour within the station waiting room before we moved onto the platform to wait for the train. The wait then was not long; I liked the darker platform better than the more lighted station. I climbed onto the train. Quite soon we were off; Perpignan was not at the beginning of the line, many were already on board; I don't know from where.

The Train to Marseille

The train was packed; standing room only! Where in the world was everyone going during this war? I actually preferred the fact that the train was crowded and I among others had to stand in the aisle. This was one of those passenger trains that has small compartments for about 6 people each, with an aisle outside of these compartment on my left when I climbed in. I notched another step in my venture when the train took off. Now the trick again and still so far was to be as invisible as I could.

In a way it was easy because, even in the aisle we were standing quite in close proximity of one another and no one seemed to stand out to be looked at. I don't know how long we had traveled so far, one hour, two, more? We traveled surrounded by a muffled sound of people in dialogue, over-ridden by the louder sound of the train running at a moderate clip. The trains did not run at the speed to which we are now accustomed in America, in Europe and elsewhere. I felt an odd feeling of near-peace, maybe it was sleepiness; I had been on my feet, had run like hell and walked a good number of kilometers and had not slept since many hours now. I had not dared fall asleep in the Perpignan public toilets. Nor had I eaten since my piece of bread in the morning. I really don't remember being hungry; I guess that without being conscious of it, I was set to not eat till I got to Marseille the next morning. It was no problem; I was not thinking of sleep nor of food as I am now that I write about it. I was rather in a state of alertness somewhat dulled by the train's moving rhythm; you know how trains in transit feel. There was more space between my standing-room-only neighbor on my right than on my left. In fact the one on my left was within two feet from me. He may have even been closer or moved closer because he quietly said to me, "Je sais d'ou tu viens." ("I know where you're coming from.")

I was scared to death. I had been running like hell, I was scared shitless much of the time up to now; this time I was petrified. I had not gone that far on my journey. To be sure, this was the end of me. I was never this close to filling my pants with the contents of my nearly empty gut. He must have sensed or seen it because he said, "N'aies pas peur, n'aies pas peur." ("Don't be frightened.") He was reassuring. His tone gave me the courage to hesitantly look at him. " T'as faim?" ("Are you hungry?") Dramatically relieved by his look and tone, I nodded my head. He must have looked me over well and for some time to so sharply get to the core of my problems: I know where you're coming from and are you hungry? He was, I would guess from his observations and his approach to me, a fairly well-schooled man. He knew, I did not, that we would soon be making a stop of substantial duration. Looking back on my journey, on a map, it is clear that our stop was in either Montpellier or Nimes, another of the facts I can't remember. One fact I remember with distinction is that he provided me with my first meal in 9 months—in the train station restaurant.

Like in train stations of years ago, the restaurant was in a rather large open gray hangar-like space, I felt uncertain still of my newly-met traveling companion, but his demeanor and what he did, in the end made me feel more than grateful to him. I ate—a whole meal. He didn't eat; he may have gotten a coffee. I don't remember what I ate; I know there was meat and vegetables. Rabbit or horse, I would guess. It was war. I was surprised when he pulled out his food ration book—first time I learned that food was being rationed in France—and the waiter tore out pieces of it as part payment for what I had consumed. Even then I realized that he had given me some of his monthly allotment of food. He did not look starved, but still, even people who weren't skinny like I was got hungry. He did not have to do this or anything; he could have just turned away and looked elsewhere. What I best remember is his sympathetic reach toward me, and what the man did. Other than that, a big "that," there was nothing remarkable about him, an average enough office employee or businessman or who knows what. I also remember that he did seem to know what I was about, and that I felt protected with him in the station. He also helped me understand at least what some of the many travelers might be doing on this train. He was going to Grenoble to ski! While we were in concentration camps, some were skiing! Of course in the Alps you can ski in May; you can pretty well ski anytime. Not all evil people, either. Life just went on, even while so many of us were imprisoned and starving in camps! I suppose that a number of the passengers were going to Grenoble too, because when I reembarked on our train Perpignan-to-Marseilles, many seats were now available; many had transferred to trains going elsewhere—which is what makes me think this was Nimes and not Montpellier. From Nimes railways fan out, going further East-slightly-bearing-south along the Méditeranée coast to Marseille, or fully north toward Paris and midway a twist East to Grenoble, or West toward Toulouse and Bordeaux. Not so for Montpellier. I ate in Nimes.

I was unpleasantly made aware of my arrival in Marseille by the train ticket collector's not so gently waking me. I am not surprised that I had fallen asleep. To this day I don't know what went through his mind. I can't be sure whether he looked annoyed or just surprised. I guess, it was a night train and he was just going through the wagons looking for passengers who like me had fallen asleep and had to get out. He might have wondered what hole did I come out of in such a state of dress. But scowling some, I thought, he just wakened me and seemed ready to move on. I quickly got out of the train; I didn't look back.

I had arrived in Marseille, yet another successful large step in my plan. It must have been past 9 in the morning, as what followed would indicate. Even now I wonder why it took so long to get from Perpignan to Marseille, from 11 or so p.m. to about 9 a.m. Except for the German army then, we did not travel then as fast as we do today. In any case, thank heaven, I got there. I knew the address I was looking for since I had left Rivesaltes, though I did search my pocket for the piece of paper on which I had written it. I asked someone, no doubt I selected a kindly disposed face, I didn't ask a gendarme or such figure, if he or she knew—can't remember if it was a man or a woman, I probably would have selected a woman—for the whereabouts and directions to my destination. My destination according to Vivette Samuel's Sauver Les Enfants, the OSE Bureau in Marseille, was on rue de l'Italie. Another piece of luck, the Bureau OSE was quite close to the train station and easily accessible. I'm pretty good with directions, so that was no problem. The problem, as it had been since I left Rivesaltes, was to get to the OSE Bureau without running into a life-spoiler. I got there.

Chapter 4

Safety – The OSE Homes

Le Bureau d' Oeuvre de Secours aux Enfants (OSE) – Marseille

As soon as I entered the room, protective arms were around my shouders. The return of the prodigal son, the return of Odysseus—except that I was unknown to them and they to me. But, what a welcome—home. I have felt this on a few occasions other than when it really was home. I felt this "welcome home" in a strange land when I got to this OSE Bureau in Marseille, and when I first visited Jerusalem, many years later. I don't know whether it was one or two of several people in the Bureau who were immediately at my side. I doubt that I even said who I was or where I came from. They knew. Of course after that reception, I immediately told them who I was and where I had come from. It was 2 May 1941. I was there for only a few hours. I am certain that they had been through this kind of thing before and by now the channels were well traveled: this kid we send to this or that OSE home. Most likely space availability and proximity to Marseille determined which OSE home.

I had the good fortune of being sent to the home in Boulouris on the *Côte d'Azur*, between Toulon and Cannes, much closer to Cannes than Toulon.

Boulouris – *La Feuille*

The OSE home in Boulouris named *La Feuille* (the leaf) was an asylum and oasis, I mean asylum in the generic meaning of the word, not like it has been used to mean a hospital protective for mentally ill people. Almost from my first day there, the protective ambiance, the people in it, devoted, determined, caring social-service-type people and the refugee kids like me, my insides calmed. The inner strain, not that gripping gut twisting I experienced escaping, but that entire body strain which had taken hold of me since we left Bruxelles—except for some time in Village—left me. Even though I was separated from my mother, this felt really good; no doubt the vice-gripping stress of escaping had rapidly relaxed and now was over.

The OSE's protective hand; overnight I felt good. I felt that since I had escaped and did have the feeling that I was in protective custody by some power that could counter or at least withstand Vichy-France's miserable actions against Jews, I knew that my mother could escape and would do so soon. I felt relief.

Boulouris, then, was no more than a village, not large enough to be considered a town. Now 60 years later, it is lost within the melding of one village to the next by the massive expansion of vacation homes and tourism on the Cote d'Azur. Boulouris was a haven, well deserving, then even more than now, of its reputable balm and beauty. La Feuille was situated on a curving small macadam road—the road elevating slightly from its origin to its meandering end somewhere—behind a low wall close to the road. One went into a rod iron-gate that I think was always open. A sandy-graveled substantial court was the entry area to the Home. It was an old, long established villa-type, with massive but house-proportioned stone and masonry structure. La Feuille, situated near the road, was set on a substantial piece of estate where many of our camp-like—wait, I mean "summer camp"-like, not the second-circle-in-hell-camp I just left behind—activities took place.

As best as I can remember, the staff consisted of 3 social-worker type adults, one man probably in his late 20s or 30s, called Mora, one woman a few years younger than him called Aranka, and one senior, admirable woman by the name of Masour, we called her "*Madame Masour.*" We called her "Madame Masour," prefaced by the formal "*Madame*" and her last name—I learned from Vivette Samuel that she was indeed Germaine Masour, a social worker who spent 20 years serving the OSE—whereas we called the other two by their first names [I think it was their first names], Mora and Aranka. I guess we sensed that Madame Masour was the matriarch of the Home, even though, I am left with the feeling that we did not see her with the everyday regularity with which we saw Mora and Aranka. Madame Masour was a warm, dignified lady who could be casual, caregiving, and comforting with you. She really conveyed a sense of secure and committed shouldering of responsibility for us; she was admirable. Mora, I hate to admit, was my favorite. He was warm, kind, engaged with us 24 hours a day. So was Aranka; I really liked Aranka too.

"Good luck for America." Aranka and Mora in front of *La Villa* Mariana. St. Raphael, circa 1941

Also memorable were two other women we saw daily. Inez was the chef, homemaker, grounds-keeper, you name it, she did it. She was warm, friendly, kind and always very nicely responsive to interchanges with me, and from what I saw, the others as well. I think she would have liked to be a man because she cropped her hair short like a man's—which was not in style then—and she wore men's clothes—also not in style then. I say this only to convey my world then. And Inez had the cutest all-chores assistant named Julie or Julia. She was about 19 or 20. She was not only pretty and lively, but she too was very pleasant with the kids.

Now, I am not delusional when I say that all these staff were felt by us to be really warm, caring, protective people. They were. Whether they were that way in their private lives, I have no way of knowing. But I say they were so with us. It may be that, in addition to their just being very nice people, the life circumstances we all experienced made for that kind of mutual caring and positive relatedness among us. Other than for Inez and Julia who were from the region, we were a persecuted lot, the staff may have felt we are in a time of war, injustice, maltreatment, and hardship, and they were committed to make life as good for us kids as they could. They knew our lot, the kids'. Each of us was a "war-orphan" for the time being. Some may then already have become "war-orphans" for always. Some of us were so only temporarily. Combining with this warm ambiance was a sense that in this home we could be shielded and defended against the malevolent authorities that could put us in hell. Since Récébédou, and especially since Rivesaltes, I no longer felt secure in Vichy France, even in the face of my mother's efforts to be protective. Even with her Vichy France could put us in hell; my mother was still there.

Here, I somehow felt those who could harm us could not reach into these walls; I felt safe; and, devoted, good-hearted, responsible grown-ups surrounded us.

The kids there contributed to the character and quality of this environment. I may have come away from my experience in the OSE home(s)—there was another one I'll get to shortly—biased favorably beyond its merits. But I do not think so. Whether we felt we were all in this boat together, which we were, or what benevolent forces were at play in this time of malevolence toward us, we kids got along. I'm sure there must have been the normal childhood rivalries, envies and jealousies. We all had suffered much fear, threat, distress, let alone now one year of hunger, homelessness, loss of family, and more; and there was very good psychological explanation for the accumulation of plenty of hostility within us, each of us. But it did not get expressed toward one another. It may have when I was not there, yes; but I would have known if it had because then one feels it, it's in the air, on people's faces, in their voices or in their silence. It's unusual for a group of kids; I never heard about or heard any talk of fights between two kids, between two boys or between two girls. We were living in unusual times, in fact for Jews and other persecuted minorities these were awful times and they were yet to become as bad as we all know they got. Maybe the unusual times did it. The best I can come up with now for this remarkable peaceful co-existence within a population that quite normally could be expected to at times come to clashes, is that we were all turning toward one another with good will, almost to protect ourselves and one another against a common dreaded external enemy. Anna Freud and Dorothy Burlingham, two Child Psychoanalysts in London at the time, found and later reported how among very young war-orphans, even two and three year-olds turned to help each other in times of distress among any one of them. The type of explanation I just put forward has been given by other psychology-types like me. The explanation has much merit.

But as I think of it today, perhaps yet another thing operating in my experience then made my being in the OSE home so positive. There were stark differences between récébédou-Rivesaltes on one hand, and Boulouris-St. Raphaël on the other. The most stark was this: when we left Belgium, we had sought asylum in France and we were treated with shameful indignity and incarcerated in two stations into hell; we were

Les garçons—Boulouris—2 June 1941—"La Feuille"
Mme. Masour (back row, second from right); Henri, 12 (first from right with saluting friend on his shoulders), three months after the escape from Rivesaltes

put there against our will by reasons of malignant distortions about us, by malignant prejudice. And then, trusting my mother's wisdom and wishes, when I sought asylum at the Bureau OSE, I got genuine asylum, not prison and rationalized, programmed degradation. As I look back and try to grasp the differences in what I experienced in Rivesaltes as compared to St. Raphaël—*La Villa Mariana*—in Rivesaltes I was dumped into muddy gray misery—hell is not just fire—whereas in St. Raphaël, even separated from my mother, I felt I was in a protecting, caring, and even healing environment.

There were about 25 kids in the home, most between the ages of 6 and 14. The two oldest among us, two girls about 13, 14. Though we were all together in most activities from eating to just lulling about, these girls were somewhat separate from the rest of us, I don't know just why. Maybe because they were really starting to become young women, in terms of their body changes. Of course, boys and girls slept in separate rooms, rooms of boys and rooms of girls; there was no large dormitory-like room. There was increasing familiarity among us since there were no kids leaving and there were no new arrivals after I got there. When I got there the kids seemed already to be a group with some cohesion though true, more the boys with the boys and the girls with the girls.

We ate together. Food was no doubt scarce even among people who were not interned in concentrations camps, as I learned in the restaurant in the Nimes train station. But given what I had learned in that restaurant, even though food was rationed, I knew that most French in Vichy-France were eating much better than we were. And no doubt some French were eating quite handsomely, even shamelessly. There must have been some explanation why dinner often consisted of only one vegetable; and why that particular vegetable featured as dinner day after day. Fortunately, not rutabagas or turnips. Actually, a very good vegetable to my taste, chickpeas, was the one I remember best. We had chickpeas many times. Food portions, of minimalist dimensions, were much like in Rivesaltes but somehow it seemed altogether more bearable. We ate the little we ate in our OSE "home," not in hell. It may also be that by now I had come to not expect more. And eating in the home was not an isolated, hoarding type of experience. We were all together, talking, laughing, eating chickpeas in a caring, congenial environment. This is not so surprising to me. We know in my line of work that the emotional environment in which the child is fed is more critical than what the child is fed, so long as there is enough to meet the child's physical needs. Well, I found out that this does happen even if there isn't enough to meet the child's physical need. So, even when half starving, in a warm, loving environment, kids can laugh and enjoy living. We all go a long way on good emotional fueling. I really don't recall any complaints of being hungry, of wanting more than one was getting. There may have been; I didn't seeing any. Was this factual? Is it my wishfully ameliorating what it was like? That is possible. But I have to trust what I remember. As we say in my work, within actuality-bound limits, the reality that one perceives is psychologically more real than the actual reality. Sometimes that's good; sometimes that's bad. It's like Rashomon where three observers of the same reality report it quite differently; but none of them invents that a murder happened. On that, they were in accord. The Holocaust happened! I didn't dream it.

Speaking of eating one of the things I, and no doubt we all, enjoyed, there was joining in on the various harvests of edibles that occurred in the regions at their appropriate times of the year. One I associate with Boulouris was the fig harvesting. I may be wrong, the season time does not associate well with what I believe happened, but I associate figs with Boulouris and grapes with St. Raphaël. Whether it was in Boulouris or

St. Raphaël, I do see myself in a fig tree gathering figs, gently when they feel soft; even more gently when they are not yet soft so as to not disturb them; and less restrained when they are full-bellied and though close to ripe ready for the picking, by the hands-full, eating some and putting some in a basket. Everyone knows figs and fig-tree leaves. But not everyone knows that some fig trees are small and some are large. These were large—for a fig tree—and you climbed into them to get the fruit. We had earned that work opportunity, gathering luscious fruit, when we were near-starving. But like with everything else in life, too much of a good thing tends to backfire. With figs as compared to grapes—which I'll get to shortly—a belly ache is more likely than diarrhea for which grapes are well known. These were really good figs, whether you were hungry or not. I must say though that I have infrequently met a fig that was not really good.

Given my skin reaction—which has waxed and waned in the course of this writing—I must say a few words about our sleeping accommodations. We each had a single normal bed (not thick wires stretched between two-by-fours), with a real everyday covered mattress (not a straw-filled skin excoriating sac), we had sheets and blanket(s), the sheet protecting me against attack on my skin by direct contact with wool. For me, this was not just a trivial difference between Rivesaltes and the OSE Boulouris-St. Raphaël home.

Another notable difference between the OSE home and Rivesaltes was that in the OSE home I was provided with clean clothes and a pair of shoes. Those not accustomed to walking barefoot—not that this would have been wise in the cold of winter in Southern France or in Boston or Chicago—or who wear shoes made of wood or of blanket material, know what a marvel a regular pair of leather shoes can be. It makes much sense that, like we see in some war movies, soldiers in the field of battle will rob the dead of their boots; in time, shoes and even boots do wear out. By the time I arrived in Boulouris, my blanket-cloth shoes were ready for the trash can; happily they gave me a decent pair of leather shoes. Of course, even though the double layers of clothes I put on to travel from Perpignan to Marseille lasted me for some time beyond my arrival in Boulouris, in due time I was supplied with a very reasonable wardrobe equipping me quite well to accommodate nicely to changes in seasonal climate.

For reasons I can only guess at, actually they may have been positive reasons, we moved from Boulouris to the environs of St. Raphaël, some 5 to 10 kilometers closer to Cannes. This may have been in July or even as late as August 1941. Several possible reasons present themselves. First, I think that the estate, I would call it, into which we moved, *La Villa* Mariana, was larger and better situated for a bunch of children than was La Feuille. For instance, getting to a swimming cove tailor-made for kids, a really magnificent and protected jewel of Mediterranean Cote d'Azur—I see it now and will always remember it for its unique beauty and variety of water offerings including water play in shallow areas, deep swimming areas around the horseshoe-shaped cove, protected from the outside world by magnificent walls of rocks on each side that rose to one hundred feet above water from which now and then someone would do a breath-taking swan-dive, an awesome sight—was less than a mile from *La Villa* Mariana. Second, once the school term started, I think in September, we were registered to go to school, and the school in St. Raphaël was located within reasonable walking distance from *La Villa* Mariana, whereas getting to school from Boulouris would have been a much longer trek. Exactly when we moved, I don't know. Perhaps two or three months of my getting to Boulouris. I liked La Feuille, but I liked *La Villa* Mariana more.

St. Raphaël—*La Villa Mariana*

La Villa Mariana was a nearly-cubic structure, elegant, I would guess with rather substantial stucco-covered stone blocks used as bricks might have been. It was really a lovely old, I thought then a quite large Villa. I have a photo of Julie sitting on the banister of the broad front porch. To move there in the summer time—today I might think of it as going for a summer to the *Côte d'Azur*. That's today. But even then, in 1941, even with the threat of Nazism, German, French, Italian, Hungarian Nazism, European Nazism in brief, on a *pois chiches* (chickpeas) diet, with the ambiance we brought from Boulouris, all of us together, no one being left behind, it was lovely. Amazing how, being away from descent-into-hell-Rivesaltes, could make *La Villa Mariana*, with the people and the emotional surround we all brought to it, even without my mother there . . . could make *La Villa* be such a haven. I am not the only one to speak of the OSE homes this way; there were quite a number of us, kids then, who found the same life-saving experience there.

Other than being translocated from Boulouris to St. Raphaël, it was he same OSE universe. No character changes, no ambiance changes, only the physical surround. But I do remember the surround quite well. I will admit to the possibility, the probability, that in some details I am mistaken. Wait! In no way do I mean that I am inventing anything. I am inventing nothing. It happened. This story happened. The details are somewhat trivial against the facts that are, I know, unequivocal: the Germans marched into Belgium, we ran for asylum to France, we went to Village, then we were ordered by the powers-that-be, the government of Vichy-France via the local *gendarmerie* (police), to show up in an appointed place at an appointed time in Toulouse, then were transported to Récébédou, then Rivesaltes, and I escaped from that downward-into-hell hole. The details to which I am referring are: where did we get heat in Rivesaltes? Was there heat? Was there a pot-bellied stove? No. There was heat from a small wood fire made outside the barrack. Was there a stove in Récébédou? Of that I am not as certain as I like to be. I have written what I have imbedded in memory and believe I experienced; this is not an invention. If I am mistaken about some details, I am not about the picture.

I do remember a number of things about St. Raphaël, even to my own amazement. Life was bearable in St. Raphaël, even though I was separated from my mother; those who made up St. Raphaël made life actually better than just bearable, in a number of ways they even made it good. I will remember St. Raphaël always; but the way it was then, the way it still was in 1953 when I visited there and took a few photographs; not the way it was when we visited in 1997 when it was saturated with houses and milling people and snarling traffic, over-crowded in ways typical of many vacationing areas today.

Thank heaven the sleeping accommodations did not change from Boulouris to St. Raphaël except for the place, the location. My group of boys, it may actually have been all the boys, were housed for sleeping purposes in a small house-like structure separated from the Villa proper, like a larger than average garage or carriage-house. The entire structure was committed to being our small dormitory. It was situated at the left side of the entrance of the "estate" in front of the Villa. The girls' sleeping area was in the Villa. Nor did the diet change from Boulouris to St. Raphaël. Actually, it's at *La Villa Mariana* that I especially remember the *pois chiches* (chickpeas). But I do remember distinctly a time when our diet was temporarily modified.

I suppose it was in late September or early October 1941 that we were invited to supplement our chickpeas diet with grapes. It was grape-harvesting season and a substantial vineyard owner welcomed cheap help to make his harvesting as inexpensive as he could. We learned from one of our guardians Aranka, Mora, or Mme Masour that the grape-grower had asked for help and was looking to hire some of the hardier kids who would be willing to work, for some small monetary remuneration in his vineyard. The contract as I think of it today probably was something like, help us with our grape harvest and we'll pay you a small amount of money for your labor. In addition, and this was the drawing card, you can eat all the grapes you want. Wow. Tell starving kids they can eat all the grapes they want. I remember, we were enthusiastic both in grape-picking, and not so wisely, in grape-eating. It really was a pretty good deal, quite pleasant in fact, except for the price we paid, diarrhea! Fortunately, it was not an infectious process, just some hungry kids overindulging on a natural laxative.

Starting sometime in September 1941, some 18 months after we had left Belgium, one of the everyday highlights in St. Raphaël was that we went to school, to an established French school. I liked school from my earliest beginnings; I took to studying and learning well from the start. The war hit Belgium just after I had finished fifth grade. Since then, end of April 1940, the next time I had anything like school, was the last months we were in Récébédou, I would say October-November 1940. A group of grown-ups from among the interned in récébédou organized a few classes a week, which I attended and constituted a genuine effort to keep the children's learning and studies going. To what degree the classes continued with regularity, how large the classes were, what grade levels were taught, all that I do not remember. It was an amorphous but dedicated kind of effort at giving us some schooling. But I can see the school we attended in St. Raphaël. I can see it in the fall, trees with browning leaves; a long-standing, typical, anywhere-in-Europe school, gray and wearing years of weathering; adjacent to it a quite pleasant school yard, it too a gray-but-not-drab cement surfaced area surrounded by a high fence, some stretches stone, some wire. It was good to be in school. I remember how just getting there was a gem of experiencing

I guess I really liked behaving like a Boy Scout in St. Raphaël; it really was not as good in Récébédou. I liked the march to school and back to *La Villa*; why I did is stacked with reasons. First of all, in that day, 1941-1942, walking-marching as we did along the shoreline, on a two-way semi-macadam road, lined with palm trees, a magnificent sun in fall, even in winter, and certainly in spring, this of itself made it memorable. This shoreline is what made the *Côte d'Azur* what it is known for. Then add the fact that, since I was one of the older elementary school age kids, and evidently, Mora, Aranka, and Mme Masour thought me capable of taking the group of about sixteen to twenty of us to school and made me the "group-leader"; I made it the "Scout-leader," for want of a better term. I was made responsible to march us all to school in the morning, a distance of perhaps 5 to 7 kilometers (around 3 to 4 miles) and then, mid-afternoon, back to *La Villa* after school. Even in winter I don't remember any terrible weather day. It could be that given the misery we were all going through, Mother Nature gave us a break. I must say, to this day, I think that possibly the best part of it is the way we agreed to sing as we marched to and from school. Singing, in a group, is a key piece of camp, summer camp! life for children in Europe. I suspect we sang better in the morning going to school than in the afternoon after having labored there. No doubt we were then quite tired, by mid-afternoon, kids who were skinnied by not enough food for many months by now, since September 1940, and here we were marching to school from September 1941 to April 1942. We sang better and more in the morning.

To this day I see us marching, boy-scout fashion, not like soldiers, that is, not crisp, not regulated, not so in step to the beat, singing as we went.

> *"Une fleur au chapeau, a la bouche une chanson,*
> *Un coeur joyeux et sincère,*
> *Et c'est tout ce qu'il faut à nos filles et nos garçons*
> *Pour aller au bout de la terre.*
> *Vous qui nous regardez passer sous le soleil et sous l'orage,*
> *Peut-être bien que vous pensez que nous avons bien du courage . . . ."*

> (A flower in your cap, a song on your lips,
> A heart joyous and sincere,
> And that is all that is needed for our daughters and sons
> To go to the end of the earth.
> You who watch us passing by under the sun and in storms,
> Perhaps you think we have a good deal of courage . . .)

And there were others like,

Un kilomètre a pied, ça use, ça use,
Un kilomètre a pied, ça use les souliers.

(One kilometer on foot, that uses, that uses,
One kilometer on foot, that uses up your shoes.)

This is followed by a progressively funny, repetitive refrain that goes to the point of one's wearing down one's toes. The song was funny then, but I would not have sung it when I had only cloth shoes.

There were more boys than girls in *La Villa*. In fact, there were about 12 boys close to my age; I was among the older of them, most of the others were anywhere from 1 to 3 years younger than I. From my experience, as I said before, we got along fine. I remember it as normalizing, I guess, that we would gather in the morning at *La Villa* and march to school and that we would quite predictably meet in the school yard for the march back to *La Villa*. There was a nice feel about it—at least for me and I know for two of my closer friends, Armand and (I can't remember the other's name). I do recall a couple of younger kids who seemed quite more troubled than the rest of us, I don't know why. But no doubt, they had strong reasons.

Through the cloud of years, I remember the classroom they put me in, just large enough to accommodate maybe 25 individual student, each with his or her own desk. Just continuing my pattern of doing well in school in Bruxelles, I did well in school in St. Raphael. In France in that day like in Belgium, the three top-graders got honors; being second, I remember, brought me much pleasure. This is where I memorized "*Le Corbeau et le Renard*" (The Crow and the Fox) by Jean de la Fontaine—which I remember to this day and with which I delighted our middle son, Karl, when he was taking French in high school, in waking him some mornings by reciting it to him, with due characterization and inflection, of course. I enjoyed it as much as he, at the very least, as he would smile even before opening his eyes, probably entertaining me as much as I did him. Even to this day, mention of it by either of us makes us smile.

I also smile when I think of my misadventure with those two pretty older girls in our OSE group of kids; they were probably 13 or 14. Their development suggested that; I don't mean their psychological development. Of course, being a normal boy I tried to impress them, as did Armand, and several others among us "older" 11 and 12 year olds. One of my efforts to impress them met with some near-disaster. Of all places, this near-disaster took place in that beautiful Méditerranée cove in St. Raphaël. When they asked me if I could swim, of course, I told them I could. They could; how could I tell them that I had never had the opportunity to test whether I could swim or not—the wave-surging waters of the North Sea near Ostende which we occasionally visited did not provide me with swimming opportunities. Besides, swimming really looked a no-brainer; why, all you need to do is flop your arms and legs around. So they innocently enough invited me to join them in what turned out to be the "deep end" of the cove, if one can think of it that way. I very quickly learned that the no-brainer of knowing how to swim was, while perhaps not requiring great skill, nonetheless required a necessary modest capability I had not yet had occasion to develop—in fact, I did learn very quickly after that. Fortunately, they were nice kids, and didn't let me drown. I am guessing that as soon as they realized that I had hoped I could swim but could not, they rescued me. Perhaps they were sufficiently satisfied, as many girls are, when they see a boy who has to uphold his macho foolishness which he mistakes for dignity and manliness, has to face the fact that he really is not that big and capable. They were even solicitous; impressive generosity on their part. And we remained friends; and though I well deserved it, they didn't tease me even once.

Life went on in St. Raphaël as it also had in Riversaltes. This time life's going on took the shape, of all indignities visited on me by my own body, of my having an inguinal hernia. It had never come up before. But I guess I must've had some abdominal symptoms or I felt some uncomfortable bulging in the lower left hand quadrant of my abdomen, as we say in medicine, for this problem to be uncovered. Very simple and not very successful treatment then, though I have seen such in movies of the 19th century: bed rest and a support-belt like contraption that is intended to contain abdominal contents within the abdominal wall. It's not regaling to further describe, so I won't. Altogether it was not pleasant, but it was not so bad.

But there are things that matter more to a boy than just some abdominal ailment problems like the one I just described. St. Raphaël is among other things, the place where I had my first girlfriend, Sara. It was not a serious affair. It did though, bring with it very nice discoveries and feelings. I can almost see her. But I do remember distinctly that feeling that having a girlfriend, in my series of six in my romantic life history, brought me. This is not the place to go into details. It is a very nice feeling, very nice; enough said.

I turned 13 at the end of December 1941. I was 11 when the war started for Belgium; since then where we went, we did so in transit to somewhere yet undetermined. I take this narrative break here to take note of the fact that, of course as a Jewish boy, turning 13 is a significant traditional occasion. It's the day they say when "you become a man." This is, as so many know, when a Jewish boy has his Bar Mitzvah; in Europe, during the 1930s, 1940s, girls did not similarly celebrate their Bat Mitzvah—simple male chauvinism so prevalent among Jews in the Europe of that day. But during these war years, there was no talk of Bar Mitzvahs around me, not mine, not anyone else's that I know of. I had been reared in an Orthodox home where food laws were observed, Holidays were observed, so was the *Shabbat*, though my mother and I or my Aunt Esther and my cousin Joseph with whom we lived, did not attend Friday evening or Saturday religious services. My Uncle Frenkel, my favorite uncle of my favorite family—where my mother and I spent many a Shabbat dinner and with whom we had increased contact after my mother and Aunt Esther parted ways—was a quite religious man who set *tefillin* twice daily and prayed. I attended *Shul* (Synagogue) with him on a number of occasions and was significantly positively influenced by him, though I never gained his fervor for the classical religious man's attending to daily prayer and ritual. While feeling deeply Jewish from my earliest years, I never felt deeply religious. I know that in my younger years in Bruxelles, I "believed in God" as we say; but I was not avidly interested in prayer.

But everything was turned upside down with this war. For many of us. I turned 13 while at *La Villa*; no question of a Bar Mitzvah. I was not thinking Bar Mitzvah; I doubt anyone else in my environs was thinking, or at least no one even raised the question with me; and I certainly did not raise the question. And, my mother was not there. When my mother and I parted with my escape from Rivesaltes, we had not talked about the fact that I would be turning 13 in eight months. Maybe she didn't

Uncle Maurice Frenkel (given to the author 23 May 1940)

dare talk about it with me because she was not certain that we might be reunited by that time. I didn't think of my having a Bar Mitzvah at the end of the year; given our life condition, a Bar Mitzvah was not a pressing thought; we had far more mundane survival matters on our minds. In my universe of the time, other than compliments of the Rivesaltes authorities who acknowledged our Jewishness by degrading our miserable living conditions further in honor of our Passover 1941 observation, there were no religious observations. For me and those around me, there had been no religious observations that I know of in Récébédou, nor in Rivesaltes, nor in *La Villa*, Holidays observations yes, though not with religious services, and I knew of no Sabbath services. So my 13th birthday came and passed silently. I don't recall anyone's birthday being observed in *La Villa* Mariana.

I had been in the OSE home since May 2, 1941. Some time in March 1942, I believe it was Mme Masour—though it might have been Mora, I think not—sought me out to talk to me. With some seriousness but also a good feeling, Mme Masour told me that I was to leave St. Raphael to go to America. I did not initially grasp what she was saying. How is this, I would be going to America? What was I to make of this? How did this come about? Mme Masour told me that my mother, from within Rivesaltes had signed me onto a list for children to go to America. On inquiry, she told me that no my mother was not going to go with me; that my mother wanted me to go with other children. She could not go too. What next? I can imagine what I would feel now, and think it very likely that I didn't know then how I felt about this. I had no access to my mother, so we couldn't talk about it. I did feel, no doubt, looking back, that she would have made a strong argument for me to go, that she wanted me to go. Like she had presented me with regard to escaping from Riversaltes. Escape from Rivesaltes that's one thing; that she would also escape from Rivesaltes I found believable. If I could do it, it was automatic that she could do it too. Was my mother going to come to America too, separately, later? Mme Masour did not seem to know. Or, as her behavior indicated, so I thought. I say this now knowing from Vivette Samuel's book that at this time, beyond January 1942, the OSE was outright committed to separating children from their parents even in the concentration camps, even in Rivealtes where Vivette Samuel volunteered to be interned. They did so in an attempt to rescue children from slaughter by separating them from their parents and sending them to homes and eventually to real asylum like to America. Mme Masour no doubt knew that the reason I was going to America was that the OSE knew that the Jews in France and elsewhere were targeted for extermination—the Wannsee Conference that unleashed "the final solution" had taken place on January 20 of this year. Children who stayed with their mothers—children under 13 since those older than 13 (it may have been 15) were, by French legislation or by camp administration, separated from them, an ironic recognition of Jewish ritual [Bar Mitzvah]—were slaughtered along with them. We were now in March 1942; the slaughter was going on; Mme Masour knew; but, understandably, she would not tell me that. Mme Masour was very sympathetic, really; she didn't try to avoid my obvious dilemma; she just repeated some phrases, conveying to me that this is what my mother wanted me to do and that this was a very good thing to do. As I reconstruct a bit what happened, Vivette Samuel and her co-worker, both OSE workers, sought parents out and informed them of the possibility of sending their children to safety in America and elsewhere. I assume that this is how my mother put my name on such a list, and why I was going to America. Mme Masour, withstanding my questions with patience and kindness, did not promise that my mother would follow me, she did not know. In the end, again, I accepted my mother's assignment.

The days that followed are a blur. When the time came for me to go, the school year was not yet terminating. Even though unfinished, it had been a good year. I had done very well, holding my second in the class position to the time I left. I had had the sense that my attendance in that school was temporary, and it was. Of course, it quickly got known in our small Villa community that I was going to America. I don't remember any great cheerfulness at my going, nor any envy of my assignation by anyone; what I remember were a few photo exchanges, wishes, hopes, goodbye interactions, assumptions that we would see each other again. Even though without speaking of it we all experienced that our relationships were transient, goodbyes did not feel final. The times were in flux, transient; nothing was definite or predictable.

I remember well Mora's taking over the task of trying to facilitate my taking to the idea of going to America, and his efforts in making it sound like a cheerful and lucky prospect. He took it on himself to try to teach me a few words of English. I remember a dialogue he developed with me, of course with my input. Writing and speaking in English it went something like: "Hello, Henri, how are you?" "Oh, hello Mora, I am very well thank you. I am a doctor now." "Oh, Henri, that is wonderful." Not a brilliant conversation, but it carried Mora's efforts to make me feel that the prospect of my going to America was a very good idea and would end up to be a successful undertaking. In part, Mora succeeded. Even with much trepidation, I did feel ready to go; just where, I did not know. America is all I knew.

When the time came, I believe in about mid-or-late-March, here, as compared to my exodus from Rivesaltes, the goodbyes were out in the open, with mixed feelings on my part and on that of some of my kid friends, Sara and Armand especially. The grown ups, Mme Masour, Mora, Aranka, Inez, and Julia all seemed very certain and cheerful about what I was doing. They all really sent me off with warm good wishes; their hopes and wishes of good-fortune carried me on the way. And moving me on, was my mother's wish that I go to America; among us Jews it was the land of hope. Israel was not yet what it would become.

Chapter 5

Going to America

Our Brief Sojourn in Marseille

I can't remember who brought me to Marseille, I guess I can say, "brought me back" to Marseille. Struggling to remember if it was Mme Masour or Mora, I come up uncertain though I am inclined toward guessing it was Mme Masour. My return to Marseille was under very different circumstances than my first-time arrival there. I was not returning from St. Raphaël to Marseille the conquering hero, but I was not returning the runaway prisoner. I returned to Marseille in safe hands. The place to which I returned was not the OSE Bureau itself, but it was in some way part of it. There were dormitory and feeding accommodations, not that there was any more food here than in St. Raphaël. The warm protective surround of St. Raphaël was modified; though feeling protected, the surround was unknown, anxiety and strain in the air, and there was that distinct familiar feeling of transience. I knew that we would not be here long; this was the starting point; we were about to be launched on our voyage to America. There was some excitement, mostly coming from the shepherding adults around us; but if I generalize what I felt, the kids were somewhat bewildered, anxious. This activated my tendency to look at my surround, at all its dimensions, environment, people, situation/event, in an effort to master what was happening to me in my ravaged world. This tendency goes way back with me; often, quite often, I was an observer. Here now, I most remember scanning the surround, searching about for any familiar face.

I am not certain which one of us came to Marseille first. Even though I was searching expectantly, I remember well my immeasurable surprise when I saw him. Just as he was in Rivesaltes, even though this was a year after my escape from there, there stood my Rivesaltes friend-musketeer, Savic. We saw each other at the same moment; one of us walked into the room where the other was; what a momentous reunion! Savic and I were going to America together! What an unbelievable moment. I was not going to America knowing no one; I was going with a Rivesaltes musketeer. I had known I was going to America with other kids. But I knew none of them. That now was changed. Savic and I had known each other in Rivesaltes for 5 months. Under conditions like those that prevailed there, you can be with others for months and know no one, or you can be with one of them for a few days and endow that person with specialness. Savic was special. Evidently we were so to one another.

We were photographed for our visa and exit papers. In my photograph I think I look quite nice, with a blazer and a white shirt, with my shirt collar pulled out and framed over the collar of my newly gotten blazer, European style of that day. But my eyes have the look that, according to Judy Kestenberg and Ira Brenner,* a Warsaw ghetto doctor, Dr. Adina Blady Szwajger, found and reported that she saw many "children emaciated by hunger, 'with the eyes of adults.'" I know what she meant. When I look at that photo—happens infrequently—it brings it all back.

As we were being prepared for the voyage to America, among the many steps taken by those who were shepherding us, one stands out. I am totally ignorant as to how the OSE and whoever else was involved—the Red Cross, the American Quakers—worked it out. Parents of those among us who had not seen them for some time were brought to Marseille, for me, all the way from Rivesaltes to Marseille, to say goodbye. It is likely that they did the same for children whose parents were in other camps. I assume that in the case of Savic and others like him who came directly from Rivesaltes and from other French camps, Savic and they had said their good-byes before leaving theirs in Rivesaltes or Gurs or elsewhere. I assume that a number of the children were war-orphans. I was stunned when they informed me that my mother would come to say goodbye. How did they do that? Why would she have to go back? I just did not understand this craziness. It was only much later that I learned that negotiations by international organizations like the Red Cross, the American Quakers, the YMCA, as well as Social Service agencies, Jewish and Christian, and who knows who else had negotiated

* The Last Witness: The Child Survivor of the Holocaust by Judith S. Kestenberg and Ira Brenner published by the American Psychiatric Press, Washington DC, 1996, page134.

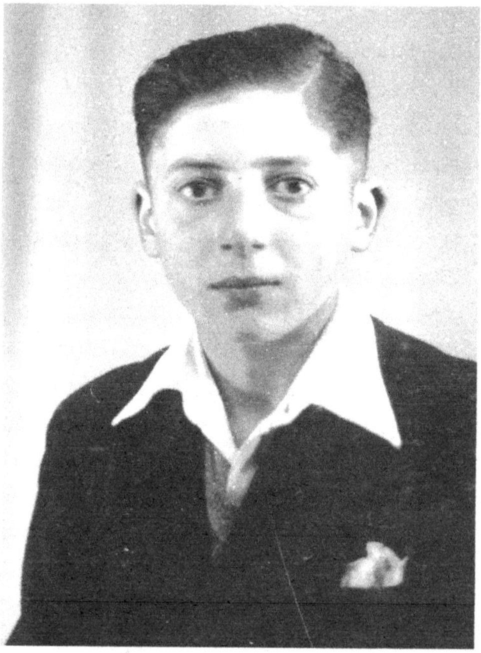

"The Eyes of Child Survivors"
Visa photo of the author, age 13 (April 1942) about to leave for America

with Vichy-France to permit the children to leave this misery-embroiled country, but that their parents had to stay!

I have to wonder if I was stunned because I had not anticipated that the OSE might go to such lengths or that they were able to do so, to bring my mother out of Rivesaltes just to say goodbye. Or was I stunned because of the implication that effort contained. The OSE felt it important that my mother and I say goodbye. As I learn from Vivette Samuel's *Sauver Les Enfants*, in early May 1942, the OSE got special permission from the Vichy-French authorities to allow the parents of those children who were to be convoyed to America to "assist in the embarquement of their children in Marseille at the time of the departure of the third convoy" (my translation). Evidently the authorities were worried that some of the parents would escape, not return to the camp. Samuel writes: *"Le 15 Mai, j'écris: 'Les enfants sont partis heureux [!] et toutes les meres sont rentrées au camp. . . . Elles se demandent aussi quand elles pouront revoir leurs enfants. . . . Sur ces dix femmes neuf furent deportées et aucune ne revint'."* (May 15, I wrote: 'The children left happy [!] and all the mothers returned to camp. . . . They wondered when they might see their children again. . . . Of the ten mothers, nine were deported and none returned.)

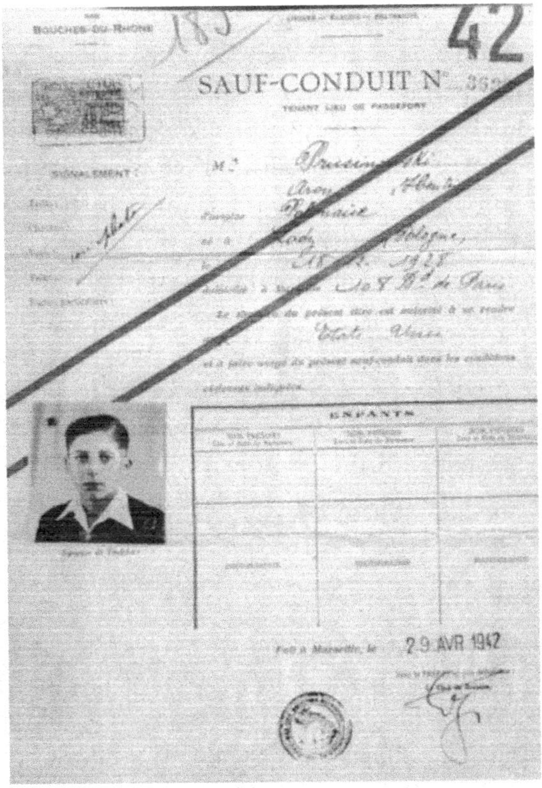

BOUCHES-DU-RHONE

183

42

SAUF-CONDUIT N° 36…

TENANT LIEU DE PASSEPORT

SIGNALEMENT

ENFANTS

29 AVR 1942

The author's *Sauf-Conduit* (travel paper) for the U.S., 29 April 1942

I was not ready to say the type of goodbye that, looking back on it, the OSE had in mind. I expected that, some time, my mother would follow me. Out of Rivesaltes, to America, where I was going.

It was so good to see my mother. We were so happy to see and feel each other. Many questions were asked, both ways. This is when I learned, from her that she had in fact escaped from Rivesaltes. But she had not communicated with me since she herself could not write—in the early 1900s, many Polish Jewish girls from merchant families did not go to school—and she could not turn to anyone to write for her, which is why I had not heard from her or known of her escape. She was found, I suppose by the police, quite possibly due to the identifying papers she carried or by having been reported by some Vichy-France-loyal citizen, and was returned to Rivesaltes. The visit is a blur now; it seems to have been just momentary—though no doubt it lasted a number of hours.

That I experience it as a blur now reflects the conflicting mix of feelings that came with having to say goodbye. I understand those among us who don't like good-byes sufficiently so to want to avoid them, or cut them off quickly, and leave without looking back. I don't do that; I am not sure though that I did not do that then. The problem is this. When we said goodbye, I had it in mind that my mother and I would be re-united, where ever that might be. It did not occur to me, it did not register in my soul that this could be our last goodbye. It was a little more than a decade later that I learned that with this visit I had seen my mother for the last time. It might have been better if I had known. But none of us was privy to that. I did not consider that it might be so. I do know that, even though I did not feel that I would not see her again, she did seem to leave me with the unspoken dictate that "life must go on; Aron, you must go on." The next thing I knew, we were embarking on Le Maréchal Liautey.

Marseille to Casablanca

Le Maréchal Liautey, the ship that would take us for the first of two legs of our trip, I later learned was the flagship of a major Mediterranean commercial line with home-port in Marseille. We were not treated to its more luxurious travel levels; we went into the belly of the ship. We were on deck when we left port; it was a sight seeing this large ship very slowly glide its way out of its tight berth and then to see the port move away. I have always marveled at large structures, at large vehicles moving about, at large buildings—I really had one of those "large" surprises of a lifetime at the end of our Atlantic crossing: New York. Leaving Marseille, soon after we were out of port, I got reminded that I had never been on a ship that size nor had I traveled on the high seas before, nor had I planned for what I got. I was shocked and dismayed at what, after several hours of it, I felt was an absolutely unconquerable sea-sickness. I was really surprised by this "sea-sickness." I had not been warned that this might happen; I guess those responsible for us had many other things in mind and to deal with. I doubt their agenda would have included, consider the possibility that some of your charges might get seasick. I don't know if they knew of dramamine then. For the uninitiated, what causes sea-sickness, I say not as a physician but as a kid who first feels it take over his body, from the pit of his belly up, is that the ship wont sit still. It just keeps going up and down, endlessly, mercilessly. This up and down movement feels like waves of feeling your insides mount up inside your body and then slowly, sickeningly sink; up, down, up, down, slowly, just at the right rate to make you sick. I was not the only one; but I felt sure that I was one of the best models of this transient disorder. While awake I spent more time in the latrine throwing up than on deck. I don't know how or whether I slept that night. Needless to say, I was totally unable to even think of eating anything. For the uninitiated let me say that even if you are starving, you don't want to put anything destined for your sick-stomach into your mouth. Fortunately the next day we arrived in Casablanca. I was very happy to get off the ship, not happy with joy, happy to not feel seasick. What a relief to again be on soil that didn't move—well, I mean on soil that by virtue of gravity and its being in a solid state one does not feel to be moving.

I was also beginning to feel a mix of residual physiological malaise and excitement at what was happening to us. Talk around me seemed to turn to America and with it, excitement about going to this land of ease and good stuff, even then no one was so stupid as to say milk and honey, but some came pretty close to that. I think now, that despite a psychological baseline, a constant state of feeling traumatized and low-level depressed, we all did a pretty good job of avoiding talking—probably also avoiding thinking—about what we had just left behind, most especially for those of us who had them, our parents. We didn't even talk of leaving Rivesaltes or other camps, nor of leaving OSE homes; we were bent, it seems now, on looking ahead, on going to America. It was not difficult coming from Europe in those days, and certainly not under the conditions that surrounded us, to think of America as the land where things would be good, you could even get rich. I guess we might have meant that it was a land of opportunity, as it still is today, but that to kids who could not even let themselves think of the misery they just left behind, coming to America penniless, it is not surprising that opportunity might translate into getting rich. After all, we were jut kids. And maybe that explains why we didn't talk of going to America for the reason so many had gone to America for, long before we did and have since: because in America they don't have pogroms and they don't persecute Jews the way they do in Europe, nor do they persecute Catholics or Protestants of any denomination; then they only persecuted and acted criminally against Blacks, Negroes to be in keeping with the times. And since this is post "September 11," while Blacks are being persecuted less, are we

Americans now looking to another ethnic group to afflict with ready-to-dispense malignant prejudice?

To listen to it, our conversations about America were not elegant; we were young kids. In fact, we were 50 kids being escorted to America by one adult couple. Remarkable that we were shepherded to America by one couple, one man and one woman. Of course there were no little kids among us, we were all from about 7 to 13 years of age, at most 2 or 3 were older, and we seemed to know the seriousness of our mission because we were quite cooperative. In fact, I am not aware of any kind of discipline problem, any behaviors impossible for one couple to handle—all said with enormous appreciation for that couple that brought us to America. Of course, as I shall turn to shortly, there was some activity that might have raised some eyebrows or even concern. We were 50 kids, I think mostly Jewish kids, but there were also some Spanish kids, refugees without parents or whose parents, like my mother, wanted their kids out of Europe, a continent that seemed then to be going to hell. We were 50 refugee children being brought to America for a better life by some very good community-minded people, very good people like Social Services people, certainly Jewish Social Services, American Quakers, Eleanor Roosevelt, the YMCA and others.

We were in Casablanca for several days only, ready to go as soon as we learned that a Portuguese vessel, as was planned, would come by Casablanca to pick us up, perhaps others as well, and then cross the Atlantic to New York City, the land of many good things. For us, Casablanca was just a waiting station. We stayed pretty well confined to our temporary shelter—which I cannot see at all. In retrospect it would really have been neat to go to "Rick's" and maybe catch a glimpse of Ingrid Bergman or Humphrey Bogart. No, no Casba, no Charles Boyer or Hedi Lamar. Just in some refuge from which we didn't venture out, for reasons totally unknown to me. I believe we were traveling with Vichy-France's knowledge and acquiescence, I doubt we had their blessings. As I later learned from Samuel we were the last kids to come to America in this way; the Germans stopped the next planned convoy. Perhaps it simply would have been quite a task for one couple to take 50 kids to the beach for some water play. Whatever the reasons, we pretty much stayed put.

Once my residual seasickness malaise fully subsided hunger made itself felt as usual. My recollection is that in Casablanca, we had no more food at our disposal than before. I have strong evidence for that; it came in the next stage of our voyage to America. That next stage was announced to us as good news. We were going to America the next day or so, on a Portuguese ship, the *Serpa Pinta*; for us it was Le *Serpa Pinta*. Not knowing Portuguese, I don't know what that name means though, right or wrong, I translated it into "The Python."

Across the Atlantic—Casablanca to New York

We embarked on *Le Serpa Pinta,* same class as before, in the belly of the ship. It was not bad, literally the ship's lowest class traveling accommodations. Though more cramped than our more recent accomodations, certainly than *La Villa Mariana*, even more than Rivesaltes, none of us complained.

We knew this was wartime; we had been in it now for 2 years—a long time for a kid 11 to 13. This was early May 1942. The newest major change in the war then that we were all aware of was that, now America was in the war too, and of course, on our side. I bring this into view now because it had serious implications for crossing the Atlantic on its surface rather than flying over it as most of us have done now for half a century. Up to the 1950s, and even later, one crossed the Atlantic hugging the surface of the water, by ship. Even we kids knew about submarines; they like things that hug the water; that's their scavenging site. And I think we were told that we would be safe because we were traveling on a Portuguese ship, a ship from a neutral country, a ship that would not be a target for submarines. Of course, no one said some mistake could happen. But even if someone had told us that, I'm sure no one was ready to turn back. We were on the way to America on a neutral country's ship and moral kids like us knew that every country observed rules of law even during wars. It was the Spring of 1942; my peers and I, had not yet heard of Wannsee, or of "Final Solutions," or learned that in Auschwitz, the Nazis had already been gassing and cremating masses of Jews since September 3, 1941. The adults in Rivesaltes probably knew and it may have determined my mother's decision that I should go to America; but I doubt that any of us kids knew of these ongoing war crimes. In any case, we were on our way. I may have been less interested in watching it unfold, or I may have been taken by the details of the ship itself, or perhaps without being aware of it I was already thinking of getting seasick all over again, but I don't remember pulling out of Casablanca port. I do remember noting that *Le Serpa Pinta* was a substantially smaller vessel than *Le Maréchal Liautey*. But in some ways I liked Le *Serpa Pinta* better, it seemed a nicer vessel. I immediately saw that it was not made of light gray or cream-color-painted-metal everything, walls, doors as was *Le Maréchal Liautey*; *Serpa Pinta* seemed to have more wood materials, frames, doors, even some handsome dark brown polished banisters in places.

Nonetheless, soon again, within an hour of setting off, the rolling of the ship grabbed my vulnerable gut, just recently settled from its first trials. You don't have to be an astute physicist to know that the rolling of ships on the Atlantic would be of wider range than that produced by the comparatively quieter *Méditerranée*. I got sick, sick. Now here was true injustice on the part of Mother Nature! There was food on the *Serpa Pinta*. I had no idea there was this much food anywhere in those days. How could the Portuguese have food in such abundance when the rest of Europe, at least the Europe I knew, was near starvation? For us it was as if food had nearly died; certainly good food had. It looked like there were tons of it on this ship, including marvelous-looking white bread. "Marvelous-looking" because I had not seen such voluptuous bread since Bruxelles; of course in Bruxelles I didn't realize that I might some day think of bread as voluptuous, beautiful, whatever 'gorgeous' word you want to use. Except for very early there, even in Village the bread didn't look so good. Now true, my indignation against Mother Nature was not strong; I may feel that a bit more today than I did then. With a mix of today-feeling and then-feeling, what a sardonic plan by some nasty power: here was this gorgeous bread and in such abundance, as well as other eating things including meat, and I was so sea sick, I couldn't take one bite for at least 3 days! Talk of torture. Here I was, 13, having progressively starved since we left Bruxelles—except for a few weeks in Village and for my meal in the train station at Nimes—, starved for two years, and here was this luscious-looking food at my disposal and I could not eat a morsel.

Maybe, in all fairness to her, I should make mention of the fact that Mother Nature had the decency and compassion to let us have good weather. We had a fairly calm Atlantic to slice through. Fortunately, after two days of violent seasickness, a third one more moderate, my physiology accommodated to the rhythmic ups and downs of the ocean and my seasickness abated. My appetite came back little by little, counterpoint to my abating gut disturbance. The food was good. Since I could only gradually eat an expectable amount, I did not suffer from too rapid a gorging of myself—not that I saw any of my peers suffer that disorder. By the way I was not the only one frequently running to, spending some time in, and puking into latrine receptacles, or when the sickness calmed, leaning, hyper-extending over the deck ship rail. For that of course you had to know where to go to not afflict others or yourself for that matter with whatever it was you were able to project back to where it all came from, earth to earth, dust to dust.

I don't know how or when exactly, but in the midst of this quite tolerable misery—I'll take seasickness any day over the misery we had just left behind—, a lovely Spanish girl about my age, Manolita, asked me with a smile if I needed any clothes washed; she was going to wash her clothes. I don't know if she had noticed my frequently vomiting over the rail and not wrongly assumed that some of it might have undesirably come back to me, compliments of the moderate ocean wind. Or whether she was quite simply a smart kid who knew by now, everyone needed some underwear and shirts washed. Both easily applied to me. It was a truly lovely offer. I accepted it, I think, nicely. I had never talked to her before, nor she to me. Of course, this made Manolita and me friends, and we were friendly for the duration of our voyage. Looking back, I suppose she may have liked me more than just to be friends; I liked her too, but I was not influenced by feelings other than feeling friendly toward her. I don't mean that I was wise or unwise. From the little I knew of her, Manolita was a very nice girl, and she gave me a very nice moment; I remember her with warmth. None of us was rich in nice moments in that era; or more accurately, we were all wanting of so much, that all the nice moments we could get then would be remembered with warmth. Manolita proved that among the 50 refugees, we were not just Jews; some of the kids, kids who no doubt had suffered a great deal too, were Spanish refugees, perhaps orphans, victims of the Spanish dictator Franco. I can't remember, that too with some regret, where she went after we arrived in America. Maybe her gesture accelerated my conquest over my seasickness.

From about the 3rd day on the *Serpa Pinta* things improved, by the 4th day they had improved well. In good time too, because, some interesting things happened. At least they would be very interesting for a 13-year-old in that era, or in any era. I learned a few interesting things about sex on the ship. The first of these was a negatively interesting thing; the second was nearly-priceless. Much to my surprise, I had begun to eat well. Not only did I feel like eating and did, but I was also ready to take a bath, since we had learned that such facilities existed on the ship. My hygiene-impulse had yielded to my seasickness nearly as much as had my appetite; like my appetite, my wish to be clean came back too. For reasons that are a mystery to me, the powers that be made us go to bathe in pairs, not sex-mixed pairs obviously. During our trip I had befriended a boy a bit older than I, 14; I can not remember his name. He had an older brother, Jacques, I think, 16; he was the oldest among us. Though the younger of the brothers was my "friend," I chummed around a bit with the 16 year-old too. When I indicated that I was going to bathe, the older one asked if we could go together. Why he did not ask his brother to do so, I have no idea. Or, I had no idea then. So off to bathe we went. Things were going perfectly fine, we got there, started the water going, undressed and I got in the tub. I'm not certain that there was only one tub or whether there were two tubs. In any case, in the course of our talking about who knows what, he asked if I'd let him put his penis in my anus. Wow, wait a minute, I thought, where did that come from. Within a moment I told him that I did not want that; no I was not interested. Fortunately, he did not press his point. Not that he would have succeeded because even though I was always a small guy, and I did feel some fear when it came to fists, I did not back off the few times I was challenged. Boys in Europe are not different than American boys when it comes to showing their prowess or defending their honor by accepting to get into a wrestling-boxing—no kicking was allowed among young guys fighting in those days—match with another, especially if he was bigger than you. Machismo is universal among males, more so in some individuals, and in some cultures than others. I was not afraid of bigger kids because once challenged years before, in Bruxelles, I had accepted the challenge of a bigger kid, had given him a good pounding with a nose bleed that scared him, and had handled matters well. In fact, since then I had gained the reputation among my Bruxellois friends as one who could take on a bigger kid. In any case, I finished my bath as did he in pretty good spirits with nothing untoward happening. Some years later, reflecting on this event, I did curse the son-of-bitch, but did not get too heated about it since I had simply and competently put him off. He was a horny bastard. Yet, he did have opportunities as I soon found out, that I would have thought would serve him much better than I. Who knows.

Interestingly, he is the one who set up the second opportunity that presented itself for me to learn more about sex. With this one, I would graduate from the lesson my favorite cousin David David, yes, twice David, first and last name, had given me years before, when I was about 9, about masturba tion. He showed me how you do it, and tried to convince me that it felt good, as if I didn't register that fact myself. But this Serpa Pinta time the lesson was much more memorable and truly elevated my sexual experiencing. Somehow, there we were one late afternoon, on deck with Annette, interesting that I remember her name, my 14-year-old friend, his 16-year-old brother Jacques and I. The 16-year-old took the responsibility if I can speak of it that way, of bringing Annette around to his sexual interest in her. I had never been in that position before: a rather passive participant, but nonetheless a participant, in the seduction of a 13-year-old girl.

Annette was a girl just as traumatized as the rest of us, and maybe more. I really did not know her, and I am not sure that my co-conspirators, including the active, perhaps I should say the aggressive agent in this event, knew her either. It does seem to me that the older brother may have some encounter with Annette before; this was not a first time effort at seduction, for all I know it may not be the first time that this not so pleasant character seduced her. It was as if he was revisiting a known situation. He too easily seduced her into all 4 of us "playing" together. I did not know then what I know now. And this is not the way I would have written my script about getting to know what I learned then. I did not have these thoughts then; this is what I think now. Truthfully, I did not know what this 16 year-old horny guy was getting at. I was a passive though very interested participant. On my own I would not have known to go the distance he went. I had a girlfriend in *La Villa*, Sara. She was a lovely girl. I really felt very warmly toward her; I really liked her; too early to say that I loved her. But we did not progress in our romantic interaction beyond kissing. To this day, even though her picture is somewhat vague, I have warm memories of Sara. Anyway, coming back to Annette on the Serpa Pinta, our 16-year-old guide was on a quest to claim from her something he either had known before or had been striving to get to. The next thing I knew he succeeded in getting Annette to allow us to engage with her sexually. When I, following the example and guidance of my senior peer-instructor who I felt was a bit of a scoundrel, touched her genitals and entered my finger into her vagina, I had never, never touched anything as gut-stirring, well genitals-stirring, as that; it was . . . awesome. I will not describe it; I'm not sure I could. It was to my 13-year-old mind, well, maybe not just my 13-year-old mind, absolutely the most positively shivering sensation I had yet experienced. To me today, I know it was one of those meaningful moments in life that by virtue of its meaning to you gets laid down in one of your neuronal networks which then stays with you and you remember over and over when some event or thought trips that network. It gets easily tripped.

In our play-exploration of her, specifically of her private parts, which I must say she did respond to, though, no doubt anxiety played its damned unpleasant role, she increasingly yielded to the advances of our senior member. She yielded to his pressures and let him penetrate her with his hard-up erect organ. Of course there were two more of us, I being the youngest of the three. After our 16-year-old hungry member satisfied himself—no doubt only for several hours, I would guess—quickly enough, lest Annette decide she could not go on with this activity, my 14-year-old friend stood up and proceeded to relieve himself of a large load of sexual excitement he'd been walking around with for who knows how long. After what seemed to me an interminable time, he achieved his ends, and yielded. It was my turn. What do I do? I let biology take over. By the way, for reasons I can't explain, there are a lot of things I can't explain, we were doing all of this illicit but normal adolescent stuff standing up. Well, come to think of it, it was not the last time I did it standing up. But that's another story. So it was my turn and I rose to the occasion. With as much awe as when I first touched Annette, I entered my penis into her incredible body-part. I don't know which felt more mind-stirring, to touch her with my finger that first time or with my penis. No need to dwell on this question. Anyway, I did what comes naturally. But my being number 3, a number I don't strive for, Annette, who, long before I became a shrink I thought seemed to become increasingly worried about what she had allowed herself to be talked into, suddenly felt she could no longer go on with this enterprise of getting whatever it was she sought in letting herself be taken advantage of this way. Of course, I did not reflect on all this then, as a growing sex-hungry 13-year-old, as I do now. Anyway, midway in my first lesson about sexual intercourse, Annette had reached all she could tolerate of this trying to please boys stuff, or whatever it was she hoped to get out of getting into this; she feebly let me know she did not want to go on. Much to my dismay, since I had not reached my biological or psychological end point on this matter, Annette acted like she was getting frightened and, being a gentleman—mh, had I really been on that occasion?—I would not press my point and complied with her softly declared wish to terminate this project now. I backed off. I was most appreciative of what Annette had allowed me to experience and did not want to cause her further distress. I like to think that I was not as much a scoundrel as our 16-year-old anti-hero. I hope this event did not cause Annette as much trouble as I have later feared it might have, I do remember it as a gift, at a time when gifts were sparse. Like with Manolita, I don't know whatever happened to Annette; I do remember her with affection.

During the last days of our Atlantic crossing the ocean was fairly calm, all seemed quite non-threatening, even though the possibility of German U-boats was still occasionally mentioned. We saw none. Nor did we see any vessel in trouble as we went.

Our last day on ship, the morning was somewhat foggy. Once someone sighted land, the word got around quickly, excitement burst out and many people gathered at the bow of the ship, trying as best each could to find a place along the rail to see as much as one could. Once at the rail, the excitement heaved and then lessened to a hum and bustle that stayed and did not die down from that moment on. Many of us, including Savic and I, just stayed at the rail, excited but also somewhat mesmerized by the approaching land of promise. It took a while; the ship just seemed to take its time. Well, our impatience to get there made itself obvious; the ship seemed to move more slowly now. Faces, especially the grown-ups' faces, were beaming. I felt a quieter excitement; maybe some of the other kids did too.

Yes, it was good to get to America; but the conditions, coming to America without my mother, dampened the enormity of excitement this type of arrival warrants, coming to America. And then a new quite more vibrant excitement burst out with the cry "La Statue d'Liberté!" Some just have better vision than I, or maybe they are far-sighted. I started to search for the Statue where arms with outstretched index finger were pointing, and I saw it. It was a sobering moment; a different calming of the excitement, the humming around much less than before, I think a feeling of awe took over as I, and no doubt the others too, looked at it, still far off and quite small. It turned into a peaceful calm, I felt that the ocean seemed to calm some too; the land became more and more visible, the city became visible. Then as we entered the harbor, the Statue of Liberty increasingly grew and I was struck by its enormity; it was, awesome. I was a kid, 13, but somehow, perhaps because of the things I had heard said about America in years before, it was sobering, exciting, awesome to be nearing America.

Arriving in America

I was well again, no more seasickness, I could marvel at the enormity of the Statue of Liberty and soon after, marvel at the Serpa Pinta slowly getting into its berth, I assume, at one of Ellis Island's docks. As the ship was nearly into it's temporary resting place, even though it was not a large ship, it seemed to stir much activity on the dock. Looking back, I can imagine, not only was a ship coming in, but it carried people from Europe, people getting out of that place "over there"—which brings to mind Caruso's unique rendition, first in English, then in French, of

> "Over there, over there,
> Send the word, send the word over there,
> That the Yanks are coming, the Yanks are coming,
> The Yanks are coming over there . . . "
> *Par là-bas, par la là-bas*
> *Nous irons, nous irons, par là-bas . . ."*

where America again, was now at war. The Yanks were going "over there;" we were coming from "over there." Perhaps some of the people milling on the dock knew that the ship would soon unload 50 refugee children, now in America without their families. Maybe this happened those days when any ship came into America, bringing home natives who had been abroad, and wide-open-eyed, soberly excited newcomers.

We came through Ellis Island, in that era the front door into America, the land where you could get rich so you would never starve again. It did not look like the land of getting rich on Ellis Island. We walked down the plank onto the dock, and I felt again, even though I no longer was seasick, the remarkable security standing on land that stays put brings, land that does not go up and down, up and down, mercilessly. In fact, I remember feeling unsteady as I walked a few steps on the dock, having now to re-adjust that mechanism in my middle ear and brain that deals with equilibrium. It did not take long for me to accommodate to stability. We walked into what looked like a hangar, big, high ceiling, partitions guiding us through some maze, as if we had to be tested before we could get onto America's soil. We were herded into an area a bit apart from the others, and in fact we were tested, not unreasonably I must say as a physician, since those responsible needed to and indeed should have checked us out for some dread contagious disease that could contaminate New York, and more. We were all skinny, we were all somewhat sickly looking but none of us had a dread disease. Besides, even though we might have looked tired and dragged out, we were a pretty positive sounding, maybe even positive looking bunch, I sure know I felt like that. We got through fine; Savic and I agreed to stay close; no one was held back. When we crossed the waters that surrounded Ellis Island to whichever of the New York Boroughs we went, even though we did not land in Manhattan, I gradually came to see, again with awe, the large expanse and the large buildings that were New York. It is not that there are no large buildings in Bruxelles, there are, like for example, Le Palais de Justice (The Palace of Justice—The Court House). It's big. But so large an expanse of land crowded with masses of large buildings, some very tall, that was awe-inspiring. Bruxelles is not a small town; but even before I was 10 I could walk, and did, from La Gare du Midi (South Station) to La Gare du Nord (North Station), and a while later walk back to where I came from without collapsing. I could not do that in the expanse I saw that was New York. We landed in the Bronx or Brooklyn. At some point we were on a bus to our temporary destination. Another one of the indelible moments was when the bus stopped at our destination. The window next to my seat was open and I saw two kids, I guessed around 5 years of age, playing and obviously talking-shouting to each other in sounds I did not understand at all. The thought came to me in just a moment: how could these little kids understand and speak this foreign language when I could barely understand more than two words? Of course, as soon as I formulated the thought I knew the answer. But I distinctly remember my amazement at the fact that they knew English, which to me was all but totally foreign, and they were just little kids, and I, older and bigger, for all my sixth or seventh grade academic prowess could not understand a word. The lessons we learn!

Off the bus, we went into yet another very temporary asylum where we stayed for perhaps five days. Again dormitory accommodations, high-ceilinged dining hall, long tables with lots of kids. Savic and I were sticking together. I remember especially my introduction to American cereal. We did not have that type of breakfast food in Bruxelles and of course we did not have such during our starvation sojourn in France. In New York, they served this funny stuff that actually tasted quite good. I had not yet reached the point of being certain that now I would not starve anymore, so anything other than rutabagas or turnips tasted good. But this flaky stuff they gave us actually did taste good. We were eating away, and one of the nice social-work, Red Cross type women leaned toward my bowl of cereal and said, "We put milk in it; it's good with milk in it." Her gesticulations and pointing to milk and my bowl helped me understand what she was saying. I shook my head thinking, "Oh no, I can't imagine putting milk on such good-tasting cereal." The idea sounded strange to me. That was my first encounter with American Corn Flakes. Actually soon thereafter, following Savic's more adventurous example, I did let myself be convinced that it was OK to try that good stuff with milk; it was OK.

Within days of our arrival in New York we were told that we would all be going somewhere in America; we were not just staying where we now were. I can't recall if we had been told on the way over that we would be distributed to families willing to receive a refuge child from Europe, for all intents and purposes, a war-orphan, or we were told of this in New York. Wherever we were told, Savic and I decided we would stay together. In fact, that decision was quite binding. First of all we decided we wanted to be placed in the same city. We may even have said that we wanted to stay together. Savic and I had known one another for over one-and-a-half years. Even though there had been an interval of nearly one-year when we did not see each other, having shared the state of our world as we did bound us together in a special way. Being 11-12 years old, together in the same hell-hole, pretending we were "all for one, and one for all" heroic musketeers, we felt a bond that made us want to stay together. One can make friends like that under adverse conditions. Looking back now I also think that we were each, again, on the point of being separated from those familiar to us. When we left our families, our parents in Vichy-France, we all share a common major life event. It's like people who go through a nearly disastrous plane crash together; it binds. But there was even more for us. We were essentially orphans, even if only transiently. Each of us was alone, and for most normal enough kids, it is quite natural, self-preservative actually, to find someone to reciprocally attach to. And Savic and I did just that. We asked to stay together, that is, to go to the same city; we did not expect that we could be placed together in the same family. We were.

Chapter 6

The Start of My New Life

Pittsburgh, America

Savic and I were placed with the Wagner family. Good heavens, what generosity! It did not register with me when I was a 13 year-old, I was not aware then as I have been now for a long time, how enormously generous, how deeply decent, Faye and Harry Wagner were; and how lovely and accepting their 3 young daughters were, Phyllis, then about 8, Sandy, about 5, and Evie, about 2, were then, and have been ever since, in accepting two 13 year-old strangers into their home. Yes, we were Jewish refugees and quite a number of families throughout America opened their homes to us. Remarkable. Harry and Faye Wagner were not well-to-do people. At the time Harry supported his family of five by driving a bread truck route for one of the well-known Pittsburgh bakeries. Faye was a stay-at-home Mom, very common in America in those days. The house was modest; there were enough bedrooms to accommodate Faye and Harry in one, of course, the three girls in another, and there remained a very small bedroom that Savic and I shared. The Wagner family treated us really well. Savic and I had some run-ins with Harry; he wanted boys who would live up to his hopes; neither Savic nor I were such kids. For myself, I know Harry liked my making good grades, but he did not approve of my interest in music. And I guess most of all, my need then to be an adolescent who had come to be quite self-reliant and wanted to have a good deal of self-determination, compelled my bouncing unpleasantly off the program he somehow envisioned for me. I'm not altogether sure what that program was; but whatever it was, it was not where I was going. Our run-ins were occasional and never got harsh; they just could be quite unpleasant. But these did not and do not interfere with my enormous gratitude and love for him, the bear.

Faye was a remarkable woman. I loved her from the start and my feelings for her continued, and continue even now; she died some years ago. My dilemma with her was that emotionally I could not call her

The Wagner family in 1943
Harry and Faye with daughters (*from left*)
Evelyn, Phyllis and Sandy

"Mrs. Wagner," that was too removed from how I felt about her; I could not call her "Mom," that was just out of the question for me, I had a mother, and Faye Wagner in no way suggested that I do so. How I came to it I don't know but I came to call her "Lady." Now, it was not "Lady" in a distancing, or depreciating, or in any way negative; I said it with warmth, and I felt she knew it. She was, truly, a Lady. She never gave me any indication that she did not like being called "Lady"; nor did Harry say anything about it; he would have, if he had not liked it. Nor did the kids say anything or seem to object. Maybe it was plainly obvious that I really liked and respected her, and that I was very appreciative for all she was doing to make our coming to this foreign land work for us and help us get started in America. Over time I really came to love her, to love all of them. Who wouldn't be so moved, when given the circumstances of their life, this family took in two 13 year-old refugees from Europe! Incredible. Faye and Harry made it possible for Savic and me to pick up living our life, which had been so suddenly arrested by the war.

No, we did not pick up living our life; it was not that. Before the war I was in a world with my mother, my uncles, aunts, cousins, friends, my school, Bruxelles, speaking French and Yiddish. My father and my brother were in Lodz, apart but accessible, in my world. Of course this life, as of May 1942, was not the life I was living before the war. My life was taking a turn very different than I had ever imagined. I did not realize then that it really was the start of my new life; my old life had been violated, fragmented; and it is taking me the rest of this life in America to bring some closure to what happened to my life of origin. It was not until a decade after I came to America that I knew my original life was over. That it had been shattered. But as it did even in Riversaltes, life went on; and from the fragments, with the help of many on the way, it evolved into this very different, new and eventually very good life.

Two years after the war endangered my Europe, I was again in a safe land. I had been transplanted from Europe to America, with very little said and my not realizing that I was to make a new life in America. Mora was the one who, I remember, spoke to me of my life in America 20 years later. When I saw my mother in Marseille she had either been totally vague about our future and it may be, as I think of it now, that I do not really remember what we said during our visit in Marseille, our last time together. Looking back, our future was shrouded in such uncertainty that whatever my mother said to me could only have been supposition. Would I have wanted to hear such uncertainty at 13? Or any other time?

I never doubted that I would see my mother again. Then, it was not a question of would I see the rest of my family again. It never occurred to me to think that my life with my family was over. Yet somehow, I did feel that it was totally up to me, with the help of those around me, to keep my life going. If even in Rivesaltes life went on, it would go on now too.

Of course Savic and I couldn't make it work just by ourselves. We were without parents, we couldn't speak the language, and we were penniless. But, we were not alone. We were with the Wagners and we very soon found out that the Jewish Social Services of Pittsburgh, like there are such Bureaus in every large-enough city in America, had taken on the responsibility for us, those 50 kids who had come over on the Maréchal Liautey and then on Le *Serpa Pinta*. We later also found out that the American Quakers, and the name of Eleanor Roosevelt surfaced many times when those around us talked about it, also had a hand in our coming away from the increasingly more malignant conditions perpetrated by humans against humans in Europe. We had been rescued from the "Final Solution" which started in Wannsee about 4 months before, on January 20, 1942, and began to be felt in France in April 1942. Nearly at the same time as the first convoy of asylum-seeking foreign Jews was shipped by the Vichy-France government to Drancy and quickly from there to Auschwitz, Savic and I, and 48 other Jewish and Spanish children were shipped to America.

The thought stuns me to this day.

Entry into Our "New World"

Savic and I entered this "new world" with an already well exercised readiness to cope as best we could with whatever lay in front of us, or might even come from behind. For me, I can't say how Savic experienced it, since I left my mother, I feel I was determined to govern—as much as a 13 year-old can—my life, what I would do. I was prone to decide the choices I would make with fair tenacity. I felt compelled to be determined; others might have experienced me as stubborn. When I say I would "govern" my life, that I would govern me, I was not altogether free to do so: I was just as much governed by forces within me that at times seemed to have their own impetus that would make me do what I did do. I was compelled to go with them. They were that in me that compelled me to immerse myself into music. I was not conscious until later that my emotional link with my mother, for whom singing was just a natural way of expressing herself just as it was for me, organized into my need to delve deeply into music. Harry could not see that; I could not do otherwise. This had much to do with my not being able to get into the program Harry had designed for me. And the more insistent he was, the more I had to protect the integrity of "me." All in all, I was determined to do whatever I could to forge my way into my new life.

I also believe that some of my determination to be the one to govern me was at least in part driven by anxiety; without my mother on whom I could rely with no reservation, I was now psychologically alone. Of that unit of two that made my life secure, I had lost that part on which I totally relied—for nearly everything. It was not in me to just take on another such part, even when very capable and loving Faye Wagner offered herself as substitute. I could not bend to do it. My mother was not lost to me; she was just in that other part of the world now unavailable to me. For now I had to turn to myself. I did. But fortunately, my good relationship with her guided me to trust that others can be turned to, can be reliable and genuinely caring.

On entry into our "New World," though I was set to govern me, there were many things Savic and I could not do. Neither of us knew what the war in Europe would next do to our families and to the life we had left behind. Here we needed grown-ups to do what only grown-ups can do. The prime persons responsible for us were on the one hand Harry and Faye Wagner and, on the other hand, the Jewish Social Services Bureau, Director, Mrs. Gertrude Glick, and my assigned Case Worker, Mrs. Rhoda Mintzer. The Wagners saw to it that we were well fed, always with them, like one family; that we got to bed at a reasonable time, maintained hygiene practices both as we had known them in good times before the war and as they maintained themselves. When the time came for it, they saw to it that we got to school, would be fed at lunch time, that we socialized as kids might be expected to, all in all, that we led a pretty normal kids' life in Pittsburgh. The Jewish Social Services, Mrs. Mintzer, who was mostly visible to me at the beginning of our life in Pittsburgh were no doubt the ones responsible for our developmental program, such as how to proceed with our education—which I assume they took on until we finished High School—and providing the Wagners some funds to clothes and feed us—which no doubt hardly met the expenses required to take care of our needs. I for one also counted on Mrs. Mintzer to provide us with any news of my mother and Savic's parents. Social Services also took responsibility for our citizenry in America including their taking action when the time came for our Naturalization in June 1952, and the handling of all documents pertaining to our actually being on Earth, formerly in Belgium and France, and now in America. Social Services probably did other things as well of which I have never been aware. Though Mrs. Rhoda Mintzer was assigned to our case, our direct contact with her was infrequent. Interestingly, I also remember the address of the Bureau: 15 Fernando Street, in the Hill District in Pittsburgh. Am I destined to remember Social Services Bureau addresses? I know the one in Marseilles (of the OSE) was on Rue de l'Italie, near the train station. All well and good, but how do you get some foreign kids with no families of their own to start life in America? The first most basic steps had been taken. We had a foster home where we would stay for an undetermined period of time; and our papers were in order. We also soon had a Pediatrician and in time got a Dentist. The next most expectable important thing was getting us started in school.

Great! But what do you do to mainstream kids approaching High School years who can not speak English? While we might have been ready age-wise for entry into High School four months after we landed in America, there would have been no assurance that we could learn what we needed to learn to progress fruitfully in an American school speaking and understanding only French and Yiddish! So we were sent to school for one year to learn English and basics in a number of course in preparation of an American High School education. It is also a fact that during the two years from May 1940 to the present May 1942, the schooling I got was inconstant and limited. So during our first year in America, we were in a special class where in the very capable brown-spotted hands of kind, dear Miss Prosser, we learned English, how to speak, read and write it, we learned some American History, including especially Citizenship—the Pledge of Allegiance, the Bill of Rights, Lincoln's magnificent ". . . We hold these truths to be self-evident . . ."—and some math. With this year of preparation, all evidence points to the fact that Savic and I were well prepared by Miss Prosser, as we proceeded from there to Taylor Alderdice High School in Pittsburgh where we both progressed quite successfully. And we continued to progress quite successfully academically and both ended up a decade and a half later as physicians.

While Savic and I had determined we would stay together when we came to America, within less than one year our relationship suffered a number of disagreements that progressively made our sharing the same small bedroom difficult. Why this occurred between us on its appearance is somewhat puzzling because Savic and I had gotten along well since we had met in Rivesaltes and each of us got along quite well with others around us. My relationships with the Wagner family and, from all I saw, his relationships with them were good. Savic may have found Harry more difficult to accommodate to than I, but he did not make such a big issue of it. Our relationships with our neighborhood and Shul peers whom we shared were also quite good. It is true that the bedroom we shared was exceedingly small and really did not accommodate two 13-14 year-olds half-way well. But given where we had come from made this a questionable minor source of misery. Neither of us was happy with this arrangement, true, but I feel that this was not the root cause of our separation. However, being together became not only unpleasant to the two of us, but to our host family as well. Those responsible for us thought it might be to our advantage to be separated, for one of us to be placed in another home. I cannot reconstruct how it was decided; Savic went into another home; I stayed with the Wagners. It could just

Savic and the author in 1946, Juniors-Seniors in high school

Savic—high school graduation photo

as easily have been the other way. I find it meaningful that Savic and I experienced distress at being separated; no ill-feelings seemed to have been experienced by either of us. Savic settled into the other home quite nicely, from all I learned about it from him. But even to this day, I puzzle over what happened to us then; why was it that once we found asylum in America and were well on the way to making a good start in our new life, my very special friend Savic and I could not get along?

I have no certain answer to this question, but I do have some thoughts. We were good friends and have valued each other to this day, even though we have not maintained active contact. Were we to meet today, it would be a warm and most welcome event for each of us. I wonder if we found interest in each other as 11-12 year-olds stuck in the same coerced misery, liked one another, found harmony when we played together pretending we were good-guy musketeers fighting evil, two Jewish boys fighting Nazis. We were going to escape from Rivesaltes together; once our parents told us they wanted us to do so, we felt even more drawn to one another. We must have been friends then already or why would my mother and Savic's parents have even considered that we would escape together? As I said before, at the last minute, Savic's parents retreated from the plan, and my mother and I agreed that I would follow through on the plans. I escaped; Savic stayed in Rivesaltes. Then one year later, under very challenging, frightening conditions, going to America alone, without parents, we find each other again! What a remarkable moment. One year later, after having planned to escape together, one of us escaping and the other staying put in that second circle of hell, we find ourselves reunited. I was blown over by it; all signs indicated that Savic was too. It may have been at that moment that we agreed, not yet saying it, that we would come to America together, and this time, we would go to the end of the line of this voyage together. Had we without thinking it decide to cling together like two naufragés (shipwreck survivors), clinging together in a very uncertain sea? Now that our life was getting restarted, that we each were making a good start, maybe we could let go and not cling to each other, at least not be needing to be in the same family; maybe the same city was enough.

But couldn't we, not cling to each other and still stay in the same family? After all siblings don't cling together and stay in the same family. Maybe something made us need to be separated, to not see each night and day. Had we become too painful reminders to one another? Were we simply too constant reminders of who we really were, two kids who had left their families and all that went with them behind? Did we, as we were straining to cope with the many challenges we were facing, did we now miss unbearably our families and life as we had known it before this whole mess started? We were constant reminders to one another: "Heh, Savic, comment vas ta mère? Et ton père? Et Michel?" "Et toi, Henri, comment vas ta mère? (Heh, Savic, how's your mother? And your father? And Michel [Savic's younger brother]. And you, Henri, how's your mother?) Just one look was enough. How could we deal with that? We had to go on with today, and wait for time to bring our better past and better present together. We were too young to handle this without strife. Maybe grown-ups would have found it unbearable too. With deeply felt sadness I say today, we couldn't do it. And I feel sad thinking of my dear friend Savic. Savic did well academically and professionally. What saddens me is that I think he may have suffered from insecurity in intimate relationships. He married at least 3, possibly 4 times, thus finding no stability in that crucial sector of life. I wonder if having left his family as he did—as we both did—remained for him an unresolved trauma of "having been sent away," leaving him burdened with residual rage toward those he loved dearly, a factor irreconcilable with forming trusting relationships with those with whom he sought intimacy in his new life? But I am guessing, "wild-analyzing" we say—to interpret thoughts, feelings and actions without having directly from the patient information needed to do so. In addition, I suspect that the traumatizing effects of what happened to us may lie at the bottom of his leaving the U.S. and migrating to a South Pacific Island at the time when, in America, we all lived under the threat of a nuclear disaster. Anyway, many years before that, in 1943, Savic left the Wagner family. We separated; life went on.

I am certain that it was Harry and Faye who thought of it, not the Social Service Bureau: they enrolled me for Hebrew School classes, quite with my consent, in a very small Synagogue two blocks from 1119 Greenfield Avenue, Squirrel Hill, where we lived. I remember the face of the young schoolmaster, but not his name—it could have been Rabbi Kimel, but I am not certain. It was totally in my preprogrammed brain that I would have a Bar Mitzvah. In fact, with my background, my mother and my uncle Frenkel would have raised all kinds of hell, if I did not have my Bar Mitzvah. All concerned seemed quite indifferent to the fact that I was not to be 13, but 14. So, one year here, one year there, what's the big deal? Besides Jewish Law permits Bar Mitzvah at years later than 13. Yes, I had my Bar Mitzvah at 14, in Pittsburgh, Pennsylvania, U.S.A., in a small Shul I believe on Murray Avenue, with some very nice people wishing me well. It was nice, and very generous of Faye and Harry, and "the girls," Phyllis, Sandy, and Evelyn.

From these beginnings, I took off; so did Savic. We were both very committed, good students. We had no news from our parents. But we both knew we would, someday, maybe when the war "over there" was over. Savic and I, living in rather distant sections of the city now saw one another only from time to time. I guess as often as brothers might later in life, after they have left home. The homes, school, friends, summer camps, all were the American way; they were good. We grew in them well. It was the summer of 1945 when the war with "The Axis," Germany, Italy, and Japan, was finally over. I was at a party when the news came—and we really celebrated the news rollicking in the street. But as time passed, Savic and I heard nothing from "over there." For me, and no doubt for Savic, this now was getting worrisome. It was long enough already! Now the war was over; the more time passed and I heard nothing, and the Social Service Bureau heard nothing, the more my dread grew about my mother's whereabouts and fate. I had no choice; everyday, I went on living.

I can't remember when—there is too much I can't remember, and that's one of my miseries—but it was sometime in our later High School years, that Savic, exuberant, told me that he had heard from his mother. It was almost unbelievable; Savic had heard from his mother! His father had died, I believe in Rivesaltes—where many died of starvation and disease. His brother Michel was with his mother somewhere in Southern France. But the news for me was not good. Savic's mother had told him that my mother had been sent away from Rivesaltes to one of the death camps, and Savic's mother was certain that she had been murdered. Along with so many other Jews. I was shocked! Mortified!

I welcomed being pulled away from what I felt by the pre-occupations of everyday life of a 17-18 year-old adolescent well-engaged in school activities and with friends.

The mix of disastrous news and the vibrant evolving of my new life, I know, created an irreconcilable mix, a polarization of mental pre-occupations and feelings. Looking on it now, my age, my need to protect myself against excessive pain led me to suppress, set aside my mourning the loss of my mother. I had not yet become able to be close enough to someone, anyone, who could have ably helped me mourn. It is a very difficult undertaking for a child to mourn, even for a late-adolescent, without the help of a well emotionally attached other. Naively, pushed by the challenges of adolescence, I turned to my life of now, to my friends and doings—to my American blessings.

Multiplying my new life blessings, Donald Steinfirst and his family came into my life, or Donald took me into their life. I met Donald when I

The Wagner Family in 1948

Emma Steiner, High School Choir Directrice, 1948

was in 10th grade in High School. My High School music teacher, Emma Steiner, the choir director, another person I will never forget, thought I had a good voice and that I should have singing lessons. Emma Steiner, she deserves to rest in peace, was an unmarried woman, in her 50s I would guess, who just was totally dedicated to making music, to making kids learn the wonders of music, by means of her choirs in Alderdice High School. A number of us found Emma Steiner to be a marvelous character. If something got into her, if we ticked her off in one way or another, not an uncommon occurrence with this very demanding Choir Directrice, we were in for a lecture, and sometimes in extremis, we would get a harangue. At such times she would take off on her imaginary horse, and tell us, scolding, she didn't know why in the world she was subjecting herself to the torture of trying to get brats like us to make music. Why, she'd marry the first Nigger who asked her! she'd occasionally say. A very regrettable expression! It was her maladroit effort at telling us she would do anything just to not have to slave with us brats. She was a "White Anglo-Saxon Protestant," a "WASP," as is said. It may be that she was biased; though other than for that unfortunate racial slur, I never saw or heard any other evidence of it in her. This was in 1947, 1948, a time when such prejudicial slurs by a teacher in a classroom did not encounter the criticism it would deservedly get today, and should have gotten then. However, as she could be difficult, and even brash at moments, she was also devoted and committed to having the best High School choir in Pittsburgh. And she engaged with us personally, some of us more than others. I liked Emma Steiner; I did not like her tirades, but she was a top-notch musician, and she did manage, year after year, by driving us fairly hard, to have one of the best choirs in the city. It was my good fortune that Emma Steiner liked me. She thought I had a good voice; that it ought to be trained outside of school. Because I had with embarrassment told her that I had no way of getting the money needed for voice lessons, she thought that Donald Steinfirst, the music critic of the Pittsburgh Post-Gazette, might be able to help me find some funding somewhere. Through her, though I don't know how she arranged it, I met Donald Steinfirst.

We immediately liked each other. Though Donald was the Vice President of a successful roofing materials production company, his true love was music. With no formal musical training he educated himself into becoming a highly well regarded music critic. I suspect that the part of Music Criticism he liked best was not all the free concerts and operas he

The Steinfirst family, 1962, nearly 20 years after they welcomed the author into their family. *Rear*: Barbara (Dick's wife) John, (inset) Jane. *Front*: Dick, Donald, Susan

Karl's wedding day, July 1989. *From left*: Joshua, Rachel, Karl, Henri, and Erik

The author's family, August 2003. *Back:* Sophie (E), Arthur (K), and Benjamin (E). *Middle row*: Erik, Andrea (E), Lenore (J), Sabina (K), Rachel, and Henri. *Front row*: Joshua, Raphael (J), Elliot (K), and Karl. E=Erik's family; K=Karl's family; J=Joshua's family)

got to go to, nor writing the reviews, nor tapping these on an ancient typewriter at the Newspaper, no; it was entertaining some of the big stars in his home. There I met, among others, Vladimir Horowitz, and my favorite of them, Jan Peerce. Donald just beamed from start to finish at those soirees. So did Jane, his wife. What a thrill for Jane, it was all over her face, when she told of Horowitz dancing with her. Donald got me some funds for voice lessons. But well beyond that, he and Jane also opened their home to me. When I was in 11th and 12th grade, I became a rather frequent visitor to their house. Donald, Jane, Dick their oldest son, and Susan and John, the twins, were all very welcoming to me. This was just the beginning of my relationship with the family. Donald enormously facilitated my growing from adolescence into adulthood. Once I decided that I wanted to become a professional musician, a singer, Donald was instrumental in my auditioning for Vladimir Bakaleinikoff, then Assistant Conductor of the Pittsburgh Symphony Orchestra, and then with Fritz Dorian, Senior Musicologist at then Carnegie-Tech's College of Fine Arts, Music Department. A very substantial scholarship made it possible for me to get a degree in Music. Between the remarkably generous, loving, devoted Wagner family and the warm, enriching, helpful Steinfirst family, the path from my arrival to Pittsburgh, learning English and about America, going through High School and the first stage of my College education was immeasurably facilitated. Nothing can wipe away the loss of my life with my family in Bruxelles. But what the Wagner and the Steinfirst families gave me has been good for a lifetime and more.

Soon after graduating from the College of Fine Arts, in Music, I went into the Military, drafted as was then required, for 2 years. These were the Korean War years. I had the good fortune of being stationed in Europe. This is when I decided to change career path. When I came out of the Military, my whole life opened up. I went into Medicine, into Psychiatry and Psychoanalysis of Adults and Children. I married Rachel just before starting Medical School; we have now been married for 48 years. We have three sons, Erik, Karl, and Joshua. Totally objective: they are remarkable men! They are well married. Rachel and I now have five grandchildren, really, "great-children" is more accurate. As is said, things couldn't get any better. Counterpoint to all the pain of my first life, what a life in America!

Part Two

Reflections—60 Years Later

Chapter 7

Trauma in the Lives of Children

"La Condition Humaine"

For Andre Malraux, "*La Condition Humaine*" addresses, as Ferral drops into our lap somewhat derisively, the condition of being a man, which is, that man who has only one life, is willing to lose it for an idea. Gisors counters with little regard for Ferral, that it is to overcome this internally driven condition that man seeks to be God. The idea that drives man to lose his life, in Malraux's book, is set in the Chinese Nationalist-Communist conflict that despite the failure to assassinate Chiang-Kai-Chek, eventually gave way to Chinese Communism, in which in fact many on both sides lost their life.

Malraux has priority over the phrase, *La condition humaine.* But I am borrowing the phrase to carry another meaning. I am speaking of the fact, not just that we suffer, but as my own past and decades of work have taught me, that we humans create much of that suffering ourselves. That man makes members of his own Society, or equally human members of other Societies, suffer is documented by the continuing emergence of testimonies that detail some of the dreadful Holocaust atrocities survivors suffered and massacres they witnessed. These were even more odious than that we cause one another suffering in wars, in crimes against one another, community against community, individual against individual. We are all well exercised in causing others suffering.

And consider that, as we further document suffering from the Holocaust, Cambodia, Bosnia, Rwanda and Burundi, and elsewhere, in my field we find that, with intention or not, much suffering occurs in our homes. Parents make their own children suffer. And many among these children will in time make their own children suffer. *La condition humaine* I have in mind is that we humans are made to suffer by others like ourselves; and Janus-like, that, we cause others to suffer.

My Holocaust experience has driven me to labor in this arena, this condition *humaine.* And having been victimized in the Holocaust, and in years that followed seeing intense suffering in children especially, has led me to the conviction that we have only one alternative: whatever pessimism may stand in our way, we must do what we can to reduce the suffering around us, and to not let a Holocaust happen again. We have to do what we can to stop causing others avoidable suffering. In Part III, I will speak of the findings my evolving work has pointed to, that we can act to lessen societal suffering.

But first, as a backdrop to my looking back, to my reflections 60 years later, on how the Holocaust impacted on me, I want to highlight how the suffering it caused me opened my eyes to the suffering of children all around us. I can not look at myself without seeing and holding in mind the burden of suffering that afflicts so many around us, so many children.

Pain Is Part of Everyday Life

We all know pain; we know it is part of life. How many times a day do parents need to tend to their child's pain, or need to deny their child is in pain? This alone is one of the facts that make parenting so difficult. This is what makes it essential for parents to help their children learn to cope with pain, to let it guide the child into some workable, constructive solution to reduce or eliminate the child's own pain. The task becomes difficult. And its consequences are large. I'll talk about this in Part III.

If we come into the world in a well-developed state and into a family that does not have to struggle too harshly to make it, we ourselves are all able to make it. But somehow, it does not seem to happen that smoothly. Kids cannot escape torture. Something much too painful always seems to happen. Whether it's your favorite teacher who accidentally gets killed while walking on Broad Street; or a girl you really have a crush on comes to your birthday party and, in front of your eyes turns sweet on one of your friends; or from time to time on the way to school you come face to face with a bully a head taller than yourself. How painful are these? How do they impact on us? We each bring our own pain tolerance, vulnerability, the state of our self-image and our "inner-sustainment," to such experiences. Over time, all we experience, good and bad, molds us. Psychology 101.

The toll excessive psychic pain exacts on growing human beings can be enormous. The expression of pain on the young child's face is so troubling that many adults among us do all we can to deny the child is in pain. This intolerability on our part, we adults, goes so far as to disallow children to mourn even the loss of their own mothers or fathers. It has led even Mental Health professionals to assume that children cannot mourn. They are mistaken. Children can mourn; but they need a helpful environment to do so.

Then, pain requires enormous psychic energy that we put into service to cope with it. Furthermore, pain must be attended to; that's why we can't keep our tongue away from an aching tooth. By virtue of the attention and the energy it draws to itself, excessive pain robs the child of being able to attend to schoolwork, in school and at home. It robs the child of the ability to learn. In addition, by making us miserable, pain makes us miserable to be with. Our threshold of irritability drops to near-zero, our ability to tolerate frustration approaches exhaustion, we are a mess to ourselves and to others. Furthermore, excessive psychic pain causes a wide range of more intense symptoms including panic states, tantrums and outbursts of rage, terrifying dreams and other sleep disturbances, loss of appetite or over-eating, hopelessness and depression, and that is just for starts.

Excessively painful experiences vary widely. Even within the category "excessively painful," there is a range of intensity. We learned this from Holocaust Survivors. But we also have learned that excessively painful events can come from within the child's own home. Excessively painful events may come from outside the child's home, from his neighborhood, from some emotionally battered or outright criminal or starvation-crazed individual. Or excessive pain may come from the insanity humans collectively visit on each other—wars, malignant prejudice, Holocausts. Children, by chance, or too often by intention, get subjected to these. This variation in sources of pain matters. Of the types of excessively painful events a child is subjected to, those that are perpetrated on the child by her of his own parents, like physical abuse, emotional abuse, sexual abuse, tend to be the most hurtful and even the most traumatizing. It may surprise some that a Child Psychiatrist with my past might say this. To be intentionally hurt badly by your own mother or father carries with it the experience of being hurt by those who are supposed to love you, care for you, protect you against harm, and more. That they do you harm is experienced as a profound betrayal of trust, as a betrayal of familial love. I am not the only Holocaust survivor in our field who holds this view. A friend, Anna Ornstein, also a Child Psychiatrist and

Psychoanalyst, an Auschwitz survivor, holds the same view. She put it well, "Hitler never promised the Jews of Europe anything but death." Elie Wiesel said something like that too. It is probably in *Mein Kampf*. When it is your enemy, you cannot be surprised that he wants to harm and even kill you; even children know that.

But when it's your own mother! Your own father!

We have learned this just-past century that experiences that impact on us mold what of us is there to begin with, little by little or all at once. The everyday experiences that repeat themselves over and over exact adaptation by us that progressively, little by little, makes us become who we are. Those experiences that do so all at once tend to be the extreme experiences, those that fill us with a large burst of joy and well-being, and those that fill us with dread, terror, bottomless humiliation, with extreme psychic pain. Both types of modifications in our self-experiencing, at any given time combine to make us evolve into who we are. Within limits imposed by our genetic makeup and the stability of who we already are, we are changeable. Intense psychic pain carries much weight in molding us.

Extremes of Psychic Pain

And where that pain that goes beyond our tolerance: psychic pain that shocks, that scatters our brain, that splatters our body and mind, that lightning-strikes us indelibly, this now instantly becomes part of us. An event of jarring agony gets branded into our amygdala and via its projections into our frontal cortex; fixed. Often it is a series of events of body and mind splattering dimensions, each event further stamping into our brain and psyches the experience of that agony.

The coping strategies we put into effect to survive such events become part of our being. Events of overwhelming pain that drown our efforts to cope have drastic consequences. In infants we see this in extreme cases of "Failure to thrive" due to "Cause unknown"; but the cause that is unknown, we have learned, is "excessive emotional neglect"; and many of these infants die. Or, in adults like those Primo Levi, Elie Wiesel, Abraham Biderman, Rudy Vrba, Henry Krystal and others knew or saw around them in Auschwitz-Birkenau and Buchenwald, those overwhelmingly traumatized human beings who surrendered psychically, whom they called "*Mussulmann*." Under such conditions, when our efforts succeed in protecting us against lethal surrender, the psychic defenses we erect, by becoming part of our personality often bring with them ways of coping that are pathological.

But there are many who survive such excessively traumatizing conditions, and whose efforts to cope with such pain have led to remarkable beneficent adaptations. Primo Levi, Elie Wiesel, Benjamin Meed, Abraham Biderman, Henry Krystal, Anna and Paul Ornstein, and others I have known, renown, admirable examples of serious trauma survivors who have made large contributions to society. We have studied and know that adaptation to excessive psychic pain can lead to creativity—Ludwig van Beethoven, Gustav Mahler, Bedrich Smetena, Henri Magritte—, to acts of charity and human preservation—Mohandas Gandhi, Martin Luther King, Elie Wiesel—to the benefit of humans. Many less illustrious than these well-known survivors of extremes of pain have added their share of effort toward universal well being. Many try. They do not plan it; it happens, even unbeknownst to them as they do it.

There are just too many sources of excessive pain; they seem to seek out children. 60 years ago, my words to Mora, "I am a doctor," were not without meaning. Nothing we say is without meaning. Of course, by then I knew pain, in excess. Once I set my path onto Medicine, I wanted to help heal children's wounds, and particularly, those coming from their intense emotional pain. I have assumed that the path from experiencing excessive psychic pain to healing children's wounded psychic being was laid down somewhere in my brain in the course of what happened to me. I was not aware of that as it evolved.

Chapter 8

Looking Back

Sixty years later; those of us who are still here, still feel deeply pained by what happened to so many of us, so many years ago. I lament, but I am not surprised; this is how it works. You get traumatized when you're young, it's for life; for some, more; for some, less. The Holocaust is ever present, it is for life, however short or long life may be. So much so that I have not . . . done so many things I could have done, about what happened. Foremost, why did I not search for the whereabouts of my brother and my father until recent years? I am searching now to know the answer. I do know that my answer has a bearing on why it took survivors so long to speak out about their Holocaust experience.

Here I am, committed to understanding my patients, and always at hand is understanding myself, and I don't understand so much of my behavior in this regard. Well, maybe that's too strong. I understand a good deal of it.

Henri Parens, 1994

Looking back on these times, on these events, always envelops me in a cloud of aching pain and quiet rage. It is easiest when I am alone; it's easiest to let myself ache then. When it comes up with my wife or my children, I want them to know what happened; they have to know the truth. I want them to know my aching pain. But I don't want them to fume in rage or suffer my melancholia about what Humans did to us, what these Humans did to their family. I don't know how well I succeed because, I think, they are prone to try to protect me from the misery they feel. We share, but we probably all temper our feelings, trying to dose the misery we visit on each other. In public, whether in social gatherings or in seminars, discussion groups, or classes I teach about matters that touch on the Holocaust I share some of my experience globally, without detail—"It's the Nazis who did this to us; the German Nazis, the French Nazis, the Polish, . . . the European Nazis." I tend to do it as in discourse, in serious discussion, unavoidably letting a glimpse of my sad-seriousness show through. I've heard some of my Survivor friends do this too. Some of us even bring some humor into our telling, not so much to protect friends, colleagues and students—though that comes into it too—, as much as to make it possible to keep thinking and talking and not be swept into disorganization—as has happened to me on occasion.

I have been looking back for many years since the day I came to America. It is now 60 years later. As we all do, my looking back attaches to events that have gotten anchored to dates, some dates spanning an era, some vague, some marked to the day and very clear. Those marked to the day stand out. Three dates stand out for me in highest relief, May 1, 1941, early May 1942, and August 14, 1942.

May 1, 1941: 12 Years Old, I Escaped from Rivesaltes

According to Marrus and Paxton, Rivesaltes was one of the harshest of Vichy-France's thirty-one Concentration Camps. Having been in two of these, Récébédou and Rivesaltes, Marrus and Paxton are right; Rivesaltes was really a further steep circle's descent into hell. Looking back at my escape, I find it easy and difficult to answer, "How did I do that?" My friends Judith Kestenberg and Ira Brenner who studied and wrote about child survivors (The Last Witness, referred to earlier), found that many children, especially teenagers, reacted to the life situations visited on them with surprising energy, ingenuity, and effectiveness that reached well beyond what our elders, those who knew better, might have predicted. Teenagers, according to my friends, were found to have done things that in normal every day life would not have been expected of them at all; and many succeeded. Some even tolerated the stresses and strains of concentration camp, and other experiences better than many adults. A number of Survivors' testimonies suggest this as well. Kestenberg and Brenner are right.

I did not feel it an accomplishment to escape from Riversaltes. Not then; I was pleased with myself for having succeeded. Looking back on it now, I feel good about having had the guts as a kid to do it; but it was not something I chose to do, it was something I had to do. My mother told me she wanted me to do it; she conveyed with urgency that she wanted me to do so. She did not tell me that she had learned the Nazis were gassing Jews in Poland and Russia. She told me I had to go; her tone conveyed necessity. I agreed to do it. I trusted her; I knew she knew what I should do. My mother did not spin tales; she had a sense of humor and her face would then light up with a full smile; she could be playful and she could be serious. She showed that she loved, and she loved me. I knew that she meant what's best for me. It's not complicated. Many a boy my age, in these conditions, would have done the same. It was life, then. One thought survival.

Facts, circumstances, change one's way of coping, of being. Looking at it as a Child Psychiatrist, it is striking to me even today how we could agree to play Les Trois Mousquetaires (The Three Musketeers), and in a moment register the facts of our life now and shift mode into "our life has been taken away, our families' life; this is no game. Survive!" But kids do this; they can experience threat to life here and now, and yet in a stretch of hours free from alarm, they can shift into a self-protecting avoidance mode and play some simple child's game. This ability to judiciously enough defend against fully registering potentially dire conditions contributes significantly to the resilience kids show again and again. So we could play at being musketeers, but we, at least, I could when the time came, tolerate separation from my mother and take up the challenge of escaping. I did it. It did not save my mother—which fills me with tears. She saved me.

Early May 1942: I Came to America, on Convoy #3—*L'OSE* Saved Many of Us

The OSE (*Oeuvre de Secours aux Enfants*—Works [Efforts] to Rescue Children) took a decisive position on saving the children. So did other standing groups including an organized Swiss Social Service network, the American Quakers, The YMCA, as well as clusters of French villagers, and individual French Clergy, Catholic and Protestant. It justifies faith in the goodwill of humans to know that in the midst of shameless fascistic degradation of too many, many "righteous ones" risking their own lives and that of their families, fought to save many of us from the Nazis' plans. In *Sauver Les Enfants (Save the Children)*, Vivette Samuel tells us that the OSE was one of 25 humanitarian organizations, national and international, religious and secular, that pulled forces together and divided among themselves specific assignments to help the war refugees incarcerated in concentration camps in France. They were a remarkable group, these 25. Among them 9 were Jewish organizations, the OSE among them; there was an OSE branch in the United States, though it is not clear to me that they did or how they participated during the early years of the war. 16 organizations that saved Jewish children were Christian. Two American organizations stand out that were actively engaged in saving us; the Quakers and the YMCA. It was according to Samuel, the representative of the YMCA who proposed that the 25 organizations work in concert. Between October 1940 to March 1943 the Committee representing the efforts of the 25 groups met in Nimes (Southern France) once a month. Each organization was assigned a sector of concern in their overall efforts.

In its share of responsibility, the OSE carried out 3 functions in Rivesaltes. One, they provided medical aid, which consisted essentially of attempting to bring supplementary food for those children and elderly rendered most fragile by the miserable conditions they suffered resulting from the war, from their incarceration, and particularly the Nazi anti-Jewish Laws then instituted by Vichy-France. One of the OSE's prime efforts was to fight that "medical disease, Cachexia," which is profound loss of weight and sickness caused by starvation, that eventually and commonly leads to death. Their second task was to liberate children from the camp and shelter them outside (the camp) which meant taking charge of them, of their health, their education and all that goes with responsible child care-giving. Their third task was to emigrate as many as possible. Several hundred emigration-dossiers were issued. The rules were precise: only children younger than 15, in good health, and who were assured entry in the United States were eligible. Three convoys of such children left Marseilles destined for the United States. The first convoy left in May 1941; the second left between August and September of the same year. The third left in early May 1942. This convoy, and probably the ones before consisted of 50 children, Jewish and Spanish. Since my *Sauf-Conduit* (exit visa) was dated April 28, 1942, I was among this third convoy. A fourth convoy, scheduled for departure in November 1942 was blocked by the Germans who had by then broken through the armistice frontier and occupied the South of France. Furthermore, the Nazis had already unleashed "The Final Solution" and the machinery for sending Jews from Rivesaltes and other Vichy-France camps to Auschwitz had already begun. This means that here again, having been sent to America in May on the 3rd convoy, I escaped the Nazis reach by only a few months.

By means of clandestine radio and other reports, the OSE knew the dangers in the making. But I am conflicted, both as a child Survivor and as a Child Psychiatrist, by what they reasoned they must do. Grown-ups think oddly sometimes. The OSE and others of the 25 organizations assumed quite correctly that, as was happening in Poland and Russia, where the Germans had conquered the lands, if children of Jews, Gypsies, and others victimized stayed with their parents, when the Nazis executed the parents, the children were executed with them. This occurred whether executions were carried out in trucks, or in gas chambers. On first reading that the OSE separated children from their parents by plan, with this reasoning in mind, I was shocked. Was this Solomon deciding who gets the children?

The OSE and the other organizations were not wrong. As a Mental Health professional today, with our current understanding of the traumatic effects of separating children from their parents, it is troubling to think that these devoted and committed adults knowingly separated the children from their parents to save the children. Would I, a Child Psychiatrist and Psychoanalyst during the latter half of the 20th Century, recommend such a course for saving the children? Yes. The choice was dire. Many Jews predicted what the Nazis from Germany might do, Mein Kampf made it very clear; we just didn't know what methods Hitler and his henchmen would devise. What we did not expect is that there would be French Nazis who would match the German Nazis step for step, and at times be a step ahead of them.

Samuel tells us that encamped in Riversaltes as a volunteer with the OSE, one of their prime efforts was to separate the children under 15 from their mothers. Mothers and fathers being separated by Nazi wisdom—after all Jewish mothers and fathers together are a serious threat to society!—it seemed to fall to the mothers to decide the separations of children and parents. It is not incomprehensible that it would. Samuel tells us that the Spanish mothers—who like the Jewish families had sought asylum in France, they, having run in the late 1930s from Franco's fascist destruction machine—did not permit separation of their children from them. On the other hand, Samuel wrote, the Jewish mothers wanted their children out of the camp and placed in safe asylum by the OSE. Samuel is most likely right since, even though Savic's parents decided at the last minute to not let him escape from Rivesaltes on 1 May 1941—this was before Samuel came to Rivesaltes—, his parents did sign him up to come to America with the 3rd convoy. Making matters worse, was that, to legalize their taking custody of the children, the OSE was obliged to get the parents to sign over all rights to their own children. Only knowing, sensing if not fully knowing, that disaster lay ahead could have made mothers in such numbers give their own children over to another in order to save them. That the OSE separated the children from their parents to save them, as time proved to be the case for many of them, required an acceptance of causing trauma to both children and parents, in order to save the children's life.

The 25 self-determined groups dedicated to making our lot less life-threatening and to rescue as many of us as they could, whose representatives met monthly in Nimes during these dreadful years, they themselves became threatened as the Germans came to know of their activities. By late 1942, the organizations dedicated to saving us were in danger. To the point of separating children from their families to save them, the OSE and the other groups, had to counter the efforts made by the Vichy government to make sure that children stayed with their families and be deported with them. They did so in the name of family reunification. Here again, as Samuel reports, Vichy's Laval government instituted and put into action such edicts even before the Germans asked for the deportation of children along with their families. The OSE knew in August 1942 that deportation meant death. Somehow my mother knew that in early 1941. The deportation of children was formalized, Samuel reports, it was ordered. The OSE tried vainly from May 1942 on to get

* According to the French newspaper *France Soir* of June 7, 2002, in reporting on a display of the French convoying of Jews from its camps to Auschwitz, an account was given that stated the fact that ". . . 11,600 Jewish children, of whom 2,000 were less than six years old, [were] victims of the 'final solution'. In all, 76,000 Jews were deported from France. Only 2,500 would survive." (Materials distributed by Les Fils et Filles des Deportés Juifs de France [The Sons and Daughters of Jews Deported from France]; author's translation.)

"Am 14.8.1942 hat Transporlzug Nr. D 901114 den Abgangsbahnhof Le Bourget – Draney in Richtung Auschwitz mit insgesamt 1 000 Juden verlassen. (Darunter Erstmalig Kinder.) Dererfasste Personenkreis entschpricht Den gegebenen Richtlinien."

Femachreiben der Gestapo – Leitstelle Paris en des RSHA und Des Lager Auschwitz am 14. August 1942

"On August 14, 1942, transport train no. D 901114 departed the Le Bourget-Draney station for Auschwitz carrying a total of 1,000 Jews (including children for the first time). The persons involved were chosen in accordance with the guidelines that have been laid down."

Telex from Gestapo headquarters in Paris to the Reich Security Main Office end the Auschwitz camp on August 14, 1942

Convoy 19, August 14, 1942

"We found a total of 1,015 deportees in Convoy 19 . . . there was only one survivor from this convoy in 1945, Nathan Seroka."

— Serge Klarsfeld

161

POZNANSKI	EVA	14.1 .06	LODZ
PRIZANTOVA	ESTHER	8.12.11	
PRUSINOWSKA	ROSA	16.3 .01	
PREDBROSKI	SIMON	26.6 .32	PARIS
PREZEDBROSKI	ISRAEL	9.2 .37	PARIS
PREZEDBROSKI	LAJZEL	30.11.95	RADONISK
PREZEDBROSKI	BAYLA	18.5 .02	LODZ
QUELLER	BERTHOLD	9.10.93	LWOW
RABINOVITSCH	DANIEL	7.6 .85	
RADICH	ESTER	7.12.81	
RAPPEL	HENRI	5.5 .99	VARSOVIE
RAPPEL	ESTHER	24.11.98	VARSOVIE
RAPPEL	JOSEPH	12.2 .30	PARIS
RATH	MAX	20.3 .84	
RATH	MARTHA	9.13.87	
RAUCH	BARUCH	5.11.91	
RAUCH	HELENE	27.2 .01	
RECHNIC	SUZANNE	26.10.36	PARIS
RECHNIC	MAURICE	1.4 .35	PARIS
RECHNIC	CECILE	4.7 .32	PARIS

Detail from manifest.

French officials to not deport children under 16. Given Vichy's determination—most likely that of Jean Bousquet, a Minister of rank then, who is recorded photographically to have greeted Heydrich Himmler with a full smile and a thrust-forward handshake on their meeting in Paris—to get rid of the Jews' next generation, led the OSE and co-rescuing groups to operate now in clandestine ways. This was before the Germans invaded the Free Zone. Once the Germans did so, the OSE homes, now known to be asylums for orphans and children whose parents accepted separation from them, had to be closed. Switzerland, Spain, received children clandestinely crossed over their borders, and from there these countries became departure-points for those children to be sent to America and to Palestine. In this efforts, over 400 children were saved from deportation. This closure occurred about 7 months after I had left *La Villa Mariana* to come to America.

It was after Samuel had her own first child from whom she had to transiently separate to carry out her work that she came to appreciate "the actual degree of anguish," as she said, (*la mesure reelle de l'angoisse*), caused families by their giving their own children over to OSE for safekeeping. The OSE, and the others involved in saving the children were right in doing what they did.

I was saved. My mother died in Auschwitz, as probably did my father and my brother, along with who knows how many of my childhood family—like many others' families.

August 14, 1942: My Mother Was Sent to Auschwitz

My mother was sent to Auschwitz on August 14, 1942. I have repeated that sentence in an effort to inscribe it in my brain. My brain resists its inscription. But it's there, even though I often can't find it. Strategically placed markers now help me remember.

According to Serge Klarsfeld, this is the day convoy #19, carrying 991 persons, no doubt all Jews since this was part of the now activated "Final Solution," left Drancy, destination Auschwitz. In August 1942, there were 13 convoys that carried 13,123 Jews from France to Auschwitz; seemingly the preferred destination for them; Foreign Jews at first; French Jews would follow. In the year 1942, the Vichy-French government sent 41,951 persons from France, mostly from Drancy, to Auschwitz. By August 14 the Vichy-France-German collaboration in executing the "Final Solution" in France was operating well.* Klarsfeld records that transports from France to Auschwitz started on March 27 1942, this first one leaving from Compiegne carrying 1,112 persons. According to Marrus and Paxton, at the outset of their odious collaboration, the Vichy-French plan executors worked with such alacrity and efficiency that they sent their first train convoy before the Germans were ready to receive and transiently house them, causing an embarrassment for the poor German Nazis. But by August, the time convoy #19 was shipped out, the dispatching to the Death Camps in Poland of Jews who had sought refuge in France seems to have proceeded smoothly. And since the "Final Solution" once set in motion in January 1942 called for expeditiousness, no doubt the transfer of my mother and others from Rivesaltes via Drancy to Auschwitz probably took no more than two days, three at most. Once there, extermination was efficiently expedited. As Primo Levi tells us in If *This Is a Man* (retitled *Survival in Auschwitz*), in the later war years, in 1944, the killing of the incoming Jews may have slowed some in order to enlarge the slave labor corps, because the Germans were then increasingly desperate for workers and the production of war materials.

August 14, 1942, day of horror.

There were many days of horror, then.

On August 14, my mother was sent to Auschwitz. What a terrible return to her homeland. Had I not escaped, I would have returned to my birth land with her. I have thought often, "And with her to our grave."

Again, at our oldest son Erik's urging and ever-readiness to help me in efforts of discovery and recovery of information, I am currently in the process of finding out what I can about the fate of my father and my brother, Emanuel—whether and when they were sent to Auschwitz. Since they were in Lodz at the start of the war . . . they didn't have so far to travel to reach Auschwitz.

To this past year, this past August 2002 to be exact, I have not been able to remember on which day my mother was sent with other internees—like cattle—from Drancy to Auschwitz. Live stock is sent in wagons to be butchered, so that we can eat. Just to be gotten rid of! I just realized that I am scratching my arms and my head as I write this.

I first learned of this miserable day from Judy Kestenberg, a child psychoanalyst who studied effects of the Holocaust on survivors. I had long known Judy as a colleague and friend. Judy, herself a Holocaust survivor, much braver than I, was gathering narratives from Holocaust child survivors; she was one of the key American Psychiatrists-Psychoanalysts doing so. I don't recall how she came to know that I am a child-survivor. After refusing several invitations that I be interviewed by her, I consented. My memory, quite good for many other types of information, is absolutely dull when it comes to these matters. I probably agreed to be interviewed in the late 1980s. I could be off on this by as much as 5 years either way. In any case, Judy was just so sensitive, so sympathetic, so well distanced and close, so gentle and persistent, pressing for details and tolerant of vagueness. I came to so admire her work and her courage that I dedicated to her my address, "Influences of the Holocaust on development—One man's experience," which I gave in 1999 to The American College of Psychoanalysts.

Judy asked me if I wanted her to research for me what happened to my mother, my father and my brother. I had been, and to a degree still am, nigh-totally avoidant—when it comes to finding out what happened to them, my immediate family of origin. Well, that's not totally accurate. In 1953, when I was 24, I made my first return visit to Europe, courtesy of the U. S. government; I was in the U. S. Army Medical Corps for the then obligatory two-year draft; I had the good fortune of being assigned to serve in Germany rather than Korea. I say the good fortune, because this assignment gave me the opportunity to be close enough to return to my hometown; in addition, of course, it also had meant that I was not going into a live war-zone. While stationed in Bamberg, Germany, on leaves from duty, I made two trips to Bruxelles. The first was in July 1953 when I searched for and found some of my family who also survived the Holocaust, and the second was in October 1953 when I found out from a most reliable source what, most likely, had happened to my mother.

In July 1953, I found dearly loved cousins who also had survived the Holocaust.

Said aside but not lightly, I want to note here, having experienced both, that I am among those who have found a notable distinction between European antisemitism and American antisemitism. Antisemitism in America, even with its quotas—such as for admission to medical school, exclusion from certain social organizations, etc.—and its ghetto neighborhoods, did not have the public sanction, the freedom to express itself openly and maliciously in public as it did in Europe, even in France, despite France's written laws against it. True, for many in

America it was near the surface, but it generally remained covert. To a degree I have equated European antisemitism with pre-1970s American racism against Blacks. Antisemitism in the Europe of my youth was in the air, overt in the streets, on walls and posters; "Sales Juifs" easily came out of the mouths even of children. Looking at it perhaps too simply, American antisemitism is substantially more benign than the European species, especially Eastern European antisemitism, that pogrom-infected variety which, however, was notably dwarfed by that most virulent species, Nazi antisemitism. Of course, none of these species is dead, though the last is inactivated—but as I write, it has been replaced by a new brand. Before, it was Christian antisemitism; now it seems dominantly Muslim antisemitism.

In July 1953, I returned to Bruxelles for the first time, 13 years after we had left it. I was very eager to get there. Going as directly from Bamberg as I could, on the train to Bruxelles I felt a mix of excitement and muffled dread. I couldn't wait to get to Bruxelles, my first return to my hometown since we had left it in such a rush; and, I feared what I would and wouldn't find of my family there, of my old-life.

To this day I love Bruxelles, full of warm, loving family memories, modest existence. As a boy I, alone or with Felix, my best friend, would roam up to the old, always dirty-gray massive *Palais de Justice* (The Court-House) where, walking uphill from where we lived on *rue de lÉconomie* and *rue des Tanneurs*, through *La Place du Jeu de Balle*, a cobble-stone field where they played an odd type of ball game or that served as a large market place, and after crossing several streets including la rue Haute, up stone stairs to the steeply elevated Palais d'Justice, Felix and I, and a couple others whose names I can't remember, would run around or explore the old place like kids do. Or, from *La Place du Jeu de Balle* up to la rue Haute, we would turn right toward Le Rialto, the movie-house we would go to on weekends to see Charlie Chaplin or Laurel and Hardy or some French-dubbed American cowboy movie. Or from *La Place du Jeu de Balle*, we could turn left and after quite a number of winding blocks we would come face to face with the *Meneken-Pis* single-stream fountain (the Bruxelles-famed statue of a little boy arched back exhibiting how far he can urinate), and after turning the corner enter onto *la Grand Place* (Grand Place or Square). Uniquely Bruxellois, a large cobble-stoned town-square, Grand Place presents *L'Hotel de Ville* (City Hall), grand, gothic and very ornate, one square long, to the right on entry into the square, and surrounded then by smaller similarly ornate buildings, with shops and restaurants on street level. *La Grand Place* is not large like Moscow's Red Square, but for Bruxelles, it's plenty large, and uniquely old-beautiful. And I cannot leave my highlights of the Bruxelles of my childhood without mentioning *Le Bois de la Cambre,* my favorite Sunday outing park south of the city at the end of *l'Avenue Louise.* We took the tram to get there, a tram that runs in very good order to this day. To go to the *Bois d'la Cambre* was a festive occasion, and holds some of my most pleasant childhood memories, though there is one that baffled me some, that time when my mother gave me a few centimes (pennies) to buy an ice cream cone, which I did with eagerness. But when I walked away from the ice cream stand, as I quickly righted my body that had been jarred by the uneven ground, the scoop of ice cream fell out of the cone and, I was left bereft, with an empty cone in my hand. Humiliated by the event, I did not report my sad accident to my mother who mildly scolded me for bringing her back only remains of the empty come. She was not a physicist or a detective or she would have suspected that as dry an end of cone as I brought back to her looked like it had never contained any ice-cream at all, and that I should not stand accused of greediness. She didn't accuse me of that; I guess I worried she might have had that thought, though she certainly knew me better than that.

I arrived in Bruxelles. Although I was then in the U. S. Army Medical Corps, I traveled this journey as well as my second visit, in "civilian clothes" as they say in the army. Since I speak French, in France and in Belgium I had not trouble finding my way. I did not go to a hotel to secure a bed for the night or wash up, or anything; I strapped on my traveling shoulder-bag; it was not large. I had done a bit of what was necessary to freshen up on the train and for the time being that seemed to be enough. I simply was pressed to get to my old neighborhood, a bit like going directly into the lion's den, to learn more of what was left of my family and my old community. I knew I would not find my mother; I had learned that from Savic.

I had gotten off the train at *La Gare du Midi* (South Station). The station looked very different this time than it did that panicky day in early May 1940 when we left Bruxelles for anywhere in France. Now it was just a train station. It was a matter of just about two blocks to get from the station onto le Boulevard du Midi and to then reach la rue des

Tanneurs, then a left onto it and another block on rue des Tanneurs, then a right and within two hundred feet bearing left at the fork, I was on *rue de l'Economie*, where we lived with my Aunt Esther and dislikable cousin Joseph. I had traveled this path many times, twice daily, going to and from home to Elementary school which was on the Boulevard du Midi. In fact, I had just passed by the school, which I remember with good memories.

We lived on the second floor, *6 rue d'l'Économie.* It was moving, almost disturbing and yet, warming to be on this street. And it suddenly dawned on me, it struck me, that this street, and so too *la rue des Tanneurs* and the *Boulevard du Midi*, looked so much smaller than I had recorded in my memory. Now, I could cross *rue d'l'Economie* in 5 or 6 large strides. We used to play marbles, tops, and all kinds of games on this street. I was amazed at the discovery that in my child's eye, my home street was much larger than what I saw now. I thought of this many times some years later in my work with children; to the child, the world, the people in it, look much larger than they actually are; it's all dimensioned by measure against oneself.

Standing in front of the house I looked up to the second floor and stood there several minutes without moving. No on saw me, not that I know of, or they might have wondered what in the world is this man doing there? I was torn. I felt compelled to go up the stairs and look in to see the apartment we had lived in; but I was very hesitant to intrude so on the people living there. What would I say, *"Excusez-moi, j'espère que je ne vous dérange pas trop; je voulais simplement voir l'intérieur de l'apartement. Vous voyez, j'ai vécu ici quand j'étais enfant."* (Excuse me, I hope I am not troubling you too much; I simply wanted to see the inside of the apartment. You see, I lived here when I was a child.) That would be awkward. It was awkward as I slowly climbed the stairs, pushed from within by the pressing need to revisit the site, even if for one moment. As my eyes reached floor level I saw between the banister balusters that the door was open. I hesitated, but I went on, acutely embarrassed. I came to the open door, knocked and stuck my head in. There was no answer. "*Bonjour, il y a quelqu'un à la maison*?" (Hello, is someone home?) No answer. What now? I repeated my question. Still no answer. I took a step inside, very uncomfortable at what I was doing; but I looked inside. Of course the place was different, it was differently dressed, but it was the same; I recognized it well. There was warmth in it. But, quickly now

I turned around, and left. I didn't want to rush; I didn't want to give the impression if someone were to see me that I was running away. I had done nothing ill toward anyone or property. I just needed to see the place. I encountered no one on the way out; or on the street. No evidence that I had been seen.

Pensive, I automatically walked back to *rue des Tanneurs*, and automatically took a right. Walking on, I was satisfied that I had seen where I had lived. The feeling of having in some way transgressed into someone's home soon dissipated; I had disturbed no one. Turning right onto *rue des Tanneurs* was also a well traveled route for me and it was as if I automatically was going to *rue de la Querelle* (odd name, Quarrel street), where my Frenkel relatives lived, the ones we shared many a Shabbat dinner with, the uncle with whom I had occasionally gone to Shul. Turning left onto *rue de la Querelle*, and walking looking to the right, I saw that the familiar small grocery store, a simple house really, with the ground floor being the grocery store was open and a couple people were standing inside near the door. Without stopping I went on several doors further and looked for my Uncle's butcher shop. It was not a butcher shop anymore. Not too surprising that it was no longer his butcher shop nor anyone else's; it was a butcher shop 13 years before; now it was something else. Now my heart sank. What happened to them? I immediately felt what I had feared I would experience.

But wait, the grocery store, there is someone there; they might know something about the Frenkels' story or even whereabouts; they might even be the same people who were there in 1940. I walked in with a half smile, "*Bonjour, je cherche a savoir, pourriez vous me renseigner où je pourrais trouver la famille Frenkel? Savez-vous s'qu'ils en sont devenu?*" (Good day, I would like to know, can you tell me where I could find the Frenkel family? Do you know what's become of them?) No sooner had I asked my question that one of the women expressed with a mix of surprise and excitement "C'est le fils de Rosa!" (It's Rosa's son!) Suddenly filled with tears, I turned to her. Someone, someone was left in Bruxelles who knew my mother, and recognized me now, 13 years later, by my resemblance to her. I do look much like her. Two women and one man came to me. We greeted one another like those of us who remain react when we just found another one who remains, like long-feared-lost friends, even though I truly knew none of them. But one of them recognized who I was because she had known my mother. They filled me in with some of what they knew. The butcher shop was closed soon after the Germans invaded Belgium. They knew that one of the girls, Etti, the oldest of the 3 Frenkel children, owns a fur shop. I couldn't believe my ears; Etti was here! Now my heart raced. They would locate where she was for me. I don't know where they looked. They knew she was no longer called Frenkel, she was now Etti Pietruchka; she and Edouard Pietruchka, her fiance in 1940, had married. I suppose there were phone directories. They found the address of the store; they called and told her, the son of Rosa was here. They were given an address some dozen or less blocks from *rue de la Querelle*, gave me directions, greeted me again with pleasure and smiles and sent me off, as if I should rush to get where I was now going.

I had no trouble finding my way. When I got there, I was greeted by Etti who was in shock. "*Henri, Henri, mon Dieu, c'est bien toi!*" (Henri, my Lord, is it really you!) Three kisses, one on alternating cheeks, mutual staring at one another, and a big hug. My God, it was unbelievable, it was joy, it was painful-joy. I had some family left. She had some family left. Just one of me, but in '53, 6 of them. Etti closed the shop, which looked as if it was being evacuated, and it was; Edouard and Etti had

Back: Alda and Henri. *Front from left*: Uncle Frenkel, Etty, and Edouard

Cousine Micheline, 10, first seen July 1953

The author's glamorous cousins, Etti, Sali, and Alda, circa 1960

moved to a better location, *rue du Marché-aux-Herbes*, across the street of one very short 10-foot-wide ruelle, "little street," that connected *rue du Marché-aux-Herbes* and the majestic *Grand Place*. From their store, in one or two minutes you were in *Grand Place*.

Etti took me home. It was a memorable reunion. Edouard, Etti's husband, and their perhaps 10 year-old daughter, then my only child-cousin, Micheline; smiles, hugs, kisses. Then came Alda and her husband Sali, and my cousins' father, my uncle Frenkel, limping, as he long had, since his left foot had been amputated years before the war due to a serious infection that turned gangrenous. I don't think he had diabetes; however, when his infection occurred we were still far from penicillin, and then even from sulfa drugs, so that even a simple non-diabetic infection could have turned very sour. Sadly, my very much-loved cousin Joseph was away then and I much regretted that he did not join us; but he too had survived. I would not see him till a number of years later.

Joseph, who was about 8 years older than I was very special to me; of course in their own way, each one of these cousins was and is. But Joseph was especially friendly with me, aware of me, his little cousin. His sisters, his parents, my uncle and aunt were very lovely to me too, but still Joseph was special. As a young boy Joseph had been struck in the head by a horse—how I never found out—which resulted in his suffering a left hemi-paralysis (paralysis of the left side of his body, arm and leg) for which he had accommodated very well, having full use of his body as well as his afflicted arm and leg, though his left shoulder was lower than the right, his arm a bit more arched, his hand tending to hang at rest, and on walking his left leg dragged a bit, he'd slap his foot down and his body lurched a bit. He had also lost his left eye and wore a prosthesis (a false eye). With all that, he was really a vigorous young man. But his spirit was what so struck me. He was warm, friendly, outgoing, and seemed to go his own way. He did what he wanted within reasonable confines of family responsibility and concern. He really had guts. For example, I learned later that, rather than run away as so many of us did when the war against Belgium started, Joseph crossed *La Mer du Nord* (The North Sea) to England, where he joined British forces to fight. His physical handicap limited his capabilities, though I am not

*In chapter 7 of the Kestenberg and Brenner book referred to before, in which Polish Dr. Adina Blady Szwajger described what she saw in the faces of many of the Warsaw Ghetto children.

certain that those who made that determination were right, as a result of which he was taken into the Coast Guard part of the military. He later told me, true or not, that once when his ship was attacked, they had to swim back to shore. Knowing Joseph, he would have done that.

Though I felt Joseph's absence, I was grateful, I felt enveloped in family-feeling. I could not believe that here I was with Etti and Alda, Uncle Frenkel—Aunt Frenkel had died of illness a while back—and the husbands, Edouard and Sali. And, pleasure of pleasures, I had a new little cousin, one born during the war, after my mother and I had left. Micheline was then about 10, sparkling, bright, loving, a ballet dancer of some local repute even as a child. It was clear that in little time, and my cousins chuckled about it pleasantly, Micheline had a crush on me, in which I thoroughly delighted; and I was very nice to her, in fact, I adored her amply on my part. Uncle Frenkel seemed very worn. He was happy to see me but all that had happened showed on his face; he looked tired and somewhat depressed. I knew he had seen much pain, my dear almost-gruff uncle; he looked it. Thinking of him makes me think of how I look on my coming-to-America picture, "with the eyes of adults," as Judy and Milton Kestenberg wrote "eyes [that] were terribly serious, expressing the 'sorrow of two thousand years of Jewish diaspora.'"*

It was past-recapturing, a happy recapturing of what I feared might no longer be touchable; my family of origin. My cousins Etti and Alda of themselves were living access to my past, the past the Nazis shattered. Alda, Etti, Joseph, then my other younger cousin Joseph, the only one of my cousins I did not like, and my Avenue Fonsny cousins, Nellie and David, children of the David (their last name) Family whom I also really loved, these cousins were the group of my generation I knew best. Etti was the eldest of all of us. She was also, and she still is even now in her 80s, the grande dame among us. When I found them in 1953, Edouard and Etti had developed a thriving haute-couture fur-coat salon. As I saw it, though I may well be mistaken, Edouard was the artist and head of the atelier and Etti was the administrator and presenting person in the business. They had and were doing very well. Edouard, to whom Etti had become engaged just before the war broke out, was a smiling, warm and friendly guy, a pretty good saxophonist who serenaded us one evening with "Come on and hear, come on and hear, Alexander's ragtime band," the lyrics, in French of course, going through my head at the time. He was an artist through and through; no wonder they succeeded in their haute couture venture, when you add Etti's administrative brains to the mix. Edouard died not long after my 1953 visit the Bruxelles of some acute probably cardiac illness.

I later learned that during the war, Etti and Edouard had put less than one-year-old Micheline in hiding with a Christian family where she stayed for early two years, in order to prevent her entrapment in the event that Etti and Edouard were interned in some camp. Try as I have on several occasions, I have not been able to get the full story of just where and how they hid or stayed low during the war years. I am reluctant to be clinical in this narrative, but I wonder if, though they are very devoted to each other, the early childhood separation of Micheline from her parents may have played a part in the harshness that at times surfaces in Etti and Micheline's relationship. But in those dire days, parents did what Etti and Edouard did.

Alda and Sali, who are very dear to me, I found, were then working in their own two-person atelier making elegant gloves and purses that they especially liked to sell to a line of store-clients they cultivated in Italy. Which is why Alda loved to throw some Italian phrases at me, and even much later continues to entertain Rachel and me with an occasional theatrically enunciated Italian phrase. Alda and Sali married soon after the war, and my meeting

Sali was the start of a long-existing relationship of unique character, one heavily endowed with deep affection and humor.

To find these cousins, Etti, Alda, Joseph (even though absent in July '53), my new Micheline, their husbands, my uncle Frenkel, made losing my past less total. And I have wondered what happened to the David family, Nellie, David, their mother (their father had died years before the war started)? That is still an open question. I recently found out that they had left Bruxelles, that they may have survived. But I still don't know where they went, where they might be. That is stil to be taken up.

I was deeply soothed by finding these members of my family still alive. It lessened a little the pained sadness that progressively became part of my fabric after we rushed away to France, then were herded to Toulouse, Recebedou and Rivesaltes, then to my escape enforced-separation from my mother, that turned into our ultimate separation.

I left Bruxelles again by train, but this time, taking my time, a bit somber, a bit mellowed. On my way back to my military post in Bamberg, just after we crossed from Belgium into Germany, I was struck by the sight, from some distance, of the Cathedral in Koeln; it looked like it was on the railroad tracks. The train's slowing down appreciably on approach to Koeln, gave me a chance to get my camera and take a few shots of it. For a bit it looked as though we would go right into the *Dom* (cathedral), about which Heinrich Heine wrote in his *Lyric Intermezzo* and Robert Schumann put to music in the latter's *Dichterliebe* (Poet's Love, a cycle of songs). The Dom song, number VI of the cycle, the music more than the words, sat well with my mood,

Im Dom da steht ein Bildniss auf goldenem Leder gemalt . . .
. . . die gleichen den liebsten genau.
(Within the cathedral there is a painting on gold leather [of the Madonna] . . .
. . . [whose features] resemble those of my beloved, exactly.)

and the piano brings the song to a close in an extended mellowed somber passage, left hand octaves and right-hand syncopated melody, descending to the final minor cord— thinking of my mother.

Savic's mother told me what happened to my mother.

I found out from the most reliable source at that time, that my mother had been among those sent to Drancy, the detention camp outside of Paris, train-port for convoys to the death camps in Poland. These shipments of camp-internees were Vichy-France's contributions toward filling the quota of Jews the Nazis extermination machine craved. I found this out during my second, this time a 10-day furlough, in October 1953; again I went from Bamberg to Bruxelles, but this time by a long circuitous route, by way of St. Raphaël, to the environs of Toulouse, to Paris, and then on to Bruxelles.

The first leg of my trip was to St. Raphaël. Because it was on the way, I stopped in Milan for an overnight just to see it, and especially to pass by and visit La Scala. My stay there was brief; I was eager to get to St. Raphaël. I am amazed to this day about how warmly I felt and feel about St. Raphaël. That, of course, is where I stayed for nearly one year after my escape from Rivesaltes. *La Villa Mariana,* one of two OSE homes near the Mediterranee, where we survived on delicious chic peas—after the rutabaga garbage we ate in Rivesaltes, chic peas were delicious—in a warm surround of really caring adults. Then I remembered the three social workers, the ground-keeper and cook, Inez, and her cute side-kick, Julia. I remember Madame Masour visually and with positive feeling who, though I am uncertain, may not have been a constant presence in the homes, though I do have a photograph of her with the group of boys in the home. And I remember best Mora who taught me my first words of English, and Aranka of whom I have two photographs. As I remember it, in October 1953 the changes in St. Raphaël were minimal. In our visit 45 years later, everything had changed so dramatically, a milling tourist area now of melted small towns with no discernible boundaries, and to my deep chagrin, in the melt I could not find *La Villa Mariana*. It got swallowed up somewhere and even with local help, I could not find it.

But it was between my visit to St. Raphaël and going on to Toulouse that I first learned what happened to my mother. Savic's mother had survived Rivesaltes and the war. She had eventually communicated with Savic and let him know where she had gone and now was living, in Southern France. I have no idea how she selected this very small town coming out of Rivesaltes. She was working in a needle factory in this town, perhaps it would be close to a village. When the time came, I had asked Savic for her exact whereabouts, which he provided me with, and I decided to try to visit her. Savic's instructions were good. It was not difficult to find her when I got there; she was at home; had the opportunity to spend a few hours with her.

We sat at her kitchen table; she prepared some tea. I held back immediately going to the question of my mother. I asked her about herself, how she was now, what she was doing. She was working in the needle factory in town. She was of course quite older, but she seemed to be in good health. She was a small, wiry, women of vigorous stock, obviously intelligent. And she was welcoming, warm, and sad. Here husband now was dead; I didn't ask of what, how, where, when. Neither she nor I felt the need to talk about that. She was eager to know about me; she had seen Savic earlier, he had come to see her. I told her some details of my roamings, of where I was now, of what I was planning to do, by then having decided I would leave music and go into medicine. I had decided this during my two years of time to think while I was in the Military. I asked her about my mother. She told me that my mother had been sent away on one of the selections of Rivesaltes internees—everyone knew, destined for the extermination camps in Poland. I heard the jarring news. I knew the fact; but to hear her say it, she who was there, I collapsed inwardly; soon I was numb. Time slows as I write about it; nearly immobilized now, pensive, dulled feelings, heavy, sad—words don't tell well enough; I don't tell well-enough. A heavy amorphous pain, lying on top of rage that is sequestered right now. Then, nearly 50 years ago, Savic's mother was aware of my reaction; what could she do? I had wanted to know. I had asked her. She told me. She was thoughtful and sympathetic.

Our talk shifted to my trip then, in October 1953. I told her I was going on to Toulouse, then would spend three days in Paris, and then to Bruxelles to see the family I had found 3 months before. With lightening of our conversation she told me that Michel, Savic's younger brother was in Paris and would love to see me. She gave me his address; when in Paris I would see him; I wanted to, I was eager to look him up. When I left her I felt very troubled, weighted down by what she had told me, accepting, resigned, what had happened; accepting history. I was moving on, my mother had conveyed to me that life had to go on. I had to get the train to Toulouse.

My stop in Toulouse was no more than that, just a few hours there. I got out and leisurely walked the streets of that old city. I had no destination. And I found nothing noteworthy to see. I didn't have the time to go to Récébédou; I did not want to go there. Nor did I want to search out the hospital where some 13 years before, coming out of a freezing snow storm my mother and I had walked in there and they had treated my ingrown toe nail, courtesy of the Vichy-France government. My military leave time was limited and I much preferred to spend a few days in Paris and then my remaining several days in Bruxelles. I caught a late train to Paris and arrived there the next morning.

It was a bright day when I arrived in Paris. Within walking distance from the train station, I rented a room for two nights in a pension, a simple, attractive enough, 3 or 4 story house on *la Rive Gauche* (the Left Bank). Settling in was simple. It was good to be in Paris; the pleasant excitement of the city and of being there facilitated my suppressing what I had experienced visiting Savic's mother only the day before. My misery softened by being in Paris, I followed my intention and with pleasant anticipation called Michel, Savic's brother. He was excited to hear from me and we met. Two days we walked the streets of the Left Bank, we went to Montmarte, sat and ate in sidewalk bistros, talked, talked and talked. About him, his mother, Savic, me, his work, his plans, my plans;

we did not talk about his father—enough is enough. It was good to meet Michel; though I hardly had known him in Rivesaltes, a number of factors brought us together. It's amazing, though well-known, how going through hell together ties you together. We separated promising to see each other again; I believe we did once in New York a number of years later.

My pleasant stay in Paris over, I went on to Bruxelles where I stayed for 4 or 5 days. Amazing how after having found each other again just 3 months before, my cousins and I resumed our relationship where we had left off in 1940, modified only by two factors; one, that 13 years had passed and we now were all adults, and two, that we all had gone through terribly painful, very frightening times, words too thin to convey.

We have seen each other a number of times since but not without another loss of contact, most likely caused by my lack of staying in touch with them. But let me quickly add that they don't stand innocent in our loss of contact either since they slackened in their communicating with me, and between my moves from Pittsurgh, to New Orleans, to Cincinnati, and then to Philadelphia, and their moves within Bruxelles, both in their homes and workplaces, it is not totally due to neglect that we lost touch. To maintain contact during the permutation of moves on their part and mine, communication was essential; we failed. That loss of contact, however, was repaired by our son Karl during the summer of his sixteenth year, an adventure I shall touch on later.

In October 1953, like during our first reunion, I spent all my time with Alda and Sally, Etty and Edouard and Micheline. Joseph was still away; so was Uncle Frenkel. In fact, I saw Uncle Frenkel on my way back to Bamberg. He lived in Liege then and I visited him there before going on to Germany. In Liege, he greeted me at the train station; Uncle Frenkel was somber as we walked, he limped, to his home. He was not so well and skirted my inquiries into his health. He was driven it seemed to me to know one thing, how well did I read Hebrew, did I pray, did I go to Shul? I had had my Bar Mitzvah, that pleased him, but did I go to Shul? I know I disappointed him on these counts, I did not read Hebrew well as he hoped, I did not pray as he did daily, morning and evening, and I did not regularly go to Shul. I did not want to hurt him by shar-

* *Sauver Les Enfants*, page 221.

ing with him what my experiences had wrought, that at that time, while I was totally a Jew, I was an atheistic Jew. I was one of those among us who now found much difficulty with religion; we are totally Jews, but Jews with doubts, questions, and an inability to reconcile with some of the Hebraic liturgy and "the experience of God." I will talk later about what the Holocaust did to my experience of religion.

Regarding the History of Foreign Jews in Vichy-France

The timetable annotated by Vivette Samuel in *Sauver Les Enfants* does not match the timetable I have all along assumed in my own case. I know that, being quite young then, on the matter of the specificity of certain dates, I may be wrong; I know that in some way my timetable may be distorted, and that Vivette Samuel who was a young woman at the time of these occurrences is most likely right. If my timetable is simply wrong, then I know that it is the by-product of memory distortion caused by my young years and the pain, which the indignities visited on us by our host government caused us, all of us Belgian Jewish asylum seekers, and others too. Intense pain can distort not only memory, but also active and passive thinking processes and many other things, psychological and biological within us. This admission of uncertainty should not be taken beyond the way I intend it; if some of the specifics I assert are wrong, it does not extend to my being wrong about what happened to me and others like me. The Holocaust happened.

Here are some dates I remember:

10 May, the German invasion of Belgium started; we left Bruxelles by train and traveled to Southern France to a region near Toulouse. We were given asylum in a French "Village" for about 4 months. Then, I believe about mid or late September 1940, we were evacuated by order of and courtesy of the then Vichy Government and taken to a Detention Camp in Toulouse. Within several days then, *late in September*, we were interned in récébédou. Vivette Samuel states* that on *September 27*, 1940, the Germans imposed an ordinance that a census be taken of all the Jews *in the Occupied Zone* of France. If I am right in my timetable, the French were only taking a census in the occupied zone where the (German) Nazis ruled, whereas in the Free Zone, then in the hands of the Vichy-France Government, the *internment of foreign Jews was already well underway.*

Samuel indicates that on 4 October 1940—Marrus and Paxton concur—in Vichy-France, a law was passed that "authorized" the internment of "foreigners of the Jewish race" in special camps and that in October, 7,000 Jews were interned in Gurs, a concentration camp not far from Rivesaltes. My mother and I were then already in Récébédou.

In June 1941, one month after I had escaped from Rivesaltes, Vichy-France ordered a census of the Jews—not clear whether this meant Foreign Jews, French Jews, or Jews of any color, nationality, and denomination, just Jews! The Vichy Government, according to Marrus and Paxton, made a point of trying to yield up the Foreign Jews to the demands of the German-Nazis in the hopes that they might spare the French Jews. The Vichy government was then headed by Laval, no longer by the aged and ailing Petain.

I make several points here. One, is that according to Marrus and Paxton, the Foreign Jews, Belgian, Dutch, German Jews, who had specifically sought asylum in France, were, targeted for special mal-treatment by the Vichy-French Government; this supposedly in a patriotic effort to save the French Jews from the ravenous Nazis in the Occupied Zone. French chauvinism reached even to embrace its Jews. Second, that somehow, the "hidden Nazis" among the Vichy-French authorities seem at times to have been more eager than their German counterpart to rid themselves of the Jews, the foreign Jews first, but then the French Jews as well. Marrus and Paxton recorded the fact, that the first French shipment of Jews from the concentration camps in the then still "Unoccupied Zone" arrived prematurely in Compiegne, one of the three or four detention stations from where Jews were deported to Auschwitz for extermination;they thus created an embarrassment for the Germans who were

not yet ready to receive them. Such zeal and alacrity among those Vichy-French authorities! I am not totally unsympathetic toward the Vichy-French Government; these were hard times in terms of food and other life conditions, and no doubt all the foreigners who sought asylum there—one million among them, Belgians—were an enormous burden to the country, and those that governed. But this then-11-12 year-old boy knew that these were not France's days of glory. Heinz Pol spoke of it in 1940 as the Suicide of a Democracy.

My mother seems to have timed my May 1 escape from Rivesaltes with subsequently born-out well-tempered premonition. Two weeks after, on May 14, 1941, the French police arrested and interned thousands of foreign Jews. Although Samuel does not specify, I deduce that this occurred in the French Occupied Zone since these Jews were interned in Pithiviers and Beaune-la-Rolande both in the Occupied Zone. But given Vichy Government's tendency in these times to lose its moral bearings and even eagerly cooperate with the Occupied Zone Nazi authorities, it no doubt would have been even more problematic than it was for me to escape after May 14.

Again, if I am proven wrong about some parts of my historic timetable, then ascribe my error to pain-derived imprecision of memory mixed with the rage I have long carried toward the Nazis, especially toward the French Nazis in the Vichy Government who directly orchestrated what happened to us.

In addition to my Holocaust experience forging the path of my work, many memorable events attach to my Holocaust experience, like my painful conflict about my return to Rivesaltes, going to Israel, my first visit to Germany, especially Munich, and more.

Chapter 9

In The Aftermath

On My Journey in Israel

On the late 1980s I learned with a new sense of it, that I still was not ready to come face to face with some aspects of my Holocaust experience. My accommodating to, learning to live with that past has been part of my life; it is a constant. I am doing so with this writing. In 1988, I was invited to lecture in Jerusalem. I had not yet gone to Israel and was very eager to go, though obviously some unconscious force at work in me had prevented me from going there to this time. I considered the invitation to lecture an opportune time to do so. I contacted several professional groups in Israel to let them know I was coming—an Israeli colleague told me I should do so, that the Israelis want American lecturers to let them know when they come—and that I would feel privileged to lecture to them. Two other professional centers extended me an invitation that fell within reasonable time of the date suggested by my first prospective Jerusalem host. In 1989 Rachel and I arranged a trip that would accommodate my lectures and our chance to visit the country. Plans were in place several months before our scheduled journey.

Within days of the time when our plans were in place and we had purchased airline tickets, I began to develop a very unpleasant, persistent and rather intense visual light sensitivity. Any modestly intense light aimed directed at my eyes was intolerable; I had to look away. This was totally new; I had never had this symptom. My ophthalmologist found nothing abnormal in my eyes and was puzzled by my light-sensitivity. Clinically trying to be helpful, he suggested I try some antihistamine eye drops. They seemed to help, but did not eliminate the symptom. Being a psychoanalyst and in the habit of looking within minds for causes of puzzling behaviors and reactions—after years of training and doing it day in and day out, it organizes into a habit—, I began to explore what I was experiencing. I find dreams enormously useful to accessing unconscious goings on. In wondering what's wrong with me at this time, my associations took me to understand that I was not yet ready to go to Yad Vashem. I could not have gone to Israel and not have gone to Yad Vashem. I don't need a metaphor; it would have been insane to go to Israel and not go to Yad Vashem. I was experiencing my first truly allergic reaction; I was not emotionally ready to go to Israel. With much distress and some embarrassment, I excused myself to my hosts in Jerusalem and Tel Aviv; they were gracious and asked me to please let them know when I next plan to come to Israel.

What was I not ready to face in Yad Vashem? My eventual trip there in October 1999 helps to clarify. When we went to Yad Vashem, once on entry into the grounds, I felt myself shaking like a leaf. It's as if I was going to encounter ghosts of my past. I was inwardly frightened; I don't think I showed it, but I was. It's as if I was now going to get confirmation once and for all that yes, my mother, my father, my brother, others of family, were all dead, exterminated. Was I not yet ready for the whole truth and nothing but the truth? I still don't know the whole truth and I am still not totally ready for it. I knew that my mother had died in Auschwitz. Even to this day I don't know if my father and my brother ended up there too. In the late 1980s, when I had to cancel our trip, I was evidently not yet ready to go to Israel and look that truth in the eyes. No wonder I developed a visual light-hypersensitivity.

Early in this narrative I noted that in July 2002 I had developed an acute eczema. Three months into this writing my skin reaction much reduced. But it is not cured, as it has waxed and waned even through the period of my revising these Memoirs (January 2004). It is now clear, and my Dermatologist helped me to find what I believe is the causative factor in my acute (rather sudden in onset) and intense eczema. My massive skin reaction started after I made contact with some poison plant, I believe something other than poison ivy. It was treated in good time and with a good regimen but it persisted quite longer than expected. I had then started to read Primo Levi—I have read several of his books and still have some others on my coffee table at home. Primo Levi struck me. I did not then know to what degree. My skin reaction persisted waxing and waning. Six weeks later, we took me off medications I was taking known to have some dermatologic side effects, beta-blocker blood pressure medication for a moderate systolic (the upper number) hypertension, and a beta-blocker for my mysterious right eye glaucoma, the representative of some unexplained eye abnormality that has probably been with me for years. And when my skin still resisted healing, my psychologically minded Dermatologist, Bernie K. asked me, with cautious sensitivity, if I was worried or troubled about something. He, the Dermatologist felt odd asking his shrink patient, me, if I was having some emotional problems. It struck me to the core; yes, I was in the process of writing my story about the Holocaust. When I told him I was a survivor and that I had to bear witness, his eyes filled with tears. He didn't know, he said, it was a privilege to treat me. I was damned glad that he was treating me, a Dermatologist who knew about the impact of psychological stress on the skin. From that day, my eczema has been less virulent. Bernie helped me become aware that my writing this story was affecting my total self, mind and body. My wife knew it would; she told me that it would. It has taken me long to tell my story. And I had not been ready to face my truth, the whole truth in 1989; I was not yet ready to go to Israel.

Ten years later, in 1999, I went to Israel. This time going to Israel had an added dimension that made it compelling. My psychoanalyst colleague Yolanda G., member of the Israeli Psychoanalytic Society, member of the International Psychoanalytic Association's Committee to the United Nations (IPA-CUN), and on the Faculty at Tel Aviv University, had informed a Palestinian colleague of our Mental Health prevention work. Yolanda had learned of our work when the IPA-CUN had explored what efforts the members of the Committee were making or knew of that could meaningfully serve Society. By then, for twenty-five years my research team had been developing parenting education materials with the aim of optimizing parenting and thereby reducing the prevalence of experience-derived-emotional-disorders in children, including especially the development of violence and malignant prejudice.

I received an email from Abdel Hamid Afana, Director of Training at the Gaza Community Mental Health Programme. Would we come to their Community Center to help them develop programs for optimizing parenting in their community? My collaborators Cecily Rose-Itkoff and Michael Pearlman, Mental Health types like me, were equally interested in such a project. We could go to both the Israeli communities and the Palestinian community and present our research, share the prevention strategies and materials we had developed. We would then make ourselves available to facilitate their use of the materials and research the outcome of their programs. The possibility of contributing, by means of mental health prevention strategies and instruments, to the Israelis and the Palestinians efforts to live together in peaceful co-existence, was exactly the type of goal in our sights. When I felt that we might be helpful to that end, I could go to Israel without excessive trepidation. The three of us went, with itineraries to the Israeli Ministry of Education in Jerusalem, Tel Aviv University's Department of Psychology and School Counseling, to the Gaza Community Mental Health Programme, and to *Neve Shalom/Wahat al Salam* (the community where Jews and Arabs govern and live together) in Israel.

On our arrival, on our walking into the Tel Aviv airport, I was swept by a feeling of sad joy, tearful joy on seeing signs and posters in Hebrew characters; an immediate feeling of comfort set in. When we picked up our rental car I was struck by the welling of relief I felt when I saw the everyday car-rental agent write out the minimalist contract in Hebrew. *In Hebrew*! Unbelievable. Even in America this does not happen. Then, as we approached Jerusalem, the rocky sweeping hills, the far-reaching vales, the sweep of Jerusalem filled me with awe. I had not imagined it so beautiful and at the same time so grand. And it didn't take long for me to tell my colleagues Cecily and Michael that here, I felt at home. Walking from our hotel, which was situated across the magnificent wall that surrounds the old city, to a restaurant, the chatter of milling people, I felt an amalgam of feeling safe, inner calm, quiet joy. All around me, or most anyway, were Jews, just like me; like no where else I felt, I could go to anyone and say, "Heh, I'm a Jew, *Ich bin a Yid*," and feel no threat. Even in America, "land that I [truly] love," I can't do that. I could in Israel. There's nothing like it. Maybe, having been incarcerated, having smelled death, just because I am a Jew, made me so keenly aware of this feeling of freedom from fear. But perhaps too, every Jew feels this way, even the millions who very fortunately were not subjected to the sadism of Nazis.

In Israel, I felt, here I am at home. It is different than being at my real home, outside of Philadelphia, where I very much feel I am home. Returning from Israel I felt that there are two countries for which I would fight if the existence of either were threatened, and to the health and well being of which I am committed, "America" and Israel. And this

In the Hall of Remembrance at Yad Vashem (the Rivesaltes gravestone was beyond the reach of the author's camera)

"Memorial to one and a half million Jewish children who perished. . ."

I know is a major factor in my eagerness, and that of my co-workers Cecily and Michael, to accept the invitation from Palestinian colleagues to help them develop strategies for optimizing parenting in their communities. Based on our research (which I talk about in Part III), we are convinced that optimizing the rearing of children toward emotional good health would bring with it the reduction of violence and malignant prejudice. We felt that if both Israeli and Palestinian communities reared their children toward achieving good mental health, that their peaceful co-existence would be facilitated. This was in November 1999. It is tragic that extremists on both sides of the Israeli-Palestinian divide have for the past four years reduced to ashes succeeding efforts toward peaceful co-existence. By this, the world has lost a major model for resolution of conflict between ethnic groups—ethnic groups that not too long before lived in harmony, in one community—ethnic conflict, that long existing social disease that has been and is to this day spread all over the globe.

Going to Israel was most meaningful to me, and this time I was able to go without developing a psychosomatic reaction of alarm and protest. I think that feeling committed, compelled in my prevention work gave me no choice but to go. Cecily, who spent a year in Israel many years earlier has cousins and friends there. She arranged for Yochi, a much-liked friend who is a Guide to various sites in Israel to optimize our visit by helping us learn about Jerusalem. Yochi guided us through the old city, first by taking us to the model of the city, guiding us through its parts, and then by taking us through the old city itself. Touching the massive Wailing Wall brought a rush of history-feeling with it; a feeling of long, long communal reach back into time. Deeply moving.

Sustained by what we were doing there with the Israelis and Palestinians, and by Yochi's remarkable facilitation of absorbing more of Jerusalem than we could have done without her, I was able to go to *Yad Vashem.* Yochi guided us there too. As we neared *Yad Vashem*, I felt the weight of my inner misery creep into consciousness. I was overtaken with grief when I came into the darkened cave, a cemetery, I felt, with an eternal torch burning, surrounded by tombstone slabs, names carved in light: *Auschwitz, Bergen-Belsen, Birkenau, Dachau, Treblinka . . .* My memory, of just 3 years ago, is fogy here; I believe there was a tomb-slab with Rivesaltes light-carved in it. I stayed there a long time. I don't pray; I mourned. And I raged silently, like so many of us have, "If there is a God, how could You let this happen to us"! At that moment I did not remember all the other Holocausts; ours is unique, but not the only one; the Communist Holocaust, the Chinese Holocaust, the other ethnic cleansing Holocausts over the centuries. I dragged myself through the *Yad Vashem* exhibits numbed, the heaviest weight of sadness—just as I did earlier in 1999 walking through our U.S. Holocaust Memorial Museum in Washington with Rachel, who was equally smashed by it. I went to the documentation station in *Yad Vashem*. I wondered if I could learn about the fate of my father and my brother. I didn't even think then of others; only part of my brain was available to the effort. Profoundly disappointed, I found nothing about my father or my brother. But that might be good. The Nazis kept good records; I understand that the Jews in the Lodz Ghetto kept good records too. Might they still be alive? I am making that search now; better late than never; just add a large dose of self-recrimination for not having done that before, long before.

We walked through the grounds, I picked three pods of St. Peter's bread, pods yielded by a small tree, that served as food for St. Peter I was told. It is not permitted; I felt like I had in Village, many years before, stealing whatever fruit and vegetables we could to supplement our limited diet. I was troubled recently when I found that one of the *Yad Vashem* pods had disappeared.

We left *Yad Vashem*, my colleagues and I, exhausted. Knowing my story, Cecily and Michael seemed aware of my state; I noticed then that they had kept a vigilant eye on me, supporting; I had not been there alone. They were not all enveloping, my friends, providing "a holding environment" for me like Rachel does at times like these; but they were very good to be with. Once we moved on from *Yad Vashe*m, the air seemed lighter; a burden had been put down. I had metabolized something of my past. The experience of the visit stays steadfastly rememberable.

I know that my visit to Jerusalem, and especially to *Yad Vashem*, was made possible for me at this time by our mission there. We were bringing our prevention work aimed at optimizing the well being of Israeli and Palestinian children and their parents; we wanted to contribute to efforts made at peaceful co-existence in that part of the world so valuable to Jews and Palestinians. Given that, I now know, my prevention work has its origins in my Holocaust experience, and that one of its key aims is the prevention of violence and malignant prejudice, I knew I was going to Israel not just to mourn at *Yad Vashem*, but also to help protect

Gaza Community Mental Health Program—satellite site. Michael Perelman and Cecily Rose-Itkoff with a GCMHP member."

The team at *Neve Shalom/Wahat al Salam. From left*: Yochi (guide), the author, Rayet-Rizek (Secretary-General, Neve Shalom/Wahat al Salam), Cecily Rose-Itkoff, Michal Pearlman

Teaching a seminar for kindergarten teachers in Gaza City. From left: Cecily Rose-Itkoff, Michael Pearlman, the author, and Abdel Hamid Afana, GCMHP Director of Training

our people in our land. I could go not just to remember the Holocaust, to cry and curse, but to help growth in and make secure that oasis for Jews. Besides the Israeli Ministry of Education in Jerusalem, we also went to Tel Aviv, we lectured, had seminars and talked at the University there with Mental Health professionals active in the community, and we also went to Neve Shalom/Wahat al Salam, and of much importance to us, we went to Gaza City, to the Gaza Community Mental Health Programme.

In November 1999, it was intimidating—in 2003, regrettably, it is unthinkable—to go to Gaza to meet with, lecture, seminar, and talk with Palestinian Mental Health colleagues of collaboration in helping them develop programs aimed to improve the lives of children and parents. It was intimidating to walk from the Israeli side through "No-man's Land" to the Palestinian side, and wait on that side to be picked up by our host. The delay in our being picked up was keenly felt by us and was much relieved when a Palestinian taxi-driver offered to call our host to tell him we were here, waiting. Our host did arrive, apologetic, and we went to their Community Mental Health Center. We were very well received, given opportunity to lecture and present our ideas, research, and programs, and had occasion to visit another Gaza Health Center site. The prospect of collaborating with these Mental Health colleagues intent on the well being of their people was most welcome. I felt, as did my American Jewish colleagues, that we could contribute in a meaningful way to the betterment of the Palestinian parents and their children. We want more growth-promoting parenting everywhere; our research has shown that the more optimally children are reared, the less likely they are to deal with problems by violence and malignant prejudice. And we visited a refugee camp. The poverty, the dust in the streets, the transience of housing accommodations, the little that we saw, gave us much cause for pain and very serious concern. To be sure, we have such sights in America too, and there too they are cause for serious concern. In the Middle East, striking contrasts between the Israeli side of "No Man's Land" and the Palestinian side made us painfully aware of differences in life on each side that, even as they stood then, in 1999, did not bode well for the future. The problems of co-existence were palpable. We really felt that the collaboration we were seeing between Israeli and Palestinian Mental Health professionals was fruitful and could open ways for bettering the lives of the people in the communities reached.

In 2003, I am deeply saddened by the loss of such efforts, the loss of the potential they contained. But that sadness is mellowed by my feeling reassured, in awe of the fact that we Jews have a home, for all Jews. And if others close their ports to us even like my America did to all but a few Jews fleeing the threat of extermination in the early 1940s, we now can go home. Even as we have needed to fight to save our home and our people, and we know there will be attacks on us, we have a home. And we have learned to fight—going the wrong way in order to survive.

Efforts have to be made to bring us back to the constructive period in the Middle East that ended in 2000.

My Post-Holocaust Travels in Germany

I first visited Germany in 1953-54, courtesy of the United States Military Service. I was stationed in Bamberg, Bavaria, for one year. I was eager to be posted in Post-World War II Germany, though the choice between that and the alternative Korea, then actively at war, was made by the Military. I think that being stationed in Bamberg in 1953, rather than say in Munich, facilitated my being in Germany. Bamberg is a small city, with much charm, opportunity for walking, sitting on a park bench to look about, to read, to meditate. Here I was, in defeated Germany, I, in U. S. uniform. I felt protected by my uniform. I felt protected knowing that many Americans like me—well, more inborn American than I since I was then an American for only about 5 years—were there, and that they would come to my rescue were Nazis to suddenly appear and try to force me into another concentration camp. Though I felt safe, this irrational thought did at moments come into my mind. Amazing how having been traumatized, one dreads a repetition of the trauma even when highly unrealistic, nigh totally impossible.

Bamberg was pleasant; but I did avoid the few boisterous taverns near our base, even when I was with my friend Stephan, a young German doctor who worked at our Dispensary. We became good friends. He invited me to his home, out of town, for Christmas—can't recall where it was—where I was very nicely welcomed. So much so in fact, that I was given a couple presents along with the members of his family getting their fair share of gifts. They were lovely people, Stephan's family.

Bamberg also has a fine symphony orchestra and I can see the large unimpressive straightforward hall, high-ceilinged like a church, but simple. From my base in Bamberg, off duty, I visited Wurzburg several times. Unfortunately, this is also where on a rainy day, while rushing a soldier in emergency to the hospital there, our ambulance slipped on the tram rails, we crashed into a wall, and I sustained a concussion that knocked me out. I'm fine; I recovered, after ten days in the Hospital there. And I visited Nuremberg, a lovely, small city. But I also visited Munich; that had special troubling meaning.

Visits to Munich

Going to Munich, knowing its meaningfulness to the Holocaust, was and has been challenging for me. I first visited Munich in 1953 while I was stationed in Bamberg. The occasion was Pessach; the military prepared a Seder for us. Men came from stations within reasonable reach of Munich. I smile just thinking about it: the U. S. Army selecting Munich as the site for a Seder for a bunch a Jewish servicemen and women. Were they thinking what I thought? It was memorable to have a Seder in Munich, the city that above all others represents the center of Nazism, the city the Nazi Fuehrer preferred, the city that epitomizes *Kristallnacht.* We were in the military; I was in uniform—not in "civies" like when I traveled in Belgium and France—and even in uniform, I felt very uneasy in Munich, and unlike Bamberg, I did not like the Germany Munich represented to me, at least not during my first visit there. For me, Bamberg represented the city of Brahms and Schumann, perhaps because there, on a park bench, I would read Rilke's *Duino Eligies*, in German. I even tried my hand then at translating them; it was only a transient effort aimed at helping me learn German better. I have never formally studied German; but my early childhood Yiddish helped me understand a fair amount of German. In addition, my studies of Schubert, Schumann, Beethoven and Brahms *lieder* heavily engaged me to try to understand German, with ample use of dictionary too. Bamberg represented that about whar is German that I value; that by which I feel enriched. Munich represented that of what is German that frightened me; that murdered and injured so many of us; that I abhor.

This is one of my dilemmas, but it is also a large factor in my teasing out "German" from "Nazi." I am not the first to think along these lines. The "Nazi = German" dilemma. My dilemma arises from the fact that I love *lieder,* music in general, but lieder especially. Though I long abandoned singing as a career, I still think of myself as a *lieder*, a classical art song, singer. Though there is a great French art song literature, meaningful but lesser Italian, Russian, and other such literatures, the

German art song literature, including Schubert, Schumann, Brahms and Beethoven, is magnificent. German is to *lieder* what Italian is to opera. Furthermore, I think that Beethoven is the greatest genius of the fields I know and of those with which I am just acquainted.

Then came 1933. Then *those* Germans came. Many of my friends and acquaintances hate Germans, won't buy German cars or cameras or anything. Peter Gay, the renown Historian, also a Psychoanalyst, wrote this too in his memoirs of his childhood in the Berlin he loved, *My German Question* (published in 1998), his recollections as a Jewish boy in Berlin until 1939; he too has friends and acquaintances who refuse to buy anything German. I understand their sentiment. I hesitated before I bought my first BMW. So my dilemma, that of a Jew, is that I love some Germans, and I hate some Germans; I love those whose creative genius was universal and embraced the human race; I hate those who were or are Nazis, who represent chauvinism in extreme, who believe others-than-themselves should be exterminated.

But this goes beyond Germans; I also hate French Nazis, of which there were many in Vichy-France, and American Nazis (at times cloaked in Ku Klux Klan attire), and Nazi types anywhere. I cannot, do not, hold all Germans responsible for what the Nazis wreaked in Europe, nor do I hold all French responsible for what the Vichy-France government did, nor all Italians for what Mussolini did and stood for. We become culpable too when we hate all Germans, or all Palestinians, or all who-ever "all" may be, based on their nationality, ethnicity, color, religion.

My first visit to Munich was one of trepidation and conflict. I did not want to go and I wanted to go. Why I did not want to go needs no more explanation. Why I wanted to go does. I needed to see it with my own eyes. I needed to see the place, the buildings, the streets, the city squares, the Germans of Munich. And I needed to go there, feeling that I was still alive and their Fuehrer was not—though he robbed me of my first life, my mother's life, my original family's life, my community's life.

I had no trouble getting to the base in Munich where the Seder was held. Long tables, a number of them; there were perhaps a couple hundred of us. It was good to be together, having a Seder in Munich, a commemoration to having survived. It was something of a mournful victory. But it was not comfortable; I would have been more comfortable elsewhere in Germany, Wurzburg or Nuremberg would have been better.

The next morning I walked the streets to see Munich. I remember cranking my neck to look at the moving figures on the large Church's façade, staring while walking at the entrance of one of its Universities, avoiding even visual contact with the people. I was not able to look Munich in the eyes. I had no desire to stay there one minute longer than planned and caught my train back to Bamberg with relief. Munich had elicited painful repulsion.

I did not return to Germany for many years. Over the years, my work, has at times given me opportunity to lecture in Europe. A colleague from Munich, Lotte K., who occasionally came to an annual symposium in Philadelphia, after hearing some of my remarks in our scientific meetings, asked me if I would to come to Germany, to Munich specifically, to lecture at Institutions with which she was affiliated. She did not press me and did not seem surprised when I did not accept her invitation and said I would think about it. Nor, I later found out, was she surprised when I did not get back to her on the question.

A few years later, in 1991, Lotte communicated with me. Was I going to the International Child Psychoanalytic Meetings in St.Louis? Since I was, would I kindly help Suzanne H., one of her Grant Recipients who was coming to these meetings, find her way. It was Suzanne's first time on this Continent; would I keep an eye on her? Coming to increasingly like Lotte, I was very pleased to do this. Suzanne and I got along very well. As we talked, at a well chosen moment, Suzanne told me that some people in Munich really wanted to hear what I had to say regarding my work on aggression. She let me know that Lotte really wanted me to come to Munich. I do not recall how we got to it, but as Lotte later told me, I had told Suzanne that my hesitancy about going to Germany came from the fact that I am a Holocaust Survivor. This time, I cannot truly say why, I agreed to do so; perhaps it was facilitated by the fact that it coincided with other lecturing commitments I then had in Europe.

This led to four visits I subsequently have made to Munich to this time. Lotte reminded me recently that when we first talked of how I would travel to Germany I had said I did not want to fly "Luftwaffe," totally unaware that I had made a serious slip of the tongue saying "Luftwaffe" rather than "Lufthansa." I could not hide my anxiety about going to Germany. In April 1992, I first returned to Munich. I was wary; I was no longer in U. S. uniform, and I was coming alone, no Medical Corps Company to back me up. But I did have a friend and a host, Lotte K. I got to Munich in late morning, settled in, slept a bit, and met Lotte in late afternoon. My first lecture was scheduled for the evening. Due to circumstances, Lotte and I ate in a Bavarian Tavern with which she was not so familiar. That was fine with me. It could have been quite nice. But after we settled in, not far from our table there were 3 or 4 about 30 year-olds who became increasingly rowdy as they consumed more and more beer; they became loud and somewhat coarse. I think that Lotte became aware of my discomfort; she, herself was probably troubled by them. She commented on their rowdiness and apologized for having brought me here. Though I did not share this with her, I had become very uneasy when their noise turned to rowdiness. I associated their loudness and coarseness with some of the film clips I had seen of "brown shirts" brawls in taverns and on streets; and I trembled. I think I hid my distress well. And maybe not. I feel that Lotte made sure that we were out of there as soon as we could.

The fear I felt briefly in that Bavarian tavern was a blip, a spike, on the baseline fear I have felt when I have been alone in Germany. Although I absolutely insist that "German" is not equal to or mean "Nazi," that the German Government, under the Nazi regime, programmed the Holocaust for Jews, makes me more afraid in Germany than elsewhere.

When Rachel and I attended an international scientific meeting in Amsterdam, which was then followed by another meeting in Koeln, I experienced such a rush of fear as well. The morning after the symposium in Koeln, habituated to exercise, I went into the street and started my "slow-jog" trek. It was early, perhaps 6 or so in the morning. I progressed nicely, enjoying the view of Koeln in the waking hours. But as I went on my projected course I unexpectedly heard some quite loud, boisterous noises, and then noted that on my path, across the large avenue, were gathered a group of young people, men and women, probably waiting for a bus or a trolley, who had in a burst of rowdy playfulness suddenly gotten very loud and coarse. I was gripped by fear. It was no doubt my own inner stuff that got stirred up by their noises. They probably didn't even notice that I was across the street, jogging. But I felt that dread of being in danger. Just because I was in Germany and I heard some coarse, rowdy young guys!

I came to know that Lotte had not wanted such a Bavarian tavern experience for me. And of course, my fear is counter-weighted by the accumulating experiences of respect and appreciation I have received from my German colleagues who have heard my work. I remember especially the attentive

Visit to Berlin — 2001

I was invited to give a lecture on our research in primary prevention of emotional disorders in children to the Annual Meeting of Die Liga fuer das Kind which was held in Berlin in late November 2001. This was about 2 months after September 11. Lotte arranged for a young Psychologist-Psychoanalyst AnneMarie to serve as my guide, the way I had served Suzanne H. in St. Louis. I was in Berlin for nearly three days. I saw some of Berlin the first day I arrived. On first sight, Berlin seemed vastly different to me than Muenchen or Koeln. The boulevards were wide, the space was large, the air open.

Anne was most gracious and facilitating of my stay in this wide-spread metropolis, Berlin. I like Berlin; because it has long been in the fore-guard of artistic and social progressivism, because it was the home of Kurt Weil and Bertholt Brecht, and because of its many broad open-air Boulevards and its chain of communities. Not that there are not drab areas of Berlin like in all major cities in the world. East Berlin nearly depressed me. Or maybe it was Anne's taking me to the remarkable "Monument to the burning of books," remembrance of that celebrated Nazi primitive, odious festivity. The monument is buried in the center of a large cobble stone square, a barren plaza. A light surges from the ground. As you approach the source of light in the square, you see that the light indeed does come out of the ground. When you are there, a glass floor opens to view a cellar-like room walled on all sides with white book shelves from ceiling to floor. This is a library; but all the books are gone. I felt as if struck between the eyes by this stark, agonizing, starved, underground monument.

Yes, like many, I too welcomed the reminder of war, the damaged *Gedaechtsnichkirche* on Kurfuerstendamm, the bomb-damaged monumental church, left damaged as a memorial to World War II. These monuments vivified the memory of those times. But I was most reminded and moved by our visit, guided by Anne, to the Jewish Museum of Berlin, a striking metal zigzagging five stories high structure that is an art work in itself, heavy metal sheets punctured with small windows, like a massive prison. Or a tank. I was grateful that AnneMarie knew how meaningful it would be for me to go to this massive metal architectural monument to Jews in Berlin. Lotte had told me that she would ask AnneMarie to take me to the Museum. It is a Memorial, really. But, while I was struck by the imposing prison-like architectural sculpture I saw, what struck me most was the line human beings had formed, mostly Germans Anne told me, to get into the museum. We had limited time. The line extended so far; I was overwhelmed by the fact that so many people were lined up to go in, mostly Germans Anne told me, school children among them. I told Anne that we did not have to time to wait to go in, that I did not need to go in; that what I saw on the outside was so deeply moving, it was as if we had gone in and seen what there was to see. Yes, there are Neo-Nazis in Germany, there are Nazis in American, and elsewhere, but here were so many people waiting in line to go into the Jewish Museum in Berlin!

My lecture to the *Liga fuer das Kind* went very well. In introducing me the audience was told that I had just come from the U. S., two months after September 11; the audience's welcome really surprised me. Why was I surprised? I have been well received before. Fine, I did fly over soon after September 11. But was I perhaps surprised because it was my first visit to Berlin and somewhere in my head there is still the Jewish boy fearing Nazis?

My lecture in East Berlin was a much more sober affair. My Psychologist guide, an East-Berliner, educated me on some stark difference between East and West Berlin. I told her that a study devolving from her observations regarding the ways children were reared in East as compared to West Berlin would most likely document some of the harsh effects of totalitarianism on the rearing of children. The next morning I left my generous and dedicated hostess and arrived in Munich, welcomed as usual by Lotte, where I lectured on some post-September 11 reactions of malignant prejudice and potential violence.

My visits to Germany have not been easy. I was highly conflicted about it. I hold to where my ruminations on the issue have taken me: "Nazi" does not equal "German." I learned that when I was in Récébédou and especially in Rivesaltes. The Vichy-France government was the onerous authority that imprisoned us. The Vichy-France government, similarly as with the German government, was driven by Nazi Frenchmen at the wheel. Should I hold all that is French responsible for what the Vichy-France hoodlums did to us? Should I abhor the French?

Should I abhor the Germans? The Poles? The Russians? After all, the Poles and Russians, in their centuries old pogroms, over time may have outdone the German, French, Italian, and other Europeans Nazis who executed, but fortunately failed at the "the final solution." And shouldn't we also include the Italians? Ask Primo Levi; well, it's too late to ask him directly, but he left wrenching evidence of their contribution toward our extermination. And the Hungarians? They too participated in sending Jews for extermination to Auschwitz and Bergen-Belsen and Dachau . . . . Should I hate all Europeans? What do I do with my need for Beethoven and Schubert, and Rilke and Baudelaire, and Schiller with his "*Alle Menschen werden Brueder . . .*" (All humans will be brothers [siblings, really]). The question is clear, and even if difficult and arguable, so is the solution. The only solution is to do away with hostile dichotomizing driven by malignant chauvinism. People malign, torture, or destroy others because they are of this nationality or that religion, this ethnic group or that race. Blind, stupid, insane. Hate drives malignant prejudice and the destruction it wreaks; nationality, race, religion become conduits for the hate, rationalize its activation, and "justify" its discharge.

Yet with all this reasoning and my conviction, to which I hold, I have trembled in Germany. I have not in France; maybe it's because French is part of me and German is not; maybe it's because some Vichy-French Nazis collaborated with the German Nazis, but it's the German Nazis who sorted out who would go to the left and who to the right when the victims got to their death camps. The Nazi French, sadistic and shamefully enfeebled, selected and sent Jews to their death; the German Nazis, empowered by their Fuehrer and his depraved Lieutenants executed those Jews. Perhaps that is why the French do not frighten me; the Germans can, at least some Germans. And that's why in Munich and in Koeln, I felt moments of fear, real though imagined fear. It may have been my unconscious realization of this vulnerability in me that made me anxious about going to Germany. It may be that in some way that I have not yet sorted out—I think some of my faculties are dormant when I explore this domain of my life—going to Germany would have been the stage toward my own extermination in Poland, where I was born. No, I don't cherish the thought of dying where I was born, where my mother was born and died. Maybe all of this has to do with the fact that I have not yet been able to go to see the remains of Auschwitz; so many have; but I did return to Rivesaltes.

Retracing Past Travels – 1997

In July 1997, Rachel and I attended International Psychoanalytic meetings in Barcelona. Since we would then be close to Perpigan, Rachel and I decided that we would go to Southern France and then proceed on to Bruxelles. We would spend a few days at several points of historic importance to me, to us as a family. In the south of France our itinerary was to visit Rivesaltes, then proceed north and eastward on the Mediterranean coast to Montpellier, veer northward to Nimes and up to Béssèges, to visit Rachel's mother's origins. Béssèges is a village set on both sides of a small river surrounded by rather steep hills very reminiscent of the surrounding hills of Pittsburgh, where Rachel's family settled in the U.S. We would overnight there, then proceed to Marseille, on to the *Côte d'Azur* to Fréjus, a stone's throw from St.Raphaël. There a few days, and we would then return to Marseille, drop of the van we had rented in Perpignan, and go on by train to Bruxelles. We would be there a few days and then return to the America.

My Return to Rivesaltes – 1997

I cannot vaunt my return to Rivesaltes; it was not a triumphant return. I was no Rhadames returning from his victory over the Ethiopians; may be my return was a little like Odysseus returning buffeted by, into uncertain belief of, the Gods. I did not return triumphant; but I did return, some fifty-five years later, sound and sane, well gratified of life, with my dearly-loved wife, one of our sons Karl, his wife Sabina, and their Elliot and Arthur, to visit the tomb of my past misery.

On this trip, for me, for Rachel and I think for Karl and Sabina as well, the visit to Rivesaltes was the destination of largest impact. Unlike the other places where we would stop, this one was marked with painful memory, insults and dehumanization; the visit filled with trepidation and mournfulness. The day before we all left Barcelona, Karl, Elliot and I trained up to Perpignan in order to pick the van that would give us a degree of travel freedom in following our itinerary in Southern France. The start of my visit to Rivesaltes heralded by my falling flat on my face, so to speak, when we walked out of the train station in Perpignan. It was a duly symbolic welcome back to the train station from which I sprung a significant distance between myself and Rivesaltes. Perhaps it was a reenactment of my escape from Rivesaltes, replaying the moment I fell, the whole stretch of my body on the sandy vineyard ground through which

"The truest monument to the Rivesaltes Circle of Hell—its ruins."

I was running like hell toward the road to Perpignan. As I said earlier, I did not really fall on my face but gashed my knee, as I tripped on a sidewalk I had not noticed in my beclouded state. We were then looking for directions to our car rental. My fall was no big deal, the opinion of the two physicians in attendance, Karl and I; we marched on to the car rental agency. Got the van and drove back to Barcelona; Karl requested that he drive since I had proven a bit shaken by our entry into this past chapter of my life. We had gotten out of Barcelona fine; but had not taken close enough notice just where we exited the city; on our return, finding the point of entry back into it was just a bit bewildering. Which entry should we take? In any case, we guessed well on one and got to where we needed to go.

Early the next morning we were full of pulling everything together, ourselves, the kids, our baggage, and packing it all in the van. We left Barcelona; our stay there had been very pleasant. Karl wanted to drive; he felt in the right because he wanted to take charge of the vehicle with this wife and children in it; Karl, echoing his mother, often tells me I drive too fast; I don't think so. But I think Karl may have had an additional motive too; having a preview of my unstable state the day before, he knew that this trip now was not a vacation for me. Our next stop was Rivesaltes. We traveled from Spain into France within an hour; we bypassed Perpignan. Seeing the road sign "Perpignan/Rivesaltes", my mood changed; I was going to a graveyard, a graveyard that held the tomb of someone, more than one, who had been viciously murdered, someone, more than one, I loved profoundly. Grim, I wondered, What will be there, what would I see? What would Rachel, Karl, Sabina and the kids, see?

First we saw the road pointer to "Rivesaltes"; my gut sank. What an ugly name! I feel that silently now. We drove into French country, through open fields and vineyards, then into the village, Rivesaltes, looking for signs to where the camp might be or might have been. We stopped at the gendarmerie to ask about the camp, where is it? Karl, who speaks French fairly well, initiated our inquiry; I joined in. I was struck by the policeman's patient listening and sober, respectful, response. Did I expect him to spit at me? I may have; because I was touched by his slowly getting up, slowly telling us where to go, pointing as he gave us the directions. He was kind; no doubt, I felt, he had done this a number of times before. We were not the first to come to visit their local concentration camp. He seemed not at all taken aback by our inquiry.

We got into the van and now slowly, we followed the gendarme's directions. The camp was less than a mile from the village. I felt that familiar gut sink, just as much physical as emotional, that grave pensive sorrow I know, when I first saw the remnants of that hell. And I felt a sweep of gratitude; the French had not destroyed the evidence; they had not swept it under the carpet as they did of Gurs, another camp, not far from Rivesaltes. Where Gurs was, now lies a lovely village from what Sali, who had been interned in Gurs, later told me. No, Rivesaltes, the remnants were there. I was totally unaware that Sabina had taken hold of her camera and started to chronicle our approach, entry, and visit of the camp site. The countryside stretches out, in the distance, south, in a haze one sees the Pyrénnées. We entered on a short road and parked the car on the side. I dragged myself out of the car. Rachel stayed close to me; Karl, Arthur on his shoulders at the start, one eye on his wife, Elliot and me. Sabina, looking, occasionally asking a question about the camp, and as I later saw the evidence, taking pictures. Rachel looked, she knew all the answers, there was no need for questions; we stayed together. At one point I took Arthur onto my shoulders; Karl and Sabina, and at times Rachel as well, tended to Elliot, then 5, curious, exploring, asking questions, and seeing more than I had expected.

From where we stood initially, the ruins stretched out on the left side of the road that cuts the camp into two sites. On the right side of the road, at some distance, there were barracks that had been much better maintained, that evidently were occupied at this time by some uniformed groups, most probably, of a police kind, not military. The entire camp seemed to me to be 1 square mile, more or less. We held our attention to the ruins side of the road.

I felt sick. I recognized the remnants of what I had known. All the roofs of the barracks but a spot here and there, had collapsed into the shell fragmented-sections that had held up. The photos show dark-greenish coarse sparse vegetation, occasional spiny briar, the then prevalent low-growing bushes—through which I crawled—covering the sandy ground, as neglected as the barracks; the barracks remain dirty beige in the sun, gray on their shade side, orange-tan scaling walls, all looking dirty, weather beaten. Sabina caught a shot of Rachel seeming to explain something to Elliot, probably in response to one of his many questions; they were standing in front of one of the barrack-shells. Barbed-wire, rolled, crumpled together lay here and there, probably marking where the periphery stood; in one place a small stretch of it stood, leaning somewhat collapsed. In the photo of that stretch, Sabina caught a picture of me with Arthur in their backpack-type carrier on my back and, twenty feet ahead, Karl carrying Elliot. I think that Elliot must have wanted to be held by his father, perhaps sensing that this was a moment of wanting to be very close to his father. A face-on shot of them, caught by our very able photographer, showed Karl looking grim, serious and sad all in one; Elliot looks puzzled.

All the barracks had been one-level structures, about ten feet high. Among the ruins of those we saw up close, the barrack that seemed most still there, showed an entryway about 12 feet long still partly roofed, then the roofless dormitory-living-quarters stretching perhaps 60 to 70 feet. There were nine windows on each side, each nearly three feet wide, about 2 feet high, placed high on the walls, almost adjacent to the roof, so that one could not see out of them just by standing up. Of these barrack remains, the walls were a thin shell of about 8 inches—cut across—hollow bricks covered with a layer of plaster; the floors seemed to be one sheet of cement. I took some pleasure in seeing the fragmented walls, no roofs, debris scattered on the remaining floors, of the boxes that once held us captive, against our will. The shame of Vichy-France spread over it all.

And then Elliot saw a remaining structure that looked different than the rest. He had been in there and asked me to come and look at it with him. I did; Sabina caught a shot of Elliot and me, with Arthur on my back, walking down the steps of this toilet-facility. Elliot had wanted me to see it, to answer his crumpled-up-face question, pointing to the hole in the cement slab floor of the walled stall: "Zaida, is this where you went . . . ?" His question, incredulous, sad, broken voice, touched me painfully. Here it was, live; what my children have inherited, now experienced by my grandson, Eli. It's one of the most painful things in all this—what my miserable Holocaust experience has gifted my family with. These toileting facilities seemed to really have troubled Eli; they troubled me too, many years ago much more than now. Eli made reference to it again five years later when we were together again in Bruxelles. In his uniquely sympathetic, intimate manner, identifying that he was going to say something for which he felt the need to prepare me, foreseeing the pain we were about to share, he said to me again, "Zaida, was that where you went to the bathroom?" Following that with a pause and,

"You know . . . ." ['what I mean' didn't have to be said]. I put my hand on the back of his shoulder, "Yes, Eli, that's where we went to the bathroom."

Eli's questions about the toilets in Rivesaltes, the war, etc. turned more complex in 2002 when we were again in Bruxelles, "Zaida, why did they do that to you?" How do you answer your grandson who clearly needs an answer. I heeded the advice I give parents when they ask me how to tell their children something difficult to share, to explain, the best you can. Our grandchildren ask me questions about it all, the two older ones especially, Eli and Rafi. So far the two younger ones join in when the older ones ask. Sophie, our beautiful grand-daughter does not ask, I think because she would cry before she finished her question. Five years after our visit to Rivesaltes, when again, Rachel, Karl, Sabina, Elliot, Arthur and I were in Bruxelles, walking back from Le Bois de la Cambre (my favorite childhood park-associated memories go back there), Eli and Arthur were just wide open about some of their 9 and 5-year-olds' questions about what happened—their father, mother, and their Bubbie there, just holding an emotionally safe place for us, like a bubble, as we walked on Chaussée de Vleurgat to our hotel. Yes, (Eli,) those were the round holes in a cement slab where we emptied the waste products our increasingly skinny bodies found they couldn't let us keep. I didn't say that to Eli, I say it now, as I think about it again.

Other than for Elliot asking some questions, we walked through the waste land scattered with ruins silent, looking at one another at times, at times hugging to allay some of the pain. Photographic eye peeled, Sabina spotted Elliot picking some raspberries from a small bush; she then spotted a quite larger berry bush. They were not there years ago, when we were interned there. Some guilty wind might have blown some of these welcome seeds to this otherwise fruitless square mile.

The surrounding area now was lush with vineyards and some less obvious vegetation. It was already past 1 p.m., the kids, who were really great sports letting us mull all this over, were getting hungry. Karl and Sabina reasonably felt we should soon look for a place to eat before the kids have a melt down. We got back to the van and got onto the road. From the height of the van, Sabina got a couple shots of the surrounding area, cut through with train tracks, captured on film, probably in memory of my having run over these tracks in my escape from the camp. We were on our way out, but after about ½ mile or less, we saw two rocks

The inscription bearing witness on a rock—
with stones commemorating visitors to the site

into which were melded metal plaques. We stopped. The left rock held a symbolic arced metal frame stating that this is Rivesaltes and I can't recall the rest, nor can I make it out from the photograph. Perhaps it's because I was very taken with the text inscribed into the metal plaques on the right rock.

Rivesaltes, the monument.

Rivesaltes, the ruins as monument, like the *Gedaechtsnichkierche* in Berlin, but Rivesaltes and these rocks stand as *The Ruins of Rivesaltes as a monument to the ravages of French Malignant Prejudice.*

The two rocks, Remembrance monument—photos in the photos book gathered, assembled, and created by Sabina. This visit to Rivesaltes in August 1997 caused a silent storm in me. I know it did so in Rachel too, and in Karl, and clearly Sabina was deeply touched by it too. Just seeing the skeleton of barracks and walk through the coarse prickly briar, just standing there—with my wife and one of our sons, his wife and their two young children—filled me with rage, made me feel weak and nearly overwhelmed with pain. But I also felt deeply victorious: I stood here with my wife, one of our sons, his wife, and 2 of our grandchildren. Rachel and I had replenished some of what my family had lost.

And standing there I was deeply appreciative that the post-WWII French government had not erased the traces of Rivesaltes. This French government retained the ruins of the barracks and outdoor lavatories of that miserable hate-driven attempt at dehumanization of so many terrified asylum-seekers in their land. It furthermore was gratifying to see the two 5-foot brown rocks the right one of which bears the inscription, in French:

> *Thousands of foreign Jews*
> *who had sought refuge in France*
> *were arrested and interned in 1940*
> *in the Camp of Rivesaltes in the Free Zone.*
>
> *From August to October 1942,*
> *more than 2,250 among them,*
> *of which there were 110 children,*
> *were delivered to the Nazis in the occupied Zone*
> *by an act of authority, of the then*
> *Government of France.*
>
> *Deported to the extermination camp of Auschwitz*
> *nearly all were assassinated there*
> *because they were born Jewish.*
> *Let us never forget these victims*
> *of racial hate and xenophobia.*
>
> The Union of Jewish Students of France
> The Sons and Daughters of Deported Jews of France

For 50 years this fact was suppressed, even denied in France. It was only in 2001 that French President Chirac made a public apology for the Crimes committed by the Vichy Government against the Jews in France. The French have not accounted for the fact that while the German Nazis exterminated not only Jews but also Homosexuals, Gypsies, and vocal opponents to Nazism, the government of Vichy France deported only Jews to Eastern Europe for the "Final Solution." And the accounting should not stop there—America, "land that I love," looked the other way too long as well.

Standing by those rocks, Sabina caught a photograph of Karl with Elliot on his shoulders, Rachel, her face shaded by her wide-rim hat, me, my face half-shaded too with Arthur riding on my back, barrack ruins in the background. Now we are all smiling, I think even Arthur, though he may be half-grimacing of hunger. We got back into the van and moved on. Following the vineyard bordered road, we came to a fork in the road, one sign saying that along this path we would find an auberge where we could eat; the other would take us to the highway. I could not stand the thought of eating so near Rivesaltes. I said so. But in a moment, whether it was urged by the disappointed faces I saw, or it came from within me, I felt, "Yes, let us eat here; let's eat a fine meal to celebrate the fact that we are here, alive and well, and many of those who would have had us dead are gone." We stopped at the auberge and had indeed a really good, very ample meal; but I must admit, that none of us seemed able to stomach the idea of eating blood sausage, which is part of the region's menu. After this feast, not soon enough, we left that miserable graveyard.

Leaving Rivesaltes behind

We were on our way to Béssèges. Béssèges was a refreshing interlude in our tracing painful past travels. It took us away from the Holocaust. Located on a small river, substantial hills on both sides, the village with one main street, an unexpectedly massive church that serves the surrounding region, and across the river, the city hall and post office. After taking some drinks—non-alcoholic—at the village tavern, we searched for members of Rachel's family. The church priest tried to help us but even with the help of church records did not succeed in locating family members. We left Béssèges disappointed but pleased to have seen where Rachel's family came from, got overnight accommodations, and the next morning were on our way to Marseille. We went rapidly through Marseille on a major highway, and proceeded to our next destination, Fréjus, and from there, St. Aygulf, a few kilometers from St. Raphaël. Now we could relax. And we did. Sabina's photographs of us on the beach tell the story. We are relaxed; smiles. We found a very nice little restaurant near our hotel, where we liked the ambience and the food so well that we ate there all the nights we were in St.Aygulf.

While there, Rachel and I set out to find *La Villa Mariana*. I had forgotten that on my trip in 1953 I had found out that *La Villa* was then a hotel. Unfortunately, my inquiries at the St. Raphaël Post Office yielded no useful information; they knew nothing of a Villa Mariana in St. Raphaël and I was bereft. We set out to search for it, and this is when I was really made cognizant of how much things had changed, even since 1953, let alone, since 1941-42. St.Aygulf, St. Raphaël, Boulouris, etc. were contiguous, melded together, into an extended metropolis of small towns, with yet further meldings on both ends. The *Côte d'Azur*, everyone knows, has long been a highly valued resort area. St. Raphaël, to me, has lost some of its unique loveliness, though some of the locals probably do not mind. Despite my disappointment at not being able to find *La Villa*, nor of course, could we find La Feuille in Boulouris, our visit to the area was memorable. Just the memory of having been warmly sheltered there in so bewildering a time made being there now, with my family, healing, yet another degree of healing of this life wound.

We left several days later, back to Marseille. There, I was brought back to the train station where I had arrived after my then highly accelerated running away from Riversaltes. I did not recognize it at all. It too had changed much as had St. Raphaël. We dropped off the van, waited in the station, then in time, boarded out train and were on our way to Bruxelles, direct. We wanted Karl and his family, the kids in particular, to be comfortable enough during this long train journey, so we got first class tickets. Nearly the entire wagon was ours from Marseille to Bruxelles. We arrived in Bruxelles; I was coming home, my old home, my second home.

It is always good to be in Bruxelles. It was the first time, 1997, that Rachel and I were in Bruxelles with one of our sons, with Karl and his young family, wife Sabina, 5-year-old Elliot and 1-year-old Arthur. I regret that Erik, our oldest, and his family, as well as Josh, our young-

My son Karl chased by his sons, Arthur and Eli, where I played as a child—le Bois d'la Cambre

est and his family have not yet been to Bruxelles. Someday. Etti was there, so were Alda, Sali, Micheline and Jean; we even got a glimpse of Gregory, then in his late twenties, back in Bruxelles after several years in the U. S. studying, preparation for a career in Business. But I had one further regret, this one, a sad one. My very dear cousin Joseph, who had died in the early 1990s, did not have a chance to meet Karl and his young family. Joseph had been away when I first visited in 1953. Rachel and I were visiting Bruxelles when I saw him for the first time since 1940 in the mid-1980s, more than 40s years after we ran away from the advancing German troops. Our reunion in the 1980s, in his apartment in Bruxelles was intensely joyful for me and for him. I had known that he was alive but this was the first time since 1940 that I saw him. Rachel and I met his wife then, a woman who had stood by him through trying times. We liked them both. His sisters were not happy with him; we never saw them together. Joseph told us of his "adventures" during the war, escaping to England and joining in the military effort of the Allies. He had also spent several years in Israel. His health for years now had been burdened by his hemi-paresis—his left side had been all but paralyzed in childhood; but he accommodated remarkably as he grew and in adulthood was essentially left with a modest left arm and leg weakness. But now, Joseph's health was no longer in good order; we talked about that too. I saw Joseph again on my next visit to Bruxelles in April 1992, on my way back from Moscow. In terms of his health he had deteriorated substantially then, and it did not surprise me when soon after, I learned that he had died. To the end, our relationship was warm, a very special liking. To me he was a "real" human being, a man of integrity, fearless, loving, unpretentious. Rachel too liked him immensely; she too found in him the traits I had known him for, for so long; there was no mask, you got what you saw; no pretense; and an uninhibited love.

This visit to Bruxelles had an added special meaning for me: that I had the opportunity to go to one of my favorite places in Bruxelles, Le Bois de la Cambre, with Rachel, Karl, Sabina, Elliot and Arthur. This was one of the Bruxelles highlights to which my mother took me. It gave me much pleasure that Rachel and I could bring one of our sons here, and that he at the same time brought his own wife and children. It was good to see them enjoy being there, in my Bois d'La Cambre, after all, I had claimed it long before they ever came to Bruxelles. We either visited with the cousins, feasted with them, or we went to Le Bois d'La Cambre. Oh yes, we also went to Bruxelles' magnificent Dinosaur Museum; it was necessary; Elliot was then an avid 5- year-old dinosaur scholar. It was a glorious visit, our visit to Bruxelles; a victory over the odious Nazis who tried to remove me from it. It was also a balm after our visit to Rivesaltes. I went to Rivesaltes in 1997. Six years later, I went to Drancy.

On Visiting Drancy – May 2003

In June 2002, I learned that the Paris based organization, *Les Fils et Les Filles des Deportés Juifs de France* (The Sons and Daughters of Deported Jews from France), had scheduled commemorative gatherings on the 60th anniversary of each date on which deportations from France to extermination camps in Poland occurred between April 1942 to 1944. Most of these deportations ended in Auschwitz. The notice came to us too late to make feasible plans to participate in the commerative anniversary of my mother's deportation, on August 14, 2002. One year later, having agreed to give a lecture at the University of Padova in May 2003, on this occasion Rachel and I extended our stay in Europe and included a visit to Paris, to have in effect a private commemoration of that terrible day.

Rachel and I dedicated May 28, 2003, to visit the *Camp de Drancy and Le Mémorial du Martyr Juif Inconnu* (The Memorial of the Unknown Jewish Martyr). Rachel agreed to let me visit Drancy alone; I prefer to not always share my torture with my wife and my sons. After two metros and 19 uneasy stops on bus 151, I descended the bus, trembling, at *Place du 19 mars 1962.* I later learned that this is the date when the Algerian war ended. Surprisingly disoriented—I am good at orienting myself even though I have for long gotten irritable, anxious in fact, when I am lost—a couple inquiries turned me in the right direction from the intersection of rues Henri Barbusse and Jean Jaures. Asking, "*Pourriez-vous me diriger vers le vieux camp de Drancy?*" (Could you direct me to the old camp of Drancy?) filled me with near-nausea. The bus driver seemed to want to have as little to do with me as he could. He knew what I was asking; he was not indifferent in his pointing me with his head to the right; I just felt he wanted me off his bus. Is that what he felt? Or was it me? Did I ascribe to him my dread of antisemitic sneer? I know European antisemitism. It is ugly, uglier than the American brand. I was glad to get off his bus. I knew I had been riding on rue Henri Barbusse but I just could not locate the street signs. But I am not the only one among us who is disoriented in these matters. The directions to the *Le Camp de Drancy* given me by the Parisien organization *Les Fils et Les Filles des Deportés Juifs de France* had two mistakes! Yes, you get off at the metro station *La Porte de Pantin*, and you take bus 151. But it is not stop 14, it is stop 19; it is not as the directions say *Place du 19 novembre,* 1962, but Place du 19 mars, 1962. I forgave them the mistakes; I was just as fa'mished ("mixed up" in Yiddish) as they.

Stepping off the bus pained and disoriented, I pulled myself together and again asked a man to please direct me to the site of the old camp at Drancy. Since Drancy is the town, now suburb of Paris, I had to specify that I was looking for the camp. He quite sympathetically looked at me and nicely told me that it was just down the street from where we stood. That turned me in the right direction; I thanked him, he smiled, and I started in the prescribed direction. Looking for any sign from where I was, I saw nothing indicating any sight other than two to three story buildings. My disorientation slightly abated now replaced by palpable anxiety, I felt very uncertain that I had been pointed in the right direction. Three buildings-houses down the street, I asked a woman is she could direct me to the old camp of Drancy. She too smiled, and patiently told me it was just a little farther down the street, that I would not miss the monument on the left. Two smiles lessening the pain of the narcissistic injury dished out by the bus-driver, I proceeded down the street less hurt but still shaky.

About 200 feet along *rue Jean Jaures*, on the left side of the street, I was surprised by the sharply green, well-cultivated grass, surrounding equally sharply geometrically shaped flowerbeds. The green, the flowers, seemed unexpected within the surrounding neighborhood, a moderate economic environ, half stores and habitations. Sober colored flowers, but obviously well attended to. My not very steady psychic state, well enough prepared I thought for seeing Drancy, revealed itself in how stark I found the greeting grass and flower beds. Following the ground, set in a circle of stone pavement with two concrete benches, now very visible was a three-structured monument, on a trapezoid-mount stone pedestal; the pedestal rises about 4 feet off the ground, the triple-structured monument atop of it stands about 10 feet high. About 8 kids were there; one sitting on a bench, another, sitting on the steps of the pedestal talking loudly to the one sitting on the bench, and about 6 atop the pedestal, at the feet of the monument. Probably 9th or

10th graders. Writing this in English feels foreign; the memory of the experience is in French.

Coming on the green grass, the flowerbeds, and the tripartite monument, I was struck again, this time by the symbol of extermination, a horsewagon—the French specify it was a horsewagon, not a cattle wagon. It sits on train-tracks stretched some distance away horizontally to the tripartite monument. There was an inkling of Drancy! A railtrack extends vertically from the monument for some forty meters to metal steps the lead into the horizontally laid out horsewagon. Nicely painted, the printing on the wagon clear: this wagon, the type known well enough that it requires no description, large enough (or small enough—depending on how you view it) "*pour porter 8 cheveaux ou 40 hommes*" (to carry 8 horses or 40 men) printed above the sliding entrapping door! 20 meters square. Try breathing. Wagon identified as SNCF, "1" in a box (guessing, *Societe Nationale de Chemin de Fer - 1*—National Society of RailWays of France [not stated]), specific name, KKuw, 215 941. Also, to make sure the right type of animal is loaded onto it, a Star of David with the number "12" printed in its central hexagon. A basket of flowers, on the point of dying, hangs at the right of the metal steps leading to the wagon door. I circled the wagon. Came back to the steps, climbed up, sat on the upper most and leaning against the door, comtemplating what went on here, that my mother passed through such a door, maybe this door. I wrote a few notes; not trusting that I would remember the details; I wanted the exact words and letters I just recorded.

I looked back at the monument. Now I understood why those kids were there. An older man, their teacher I assume, was talking-gesticulating in a contained manner to them no doubt about what this monument, rails, wagon, plaques tried to tell the world. I was grateful that this teacher had brought these kids here and that at least six of them seemed to be paying attention. It was a lovely day for an outing. He tried, thank goodness.

But I ached: this is not Drancy. This is polished. The grass, the flower beds, the really well done three-part monument, even the horse/men-wagon is polished. Where is Drancy? Where is the dread of knowing this is the last exit on the roadway to asphyxiation and the furnaces? This place was like talking about starvation, rape and murder around an ample dinner table in a polished home. Where was the Drancy of my mother? I tried to calm myself; it worked; I had done this many times before. I became the student, the worker, which so often has helped me cope with the aching sadness. I looked at the two small plaques on the grass, one in front of the metal wagon steps, the other on the grass to the right of the wagon. Small plaques like modest burial markers. The first read:

"La Republique Française en hommage aux victimes des persécutions racistes et antisémites et des crimes contre l'humanité commis sous l'autorité de fait dite Gouvernement de l'État Français (1940-1944). N'oublions jamais." (The French Republic pays homage to the victims of racist and antisemitic persecutions and crimes against humanity committed under the authority of the said government of the French State [1940-1944]. Let us never forget.) A very small plaque; so vast a crime. Can anything the good French do, many among them "righteous," be enough for me? What can the good French do, to make up for what the Nazi French did to us? Those "righteous" French who helped us then, to them I am profoundly grateful. Am I discriminating too much? To the "righteous French of then and now I am grateful; the antisemitic French, the antisemitic Europeens, I hold responsible, and I feel hate for them. Sadly, there are a lot of them. I have not arrived at forgiveness; the best I

Le 20 Aout 1941
5000 Juifs furent
arrêtés à Paris
et rassemblés
en ce lieu
inaugurant
le camp de Drancy
antichambre de la
mort.
Pres de
100 000 juifs
hommes femmes
enfants veillards
y furent internés
avant leurs
déportation
Pour la plupart, a Auschwitz.
1518 seulement sont
revenus
256 furent fusillés comme
otages.

Ce monument
Témoigne
des Martyrs
Juifs de France
Victimes de la Barberie
Nazie
Passant
Receuille toi
et n'oublie pas.
Regardez
et voyez
s'il est une douleur
comparable a ma douleur.
(Lamentation 1:12)

can do is let go of my hate most of the time; let it be replaced by the aching sadness that remains of the terrible hurt they caused us.

The second gravestone plaque says:

"Ici, l'État Français de Vichy interna plusieurs milliers de Juifs, Tsiganes et Étrangers. Deportés vers les camps Nazis, presque tous y trouverent la mort. Nous, génération de la mémoire, n'oublieront jamais. U. E. J. F. – Février 1993." (Here, the Vichy France State interned several thousands of Jews, Gypies, and Strangers. Deported toward the Nazi camps, nearly all found death there. We, the remembering generation, will never forget. U. E. J. F. – February 1993.) My best guess is that the U. E. J. F. stands for the *Union d'Étudiants Juifs de France* (The Union of Jewish Students of France). This same group produced the inscription stated on one of the two plaques affixed on the rock monuments in Riversaltes; no doubt they were instrumental in memorializing some of the sites in France where atrocities against Jews were massive and especially virulent.

But *plusieurs* means "several, some." The devil is in the details. Why did the Union of Jewish Students of France sign onto this statement. According to Serge Klarsfeld's Memorial de la deportation des Juifs de France, 62 convoys were sent from Drancy to Auschwitz. Each convoy carried about 1000 persons; convoy 19, one of the few under 1,000, carried 991. My mother was among those. Is 62,000 sent from Drancy—76,000 all told from France—several thousand? The aches and tribulations of a nitpicker! Why did the Jewish Students put their imprimature on a misrepresenting statement, "*. . . plusieurs milliers . . .*"? Were they ignorant of the facts? Did they, to protect themselves, need to deny the facts? Were they obliged to compromise? Details! But these figures are contradicted by the tripartite monument's inscriptions.

Going back to the three-part monument, I had read the inscriptions carved into the two granite parenthesis-bracket shaped pieces—parenthesis arc on the inside, bracket on the outside—one on each side of the center-piece component which depicted adult and child size human forms intertwined in a group. The centerpiece is somewhat amorphous, intentionally unfinished in detail, reminiscent of Michelangelo's *The Slaves;* one sees that it was carved out of a granite rock. It struck me as right. Too many were sent to their death to be specific about individuals' details. The two outside pieces are inscribed:

(The left inscription reads: "The 20th August 1941, 5000 Jews were arrested in Paris and assembled on this site, inaugurating the camp of

Drancy, antechamber of death. Nearly 100,000 Jews, men, women, children, the elderly, were interned here before their deportation, for the most part to Auschwitz. Only 1,518 returned. 256 were shot as hostages.

The right inscription reads: This monument, bears witness to the Jewish Martyrs of France, victims of Nazi barbarism. Passerby: meditate, think on it; and don't forget. Look, and see if there is any pain comparable to my pain. [Lamentations 1:12].)

"Selinger 1976" is carved on the lower right hand corned on the outside of the right parenthesis-bracket monument section. So on the small graveyard plaque, the U. E. J. F. seriously understates, "*plusieurs milliers,*" how many Jews were sent to death from Drancy, and on Selinger's monument the number is overstated to be nearly 100,000. The reported numbers are closer to 62,000. Fa'mished; mine is not the only head that at moments becomes clouded, one of the after-effects of the crime committed against us.

Backing to the street, I look on again, this remnant area of what was the camp at Drancy. I am grateful that it is documented, represented; but I am troubled by its manicure, its polish, its failure to convey what happened here. It takes me back to what I saw in Rivesaltes, the much more palpable remnants of what happened there, time's material degradation being a natural monument to the degradation in humans behavior toward other humans. I walk around the grounds again, by the monument, up the rails, around the wagon, take a path behind the wagon toward the left of the site and I see children playing in a fenced playground. As I approach, I see that adjacent to the remnant of the camp de Drancy on the left are two neighboring Elementary Schools, facing them, the one on the left is the *École Élémentaire Joliot Currie* and its neighbor, sharing the same school yard is the *École Élémentaire Pablo Picasso.* Two Elementary Schools built on what no doubt was the detention camp to hell. At least, it isn't a department store or a brothel. I walk toward the street in a passageway bordering the camp site and the Joliot Currie School and see in the manicured grass yet another grave like plaque but larger.

"Sous cette allée à 1 m 50 de profondeur
passait le tunnel de l'éasion
au camp de Drancy.
70 internés repartis en 3 équippes oeuvrèrent
de jour et de nuit pour la réalization.

Commencé en septembre 1943
Long de 36 mètres, if fut découvert par les Nazis
En novembre 1943 et ne fut jamais achevé.
Il manquait 3 mères pour atteindre la liberté!

(Under this alley at a depth of 1.5 meters passed the tunnel for escape from the camp of Drancy. 70 internees divided into 3 teams labored day and night for its realization. Begun in September 1943, 36 meters long, it was discovered by the Nazis in November 1943 and was never achieved. It lacked 3 meters to attain liberty!)

I attained liberty. But I didn't have to dig a tunnel 5 feet underground; and I was not in German Nazi custody, only in the custody of less bloody French collaborateurs. I wanted to stay longer; but thank heaven Rachel was waiting for me. I left Drancy.

Two or so hours later Rachel and I went to the temporary headquarters of *Le Mémorial du Martyr Juif Inconnu.*

Le Mémorial du Martyr Juif Inconnu

The Holocaust left us not just with life-lasting ache, with memories of monstrosities and murder, it also left us burdened with paradoxes. Outstanding among these is my long silence about what happened to us on the one hand, and yet I experience the dread that it will be buried like Gurs and forgotten. Even if it is feebly represented, like Drancy, thank heaven, it is there. So too, I am grateful for *Le Mémorial du Martyr Juif Inconnu.* First, I am grateful that the post-World War II French have committed themselves to developing a Memorial and center of information dedicated to what happened to the Jews in France during World War II. Second, those who are giving life to this Mémorial-Museum are creating a repository of Shoah information with specific details of what happened to the Jews in France and how it came that so many of them were murdered. And I take note especially that, in their documentation of those historical facts that detail what happened to the Jews in France, one photograph twisted my interiors.

Our first surprise when we got there on Wednesday, May 28, 2003, was that on the point of entry into the temporary home of the Mémorial , 37 rue de Turenne, I nearly came to an argument with the man at the guichet (like a ticket sales box to a movie theater) who put up unexpected resistance to letting me and Rachel in. What did I want? Did I have an appointment? Who were we? Like, we looked like terrorists! Talking about it briefly moments later Rachel and I agreed that they are taking all kinds of precautions to defend against an act of terrorism involving the *Mémorial* . I told him my name; he looked unimpressed. *"On veut voir le Mémorial"* (We want to see the Memorial), I said with the feeeling of "What the hell do you think we want!." Not impressive on my part. He looked as though he did not understand me. I was speaking French! I told him "*Je suis un Juif; on vient des États Unis. On veut simplement voir le Mémorial* !" (I am a Jew, we come from the United States. We simply want to see the Memorial!) Whether my heat convinced him that I was one of them, I had no ill intent toward the Jews of Paris, whatever, grudgingly he pushed the buzzer that made it possible for us to enter. Great welcome. But once entered, I did calm quickly. I am still amazed at my own lability about such matters. Clearly, I was, I am, very easily jarred by unpleasant matters of Jewishness in Europe; even when it is done to me by Jews! The residual symptoms of my "Chronic Post Traumatic Stress Disorder" (PTSD), as we say in my field: low threshold for situational anxiety—like the one I am talking about now—, hypersentsitivity, occasional frightening dreams in which I am threatened, or in danger, or am robbed, some of these not terribly disguised; on top of a chronic I think characterologic baseline of low-key depression. The characterological low level depression gives me a constant low level degree of seriousness; the baseline depression, and deeply felt quiet rage gives some people the feeling that I am somewhat severe. Some of my students are intimidated by it; but those who get to know me better know that I don't bite people's heads off. My PTSD symptoms are not constantly present; certain stresses trigger them. Being in America for so long, my Jewishness does not make me labile, I am not constantly on the threshold of anxiety and hypersensitive. In Europe I have been so; I found I was so when I was in Moscow, and in Koeln, less so in Hamburg, but especially acutely so when I have been in Munich—even when I am with my dear friends Lotte Koehler and Hans Kilian. I am not so in Bruxelles, nor in London or Stockolm, nor in Italy, though I might be just as labile as I was then, entering the *Mémorial*, questioned unexpectedly as if, "Jews are not permitted here!" Amazing how a reasonably intelligent Jew can feel so even when questioned by another Jew!

Realizing that this is Europe, that Jews in Europe are more wary of antisemitic acts now in May 2003, of acts of terror, I understood; I calmed down. The fear of terrorist acts against Jewish institutions is now widespread in Europe. The synagogues I visited, as I understand is the case in many parts of Europe, are actually police guarded. The Synagoga di Roma on Shabbat was in fact guarded by carabinieri (police with weapons), and two Jews at the only open gate gave me some resistance to my wanting to come in to see the Synagogue. "*Wus is dus? Ich bin a Yid fon America. Mir vet reinkimen!*" (What is this? I'm a Jew from America. We want to come in!) I guess I talked them into letting me in. The Synagogue in Florence, a beautiful Sephardic structure, much more so than the one in Rome, was equally inaccessible and will admit one only after passing through some interrogatory, though they were less suspecting than the Romans and our Parisien gatekeeper.

Once in the *Mémorial* I felt that disorientation, like I felt that morning; I know I have occasionally felt that disorientation such as when I was at *Yad Vashem* and at the Washington Holocaust Museum. Rachel, my anchor, among other life sustaining things, was with me. We turned to the woman at the reception desk for some orientation. For reasons not clear to me, I did not identify specifically who we are, just visitors from America. Many Europeen Jews give me the impression that they like that; "Oh, you're from America and you're here." There is something meaningful in that. The woman at the greeting desk was very pleasant and welcoming. She informed us that this is the temporary home, repository, of the materials that will go into the actual *Mémorial,* which is currently under construction. She pointed to the architectural model of what the *Mémorial* will be like. Seeing our hesitancy and perhaps sensing our disorientation, she smiled and got up to show us the model. We asked a few questions. She was nicely disposed to answer us, even though she had seemed very busy when we came in. The model showed a remarkable structure; not a monument as such, a museum. I was moved to see what they were doing. "*Ce sera le Centre Commémoratif du Shoah le plus grand de L'Europe.*" (It will be the largest Commemorative Center of the Holocaust in Europe.) A large statement, given the gripping Libeskind Jewish Museum in Berlin. But the Museum in Berlin is not focussed on the Holocaust, as the Paris Memorial will be. I asked her to show me where the names of the Holocaust victims would be inscribed—I let her know that my mother's name would be inscribed there. She did not ask the name; she may have sensed my puzzling reticence to say it. She informed us that the walls of the main corridor of entry will be the commemorative walls; this is where the names of the victims will be inscribed, "*Alors, tous qui entrent le Mémorial passeront devant les noms des victimes.*" (Thus, all who enter the Memorial will pass in front of the names of the victims.) I was struck by that; awed, and pleased. Everyone who enters the Memorial, the museum, will automatically pass between walls inscribed with names of those who either died in French camps or who were knowingly, we know now and many knew then, sent to their death by the then *Gouvernement de l'État de France.*

Rachel was immediately drawn to the exhibit on the walls of the few rooms that constitute the museum's temporary home. The events of the time unfold from room to room, from the beginnings of antisemitic blaming of Jews in France for the dire state of its economy at the beginning of the Twentieth Century to the events during the Holocaust. The photos, the reproductions of Statutes against Jews, the camps in the Occupied and the Free Zones of France, a substantial part dedicated to the "righteous" French, Protestant and Catholic Clerics especially, who protected and safeguarded many Jews in Vichy France.

But equally represented and recorded on the walls were the collaborations between Vichy and the Nazis in the Occupied Zone. Daladier was among the first facilitators of the incarceration of Foreign Jews who sought asylum in France.

But most gut-wrenching was a large reproduction of Jean Bousquet greeting Heydrich Himmler in Paris. A forward thrust in Bousquet's entire body as he extends his outstreched arm to a slightly reserved, superior Himmler, Bousquet's face admiring, wanting to please, an open smile. He is meeting someone he likes, someone by whom he wants to be well-regarded. Even more than Daladier, Bousquet was among those in Laval's government who not only yielded to the Nazi demands, but even anticipated their orders, no doubt he was the one to cause the Germans embarrassment by having Jews sent to Paris before the Nazis were prepared to house them temporarily. What a painful photo: the impersonation of French Nazism.

Time passed as we looked, sat on the carpeted floor for a while—they have no seating accommodations in this temporary museum. We saw a door inconspicuous in one of the wall open from time to time, giving into a library-seminar room of good size; people were busy at some study or paper work, some were in discussion no doubt about Holocaust or *Mémorial* issues. Catalogue cases suggest that this may be where some of our information is collected. We made no inquiries; we were not there to study, just wanted to see and feel the site where my mother's name will be inscribed on the wall. We left, sat at a sidewalk café for coffee, and went on to find the site where the future Memorial is being constructed.

We found *rue Goeffroy-l'Asnier* easily enough and saw the structure in process of construction. On *rue Goeffroy-l'Asnier* we found the newly named *rue des Justes* (Street of the Righteous), the small alley-street on which the entrance to the Memorial will be situated. We were about one block or so from the Seine, not far from Ile St.Louis, a location within that remarkable area of Paris, not far from the Louvre, the George Pompidou Center, close to Notre Dame. The site was closed to visitors. One person came out of a door, automatically closing it behind him. When he saw us looking at the building in construction with interest, he turned back, checked the door to make sure it was closed. I felt the near-paranoia of the Parisien Jews, or perhaps not just Jews, but all those involved in the construction of the site. Did he think we might want to sneak in; not altogether wrong. But good heavens do Rachel and I look at all suspicious?

We were impressed with the magnitude of the structure. It will be a good residence for *Le Mémorial*. Nonetheless, tired and feeling somewhat unwelcome, we left.

So many years later, and still, each visit to sites that are part of my piece of the Holocaust has such a wrenching effect. Not just on me, on Rachel too. Seeing them, visiting there, the ache and heaviness do not surprise me. I know it will be so before I go. It proved itself too difficult the first time we planned to go to Israel. This is what has stood in my way of doing things I feel I "should" do, things I have not done.

Chapter 10

Of Burdens that Follow from What Befell Jews in Europe of That Day

Problems for My Family

One of the largest torments I continue to experience following from what happened to me, is the pain and the burden this past has caused my wife and our three sons. No survivor has escaped this; we can't prevent it; wives and kids cannot not be burdened by it. Now my grandchildren have begun to ask me, with a note of seriousness and caution, "Zaida, were you in the war?" Their fathers know that I have long wanted them to know, and now that I want their children to know, that they can say to me, ask me, anything at all about what happened to me, to all of us. In the hope of helping them deal with this burden with the least possible injury, I have tried to facilitate our talking about what happened over there. I sense that my sons have tried to protect me and themselves by taking up the past with me, mostly only on specified occasions like the Jewish Holidays.

For my wife, as I have seen again and again, she suffers that I was victimized by the Holocaust; that this happened to me. Rachel, to whom I have now been most gratifyingly married for 48 years, is not a Jew; nor as she has often said is she a Christian or anything else. As she says, she has "no religion." But she has taken on this burden of my life as part of her own. I am troubled, even to this day and will always be, by the fact that she suffers by empathizing with my pain, as it has remained in me over the years. By virtue of our meaning to each other, this letting herself feel what I feel, and empathically feel what I felt then, engenders sympathetic pain in her. She feels pain, but it is pain detached from having actually experienced what caused it. It is a mix of resonance with the pain inside me and with the pain that her own imagining of this experiencing engenders in her. I am not in her head so that even after 48 years of being together nearly every day, I can't be sure just what it is she experiences. I think though, that she experiences a mix of feelings. First, there is the "vague knowing" of what I experienced that comes from not having shared this miserable experience too. It's not knowing with the knowing that comes with having experienced it oneself. This not knowing from having experienced, especially of so traumatizing and life re-organizing an experience, creates a vague sense in one's life that I believe is at times not easy to live with. I think my sons may experience this too.

Perhaps it is just my imagining. Perhaps not everyone shares this tendency. But for those who do, it becomes a burden. Not having experienced it becomes a burden. I can tell my wife and my sons that it is not worth going through this kind of experience to know; they know this; but I think there still is the soft distress of not knowing because it was not experienced. There are many things we cannot know of our mates and even our children that we do not experience as a burden. But not having shared their suffering does. It's amazing how common and widespread this is. If someone you love suffered and you didn't suffer that experience, many a person feels I should have suffered that too; and this may bring on passive-guilt; not guilt of commission, but guilt for not having been subjected to it too.

At such moments, I have wondered if Rachel feels guilty that she was not robbed, ravaged, humiliated and starved as we were! It's the feeling "There but for the grace of God go I" amalgamated with the empathic experience that leads to feeling "It should have happened to me too." It's not wise; but empathy in the face of suffering by those we love takes us there. This can, of course, go beyond our experiencing it just with people we love. Primo Levi felt, when the man next to him was selected for death, "Why did he get tagged for the gas chamber and not me?" Passive-guilt! "I should suffer like he did." And it also becomes communal; all Jews suffer that the Holocaust tortured and killed so many Jews, even Jews unknown to them.

For Rachel, there is another factor in her feeling guilty that it happened to me. I wish it were not so, but I think it is. Regarding this guilt factor, several thoughts come into my mind. The first is that she feels guilty that she did not in some way prevent this from happening; parents feel that especially when some harm comes to their child. In the face of jarring experience we all tend to revert to some childhood ways of reacting, like magically, I could have prevented this; and if I could not then why didn't God—for those who go there.

In addition, life with its everyday difficulties makes it that she at times is angry with me and then she wishes me ill, after which, again, she is gripped by that magical thinking residuum from childhood: she dreads that her wishes are what made it all happen to me. A lot of irrational, magical, inelegant thinking goes into what makes us feel guilt. I hurry to say it's not all bad; in fact it has its advantages to ourselves and to society. We all fall victim to it more or less—well, except for those among us who have disordered or dwarfed consciences. So, I think she feels guilty that she was left out of the misery and that she sometimes wishes that what happened to me should happen to me. But my reasoning may all be wrong; I'm not at my best reasoning on this subject at this personal level. I'm better at sorting out complexities when I look at them from an optimal distance, as a shrink. On these matters, I can't do that with my wife, my sons, my family. Ascribe it to my ruminations.

It torments me that my three sons, each in his own way is tormented by what happened to me. When our oldest, Erik, was a freshman at the University of Chicago we had occasion to visit him—I was among those participating in the 50th Anniversary of the Chicago Psychoanalytic Institute. We were in Erik's room on campus, wanting to know all we could about how he was, his goings-on at the University, and all that, like all parents whose kids do so well just never tire of hearing about, and it was good and exciting. By the way, he wanted to know, who did you say we are we having dinner with? I told him we were having dinner with Sandy—the second of the Wagner girls, the one who lives in Evanston. He looked momentarily puzzled, I thought, so I elaborated, "You know, the Wagner family." He just burst into tears. I may be wrong, but I look at Erik, and can say the same for Karl and Josh, and at times I see how burdensome my Holocaust past is to him, to them.

A week ago, after telling us again that they, he, Erik, his wife Andrea and their children Sophie and Ben, would be with Andrea's Aunt Leila for Passover and not us, I showed my disappointment; I don't try to hide what I feel with my family; I'm not good at hiding my feelings anyway. For reasons I will not even try to guess—whatever my sons may think, I refuse to be a shrink with them—Erik in essence said to me, "Heh, it's all your doing. Last time you couldn't have the Seder when we could do it, so we went to Aunt Leila's" or something like that.

Two days ago on the phone, we came back to this issue. My reaction of disappointment had troubled him. He had experienced it, as he said, as if I was saying, "After all I've been through, how can you do this to me!" I didn't know whether to get angry or cry; but I sobered quickly. Our sons, Erik, Karl, and Joshua, are remarkable human beings. I have never said anything like that to them or to my wife. I have never felt, "After what I have been through, how can you do this to me." I have never felt it, I have never said it, and I never will. At those moments Erik seems to me mournful but also tired of it, I think, wishing he, could just put the thing to rest already. And I love that by some accord, some decision he made many years ago, he nearly always sits to my right at dinner—not necessarily at other meals, but at dinner, yes.

I wish he could put it to rest, and that Rachel could, that Karl, and Josh could, that we all could, already. But I hear Primo Levi's curse—my personal elaboration and interpretation of it—if you don't bear witness, "may your children turn their faces from you." And, of my own inner need, I don't want to put it to rest. I want to remember it, I have to remember it. And, conflicted, I have imposed it on my sons. The remembrance that May 1 is when I escaped from Rivesaltes is ritual. This was an occasion when Karl would cry, and Josh would cry; and yet it was also a day of celebration, of thanksgiving. And in fact, we have made Thanksgiving and Pesach commemorative occasions mixed with sadness and indeed, thanksgiving; thanksgiving for being free, in America. My sons tell me, let me know, that I have given much that is good to them. But with it, yes, my misery has left its mark on them, my sons. They have to remember. It is a responsibility; it is a burden.

When Karl was 16, in 1975, he decided and arranged to spend his summer in Bruxelles to study cello with Edmond Baert, the cellist of *Le Trio à Clavier de Belgique* (The Piano Trio of Belgium) who resided there. How he found Edmond Baert I am not sure, but I assume that he asked his teacher of that time about a fine cellist in Bruxelles. Kids are amazing; mine certainly amazed me, and still do. That's why I had the brilliant idea of becoming a child psychiatrist. Karl wanted to see and get to know Bruxelles, as I have inferred, understood, because it was where I spent the remembered part of my childhood of which I speak with very fond memories, because he knew Bruxelles means, positively, so much to me. He went then perhaps also with a secondary, or perhaps primary, mission to relocate my cousins whose addresses and telephone numbers I no longer had—they do have telephone directories in Bruxelles—as I noted before, because of their moves and my moves from the time I had found them in 1953. Considering what I am saying one might get the impression that I am irresponsible, or uncaring, or foolish. I feel secure enough in my knowledge of myself to know that I am not irresponsible and I certainly am not an uncaring person; that I am foolish, no doubt, sometimes I am. I ascribe my losing touch with my dear cousins to the pain that thinking about them, about our past has and continues to cause me. I feel much love for them and they for me, but all evidence points to the fact that the pain they represented to me, and they still do, was sufficiently great that I had avoided a second search for them. This painful research in times past had some part in my choosing to become a psychoanalyst, an explorer into individual human pasts, like an archeologist, Freud said. I had lost connection with my cousins and Karl set off "to be" in Bruxelles, to further his cello studies, further strengthen his French, and to find my again lost cousins.

It did not take long for him to find them. From his telephone calls to us and much subsequent living evidence of it to this day, Alda and Sali, Etti, and Micheline received Karl with excitement, and undertook to find him a place to stay, not that he spent much time there, to feed him, to take care of him in princely fashion. My impression is that Karl felt like the conquering hero; he had a right to that feeling. He went, found, and really conquered them. That conquest has lasted decades. We returned to Bruxelles in June 2002, for Gregory's wedding—Gregory, the son of Micheline and Jean, just married Sandra—; Karl, Sabina, and their sons Elliot and Arthur again were a big hit. But it is evident to me that while the journey to re-establish contact with my cousins, with his Belgian cousins, has given Karl much pleasure, my Holocaust experience weighs on him and intrudes in his life in a number of ways. In early 1997, as I related earlier, Rachel and I went to Barcelona for international meetings. We had decided that we would then go to Rivesaltes and St. Raphaël, in a tracing back of the path I had traveled many years before. When we told this to Karl, he wondered if he and his young family could join us on his return from South Africa. Karl was spending part of that summer doing a medical training rotation in South Africa, and since Sabina has musician friends in Barcelona she had not seen in some time—for some years now Sabina has been First Violist of the Saint Paul Chamber Orchestra—he and Sabina would arrange to join us in Barcelona. From there we could go together to Rivesaltes, Besseges, St. Raphaël and Bruxelles. Karl and Sabina—who had been in Bruxelles with the Orchestra and had met and delighted our cousins—were glad for the opportunity to make this very troubling, but then also pleasant trip with us. We had invited Erik and Josh and their respective families to join us but work conditions made it too difficult for them to do so.

As I recounted earlier, it was a memorable trip. I was aware of Karl's concern for us, Rachel and me, and for Sabina and for their two children, especially Elliot, who was then 5 and very curious about everything. Arthur was just 1 then, and of course not yet into the meaning of life and the burdens distributed to us by fate. We were all oppressed with that visit and it generated in Elliot questions he asks me from time to time. "Zaida, were you in the war?" And 5 years later, in 2002, Elliot and Arthur, asked many questions about what happened "then;" even at their young age they understand the subject without further cue than "then."

"Zaida, were you in the war?" is also a question Rafi has asked me several times. Rafi, Josh's son, is very into stories and Histories of war. Joshua too, like his brothers, carries the burden of what happened to me. I am wary of assuming that I know why Josh chose to become a scholar in Hebraic-Arab philosophic discourse, specifically the variable interpretations of Plato by Alfarabi (Arab) and Moses Maimonides (Hebraic), each a brilliant philosopher of the 10th and 13th Centuries respectively. Of course, there is more to what he is doing than I can grasp. How else do I explain to myself his focused interest in Israel and in the Arab world but that it has a bearing not only on Jews but, specifically on me, on what happened to me, his father who just absolutely adores him—and respects him so? He was the only one of my sons who had a Bar Mitzvah, all his own planning and doing after he had gone away to College, a problem gifted to him by his deeply loving father who was all screwed up about God, and about Hebraic liturgy, or for that matter any religion's liturgy; his father, me. I'll talk about that problem in a moment.

The sins of the father will be visited on the child. Fine; I understand how it happens; I am a shrink, after all! But what sins did I commit in all this? The pains of the father will be visited on the child. That's what applies to us; and it makes me weep. A father cannot have better sons than I have. And, I am really in a quandary. I want my sons and my wife to put it all to rest; but I want us to remember it, and I want to remind others of it, hoping they will not let it happen again, nor wish to perpetrate it again.

My problem with God and with Liturgy

As I said a moment before, our son Joshua was the only one of our sons who had a Bar Mitzvah. It was all my doing, not Rachel's; I am the one who was so conflicted at the time that our sons were not Bar Mitzvahed when they were of age. My torment on this question does not diminish over the years. I was reared in a Jewish family where some of us were Conservative Jews and some were Orthodox Jews. My mother was not observant, nor was my Aunt Ester; but the Frenkel family was Orthodox, though mostly it was so for Uncle Maurice Frenkel who was observant, but not Joseph or my cousins Alda or Etti. Before the war, I had started Hebrew school. The war interrupted this training and no effort was made, either on my part or those around me, to institute such training while we were in the camps. I was not an ardent religious Jew. However, as I said earlier, I was intent on having my Bar Mitzvah and did so at 14, the year I arrived in Pittsburgh. I should say that even though I was intent on having my Bar Mitzvah, even before the Holocaust I did not feel an ardent conviction about God. God was simply part of our life; no need to question. I had my Bar Mitzvah at 14, in Pittsburgh; gracious gift of the Wagners.

After graduating from High School in Pittsburgh, I spent one year at Penn State, not altogether certain that I wanted to pursue a career in Psychology. I was unhappy. I turned to Donald Steinfirst with whom I stayed in active contact. When he asked me how I was doing, I let him know that I was not happy in Psychology, that I was a very unhappy, frustrated singer. I needed to be in Music. Donald, the ardent music lover, one of my absolutely dearest friends, was something of a father figure for me—I don't say "was a father to me" because I have never abandoned the inner-experience "my father"; because I have a sense of "my father" somewhere in my psyche, though I knew him only too briefly. I think the loss of one's family during our Shoah, even more than when their death occurs in any other way, makes it that though we mourned their deaths they still are within our psyches, not replaceable. The traumatic dimension of their death makes them even more indelible than does the fact that we have known them from birth. Anyway, my father-figure

Donald arranged for me to have auditions, one with Vladimir Bakaleinikoff, the Assistant Conductor of the Pittsburgh Symphony Orchestra, at the time Assistant to Conductor Fritz Reiner; then one in the Steinfirst home with Jan Peerce, Toscanini's preferred tenor; and yet another with Fritz Dorian, Musicology Professor in the College of Fine Arts at Carnegie Tech, now Carnegie Mellon University. Through Donald and Fritz Dorian's help, I got a four-year scholarship to Carnegie Tech. The point of this detour in my addressing the question of religion is that to add to that scholarship, for survival needs, I was a Cantor in a small but well to do Reformed Synagogue on Forbes Street in Pittsburgh. I was a Cantor who gave it all he had, devotedly, lovingly, but with a feeble conviction about either God or certain lines of the Liturgy I was singing. I want to be clear. I love being a Jew; I loved being a Cantor. But I was not an ardent believer in the God about whom I sang with so much very genuine feeling. The feeling was about being a Jew; it was not about a God I love and know exists.

As a child I was not an ardent believer in God; I did not pray every morning and evening as did my dear Uncle Maurice Frenkel. But I believed strongly enough to feel as so many of us have during and after our Holocaust, "Where is God?" "Why did God let this happen to us?" God too was a victim of the Holocaust. Elie Wiesel said it better than anyone. Compelled to watch another hanging in Auschwitz, this time of a young teenager too light to be effectively strangled by his own weight pulling on the hangman's noose. Writhing reflexly to breathe as he hung, it took one half hour—and he stopped. Forced to watch, someone behind Wiesel asked, in vain, a second time, "So where is God?" Wiesel felt within himself a voice that answered, "Where he is?" "Here he is—he is hanging here, on this gallows." (Elie Wiesel, 1958, *La Nuit*, page 103. Paris: Les Editions de Minuit. My translation.)

That's one of the problems for me; I don't know if what our forebears and many today portray as God exists. I believed so as a child; true, not ardently. For years in my young adulthood I considered myself an atheist. I am now 74; I still don't know about God. I am not anti-God. I am no longer atheistic. I see God more as what I understand to be the Spinoza school of thought about God. There is something bigger than we are; "bigger" here stands for well beyond us in unique dimensions and character. What force made it possible for us all to be here? That force is clearly not man-made. How did we all evolve? The question is intended to be an evolutionary question. What force created the building blocks of whatever theory of creation we want to invoke? These questions, naïve, I recognize, leave me with no answer. There is something bigger than we are, much bigger. It cannot be humanoid, with all due respect to Michelangelo.

God is in everything, everywhere. God cannot prevent Holocausts.

I am not even agnostic; I think there is something powerful that has made it possible for us to be here.

But my problem with God is not the only problem I have with my religion. And my problem applies equally to other religions. I was introduced to Jewish Liturgy when I was a child in Bruxelles. I added to my knowledge of it beyond my studies for my Bar Mitzvah by singing in the choir in Beth Shalom Synagogue while I was in High School in Pittsburgh. While in Music School at Carnegie Tech, in addition to being a Cantor in a small Reformed Synagogue, on Sundays I sang as a soloist and in the choir in a Protestant Church in South Pittsburgh. So, I sang Hebraic and Christian liturgies. Many singers do this. Singers think of the words they sing. Singing is not just music; that's the uniqueness of singing, you sing words with the most natural, most remarkable musical instrument great pianists, string, woodwind, and brass players try to emulate. In singing the words are essential, they tell the singer how to sing. Interestingly, as a psychoanalyst, words matter just as much to me as they do when I sing. My teacher and friend Leon Saul said that as psychoanalysts "Our words are as sharp as the surgeon's scalpel," something I have repeated often in teaching. I paid attention to what I sang, to the words, and both liturgies troubled me. Jews have "the chosen people," "chosen" in everyday parlance—not like our Joshua defines it—means Jews are better than; if you are not Christian you are anti-Christ, therefore, a Christ killer; if you're not Catholic you will go to hell. I never chanted Islamic prayer but we all know these days that Muslims have "infidels," which is tantamount to being condemned to death. If you're not the way I am, you are bad news and will end up in ashes. Well, we all end up in ashes anyway, in ashes or decomposing protein and all its magnificent complements. But very specifically, as a Jew, I have serious misgivings about our being "the chosen people." Joshua, my dearly beloved son, a scholar, tells me that we were "chosen" to safeguard the covenant, the scrolls of Torah. It is not, he assures me, that we were chosen as superior to others, to non-Jews. No doubt he is right; his interpretation is much more knowing than mine. But when I say the words, I object, I don't think it's right, I don't think it's the way it should be, not in my world. We are all chosen or none of us is chosen. I can't recite such words without cringing. I cannot accept that Jews, or anyone else, Muslim, Catholic, Hindu, Protestants, and any other brand of human being is "chosen" over the others. I refuse to accept that. And that makes it very difficult for me to tend to, and attend, religious services, Jewish, or other. I am old enough to ask, "What to do with this world of ours?" We have to accept each other, every other, and co-exist without murders. I take this position personally and have done so professionally.

My questions about God, and the assertion that we are "the chosen people," make being "religious" very problematic for me, very. Arthur Mirsky, a senior colleague who died years ago, once said to me after we had talked for quite a while, "You're a very religious man, Henri." I was surprised by his read of me; I have never thought of myself that way. Then, no longer a believer in "God," no longer an atheist, I was puzzled by Mirsly's measure of me; but I took his statement positively, appreciatively; I felt he meant it that way. I'm not sure just what made him say that. But if Mirsky saw religion as I recently heard someone say as, to paraphrase him, "a personal interaction steeped in love between an individual and God," and not as bodies of liturgy steeped in divisive, chauvinistic principles and man-made laws—not that all man-made laws are bad—then Mirsky saw me. And it is not my ruminations and uncertainties about God, but the chauvinism of the liturgies and the abuses to which their malignant applications have led, that has caused an uproar in me at times in my life. Over the years since I have been an adult, when on occasion, in the service of celebration or of mourning by or for someone I value I have been in a synagogue, or for that matter in a church, I have felt distress when out of respect for others I have read or sung liturgy passages that preferentially praise the believers in the faith. I don't like being "the chosen," I don't like being threatened with the fires of hell, I don't like being an "infidel." I don't like being one of the preferred who is assured a place in heaven, and I don't like being an evil outsider guaranteed burial in hell's flames. All of this, while doubtful that there is either a heaven or a hell—though I did dwell in the first and second circles of hell.

Outstanding among these times of distress, of very conscious fairly fierce inner conflict about religion, are those times that arrived when each of our sons approached the age of preparing for and having a Bar Mitzvah. Even to this day I bemoan the problem gifted to them by their adoring father who was all screwed up about God, and man-made liturgies; their father, me. I might well have been conflicted about religion even if my life had been untrammeled, free from the Holocaust. But I know, that what happened to us, definitely has left me with the question that may underlie my doubts about God, "If there is a God, how could this have happened to us!" Not one Holocaust survivor has escaped having that thought. Some have answers. Many Jews who experienced the Holocaust came out of it more fervent believers in God and observers of liturgy than they were before. But I also know that many among us have found their belief in God fractured if not shattered. I know this from personal encounters with other Holocaust survivors—one spontaneously told me this much within one week of my working on these lines. And these Jews have as I have, abandoned going to synagogue, even on Rosh Hashana (New Year) and Yom Kippur (Day of Atonement). I am not certain that these survivors feel as troubled by the liturgy as I do; but their belief in God jarred.

I know I am trying to explain why my sons did not have a Bar Mitzvah. I am still conflicted and sorrowful about it. It may puzzle some, it may not, but I regret that my sons did not have a Bar Mitzvah. Yet, were I faced with the same matter now, I don't know what I would do. In this and it so many matters, Rachel has always been open, receptive of my conflicted wishes, supportive. She is aware of my dilemmas, of my Holocaust derived conflicts, and many other things. Our oldest son, Erik, overtly was the most distressed by my conflict with religion. He was the first of our sons to have to deal with it. When his friends were preparing for and then had their Bar Mitzvahs, there were a number of occasions when he was able to convey to me his distress at being the only Jewish kid he knew who was not having his Bar Mitzvah. It was a difficult time for both of us. I have welcomed his telling me on a number of occasions, how I screwed up religion for him. It is true. He is right. And I am full of a painful mix of feelings, some remorse, some self-acceptance, some mourning; but most distressful is having screwed it up for him. I know it is the same for Karl and for Josh. Josh and Lenny, who converted to Judaism, are the most observant of us. I truly delight in their 9 year-old son Rafi's growing mastery of Hebrew. And I wait, uneasy to see what my sons will do with their children as they approach 13. There are five of them, one girl and four boys. Whatever they do, Rachel and my acceptance and support are guaranteed.

More complex an issue, free from regret, is that I married a woman who is not Jewish. I object vigorously to any supposition that I did this with the intention of avoiding Holocaust remembrance or after-experience. Or, to dilute my own Judaism. Cursed be the one who would think this. From my first girlfriend Sara, a very low-key affair, when we were in St. Raphael, I was 12, to several other lovely girls-women over the years, and eventually to Rachel, two were not Jewish. I confess that I did not restrain myself, as do so many Jews, Catholics, Muslims, and no doubt many of other religious denominations, to women or friends of my own religion. I trace my struggle with the question of God and religious liturgies, specifically Jewish (Hebraic) Liturgy to my college years. I truly felt a need for Universalism in religion—not in the Protestant religious sense—in the overall religious sense. In fact, in college my Universalism led me to join the World Federalist movement, and while I am not now an active member—if that movement still exists—I am still of that persuasion. About Rachel, I was attracted to the person; it may seem naïve to say, to the person, not to the person configured to a prescribed doctrine. I don't find it paradoxical that, it mattered to me that the woman I loved and love would unreservedly accept the fact that I am a Jew, not a Godless Jew as Peter Gay said of Freud, but a Jew who cannot accept the constraints and biases of Jewish Laws and Liturgy.

In the eyes of some I am a religious mess, I know. I hold dearly to observing Rosh Hashanah (the New Year), Yom Kippur (the Day of Atonement), Pessach (Passover), Chanukah (the Festival of Lights), and other Jewish traditions, but I have selectively modified how our family has observed these. I don't know where my personal interpretation of God and religion might have taken me if I had been given the chance to continue my life of origin; I know that the Holocaust heavily influenced the path of Judaism I have taken. I say again, to others my Jewishness may seem incomprehensible; no doubt highly Orthodox Jews would throw me to the dogs.

I am a Jew; my position on this accepts no argument. And I visited all of this on my wife and our sons. My wife, Rachel, has fully accepted my being a Jew, has a Universalism about religion of her own. She has "no religion" and is accepting of any religion in others. My sons are forging their way through the religion problem I brought to them; they understand why and how this problem got to be what it is. Each is finding his way of living with it.

I know that the Holocaust heavily shaped my life and my personality. It has beclouded our home, our family life. It has unconsciously pushed me along paths in my work that only after the fact have I recognized derive from my Holocaust experience. I'll talk about that in Part III.

The Holocaust caused me yet another dilemma. Primo Levi's curse has long hung over my head.

Why Has it Taken Me So Long to Write What Happened to Us?

I have long been pressed from within to bear witness, to write the history of what happened to me, to my mother, my family, those around us. I am especially moved, pressed to do so by Primo Levi's admonition, well know to Survivors, that we must tell what happened to us, and that we are to "Repeat them to your children," if we do not, Levi's curse weighs heavy, "Or . . . may your children turn their faces from you." His heart was in the threat. He was right.

I still try to understand, to its bottom layers, why it has taken me so long to write what happened to us. After years of analysis, personal psychoanalysis and self-analysis, a never-ending process, I am not sure that I can answer this sufficiently well. I am troubled by my own avoidance and delay in getting to my responsibility "to bear witness" in writing. I knew I would get to it; I had to get to it. But, I have delayed until now, a detailed account of what I saw and experienced—it is not a "full" account; the details would take more time than I have left. In terms of writing about my Holocaust experience for a professional presentation, I first did so in 1999 when I responded to a request that I give a plenary address to our American College of Psychoanalysts on "Some effects of the Holocaust on development." I was asked, were I so willing, to personalize my views of the topic. I felt some trepidation about doing this. But I had now turned 70; I felt I had reached the age where I had to give precedence to my obligation to bear witness.

Why did I take so long to attend to this responsibility? I am by all family and work measures a predictable, responsible person. Why then? Some of my survivor friends tell me that they have been silent because those around us do not want to hear about it. They did not want to hear about it years ago, and they don't want to hear about it now. It is too painful for listeners, for readers.

I find this personally and I find it my field. Most of us can tolerate only so much emotional pain, at any time. To empathize with another person's pain may be intolerable at certain times; for some, those times come frequently. It is regrettable because our intolerance for another person's pain can be detrimental. For example, in clinical work we have found that parents experience much difficulty when they see their children have pain. They tell their children their hurt is not so bad—when the parent has no way of knowing how much whatever is hurting the child really hurts. Everyday.

Even more troubling is that many parents cannot let their children mourn the loss of someone they love, not just because the remaining parent is bereft, but more so, because the parent cannot bear to see her or his child suffer. Many people react to a child's emotional pain, such as depression for instance, by rationalizing that, he's only a child, of course, he can't suffer "real" depression. Well, he can. Years ago doctors thought that children do not develop peptic ulcers; they are just too young for that. Well, they can; they do. Empathizing with, letting oneself sense another person's pain, when we do just about all we can to struggle with our own, can be too taxing.

In addition, it is common to identify with those who suffered in the Holocaust, whether one is a Jew or not. What happened to the storyteller happened in some measure to the listener. We suffer individually then. But we also identify with these sufferers collectively; we suffer the agony of having "our own" being humiliated, incarcerated, abused in all sorts of ways, murdered; we suffer as a people. We just do not want to be visited by that feeling too often. All humans do this; all ethnic groups that are insulted, attacked and ravaged do. To protect ourselves we sometimes just don't want to hear more stories of our collective suffering.

So, inhibiting empathically feeling and identifying with those who suffered give justification to the coercion that we must remember. We do not want to hear again about our collective suffering when the pain we experience compels us to not remember. The pain conspires with our everyday tendency to forget. Memory fades. This is so even though experience and especially trauma that happens to us makes a lasting impression. We now know that trauma gets recorded in the ancient part of our brain, in the amygdala and the hippocampus, and connects to our new brain, the frontal cortex. Trauma gets thus inscribed in the brain and even if we don't think of it consciously, the remembering is there and affects us even from its hidden recesses.

But if the trauma happened to you and not to me, though we are kindred by virtue of our history, religion and ethnicity, and I do not want that trauma inscribed in my brain, please don't push it on me and demand that I remember it. This is not disloyalty; it is simple self-protectiveness that operates out of our awareness.

In my personal life, I find that "just not wanting to hear about it again" occurs sometimes with my wife; and I have some evidence that my sons at times experience this too. I do not object to this; I do not recriminate against Rachel's occasional protest about my wanting to go to yet another Holocaust movie or Holocaust commemorative event. But I cannot lay the blame at her feet, or at my sons', that their occasional pain saturation is what has delayed my writing my witnessing. Totally to the contrary. Rachel is encouraging me, supporting me, in fact admiring me for writing my story; and she impedes some of her own interests in my behalf—such as not listening to the radio for news while she is preparing dinner when I am writing within hearing distance of the kitchen. This is not minor; she has an avid interest in current national and international events. No, Rachel is totally in support of my writing about what happened. And my sons and their wives are equally encouraging, solicitous, and supportive.

Others not wanting to hear my Holocaust story is not what impeded my writing about it. I have to look elsewhere. Two factors stand out. One, I do not want to burden others for whom I feel a large degree of responsibility with what happened to me. Second, I think the more important, I have just not been emotionally ready to write about it. That I have not wanted to burden those for whom I bear responsibility of course does not include my family. As I have said, one of the most troubling after effects of my having been swept into the Holocaust is the awful burden it has become for my wife and our sons. One cannot silence the Holocaust experience and therefore, one cannot spare one's family. In fact it is not to our children's advantage when parents who are survivors are silent. We have found that those Holocaust survivors who could not talk to their mates and their children about their experiences burdened them much more than they realized. Whereas those Survivors who have talked about what happened to them with their families have made their burden of it lighter. One cannot keep secrets within families; children have some uncanny radar for their parents' secrets. Furthermore, if we are silent, we are likely to impede or even to disallow our children's efforts to deal with this burden constructively. So I have not tried to protect my family from knowing what happened to me.

But being a physician who delves into people's psyches and in consequence becomes personally important to them, I have long felt that a doctor's problems should never become a burden to his patients. This is the most conscious of the reasons that held me back from making my story public.

The Doctor As Burden to His Patients

Maybe this conscious factor has conspired with my own efforts to contain the reverberations of my past misery by being silent. I have reasoned and truly feel however, that I have not wanted my patients to know more about me than they might learn from my behaviors in the course of our work together. Patients learn much about their psychoanalyst or other psychotherapist; this happens more than with an internist or a surgeon. Patients learn how we interact with people over time, whether we are pleasant or unpleasant, considerate or inconsiderate, sensitive or rash, dismissive or accepting, whether we are happy or sad, grim or congenial; in time they find out many of our quirks and our vulnerabilities. Patients come to know much about their psychotherapeutic healers. We therapists cannot keep such knowledge from them. Yes, there are many things our patients cannot know about us simply from our behavior. For instance, they cannot know our histories and past and current life situations. Adding to this, those persons I analyze who are clinicians-in-training, would learn about me not only in their psychoanalyses but also in the course of our running into one another in our Psychoanalytic Institute, or hearing me speak at meetings, local and elsewhere. A large factor operative in my public silence, a factor I hold to, is that I have not wanted my patients to have to deal with the fact that their analyst is a Holocaust survivor. Here is why.

During the extensive course of a clinical psychoanalysis, the patient develops a unique relationship with the therapist. The therapist by his clinical stance facilitates the tendency in the patient to invest the therapist with what the patient has internalized of his or her childhood relationships. This normal tendency to bring to new relationships what we experienced in our past relationships creates what we call "the transference," a phenomenon essential for the therapeutic effectiveness of a clinical psychoanalysis. The issue here is that the assumption that the transference resolves with the termination of the psychoanalysis is not true. We have found that even after the treatment is terminated, this transference relationship to the analyst seems to never be fully metabolized and dissipated. There are good reasons for this.

In the course of treatment, the patient relives in interaction with the analytic therapist, crucial internalized past experiences. As these are repeatedly externalized into the patient-analyst relationship, the patient experiences these in the here and now, and is helped to emotionally, psychically review what was experienced in the past. As the analyst reacts to and adds to the patient's review of his or her past and present experience by interpretations of what is re-experienced and reviewed, the effects of these current patient-doctor interactions then become internalized by the patient. What is internalized now modifies what was internalized before. In this, what is internalized currently includes how the analyst reacted to, and what and how he or she interpreted, of the patient's "re-experiencing the past in the here and now."

Progressively, the patient's experience in analyzing his or her past achieves continuity, and this stabilizes what has been reviewed, modified, and re-internalized. The basic individual remains the same; basic personality does not change; but the old long-established patterns of reacting, experiencing, and coping become constructively revised and modified or even replaced so as to serve the patient better. Just as all the relationships and experiences we have more or less leave their mark on us, so too, the relationship with the analyst remains with the patient, side by side with all that came before, even though the effects of what came before are now modified. This is what makes the responsibility of being a psychotherapist, a psychoanalyst especially, so large. Most important is that when the patient has concluded a clinical psychoanalysis, elements of the transference relationship remain. This means that while the patient may have gained much from the treatment, the patient also now holds within, what remains of her or his individual transference to her or his analyst.

Patients come to us because they have hurtful and handicapping problems of their own with which they want us to help them; they do not need, in addition, to take on their analyst's life burdens. This is why the analyst's own life burdens, and we all have them, and the problems these burdens cause the analyst should not be brought into the clinical situation. In my case then, it would have been, among other things, that my patients might be burdened by knowing that I had suffered consequences of the Holocaust.

I do not want the reader to push the point too far. The experience of the patient who comes to know that his or her analyst is a Holocaust survivor is not as brutal, not as intense, not as long-term, not as psyche influencing as befalls the children of survivors. First, the patient and the analyst are not child and parent. But also, the patient as an adult seeking treatment is beyond the childhood developmental years, those years so crucial to emotional development and the formation of personality. Those early years are the years when the impact of a parent's Holocaust experience would most leave its mark. Also on this point fortunately, in the clinical analysis of children, the transference does not develop as fully as it does in the analysis of adults. This is because the child's relationships with his or her own parents, pre-empts a full development of transference relationship with the analyst. Thus children are more protected against fully experiencing the relationship with the analyst than are adults.

My point simply is that if my patients knew that I am a Holocaust survivor, this might burden their transference relationship. In addition to its giving shape to that relationship, this might too strongly interfere with the patient's externalizing onto me some aspects of that patient's internal representations of relationship experiencing with those vitally important to him or her in the past. For example, a patient feels guilty at hating the mother or father the patient also loves. This is the most common internal conflict humans experience, everywhere, in America, in Europe, in Asia, everywhere. In the analysis, triggered by some aspect of a current event, or a dream, or a fantasy, in resonance with this aspect of the event, arising from the internalized hate the patient feels toward his or her mother or father of old, the patient now externalizes this hate onto me. If the patient knows that I am a Holocaust survivor, whatever the patient externalizes onto me at a given time that leads him to feel anger toward me, knowing that I have suffered in the Holocaust, might intensify his or her guilt at feeling angry with me. The patient feels then and there, more guilt than he or she might just on the basis of the original anger felt toward the parent of years ago. In some patients it would prevent their ever being able to be angry with me; after all how could they get angry with a Holocaust Survivor?

In yet another patient, knowing my history might intensify the patient's sadism beyond what is internalized. This could confirm and exaggerate the patient's belief that his or her hostility and hate are dangerous, which, at some point, will likely create more intense guilt or even psychic paralysis. This then, of itself, will make the patient's life more miserable—unless the analyst perceives the problem and works with it. Thus due to its possible interference in treatment and that the transference does not fully resolve, I have felt it best to not burden my patients with my Holocaust past. It is predictable that patients would want to read what they can about their analyst's life. And this causes me some concern as this book is soon to be open to whoever chooses to open it. Enough that my wife and my children are burdened by it!

But I assume that this is just one of the factors that have delayed my getting to this writing.

My Resistance to Writing My Witness Report

My own struggle to cope with what happened to me is the largest resistance factor. Paradox. I write quite comfortably, with some ease, on psychoanalytic and developmental issues. Yet, I have not until now been able to set my history on paper. I have been preoccupied with the Holocaust. It's in me; it's part of me, part of our family; it has been the miserable part of my life. It is omnipresent, even when all is well. I have analyzed and re-analyzed, and it goes on. I have read and studied books on the Holocaust. I have watched movies of all kinds about the Holocaust. So why have I not written about it till now?

Not only have I not written my story, but, although I have lectured and talked in many places, it has taken me a long time to speak publicly about my having been swept up in the Holocaust maelstrom. I have talked to close friends about it. Also when I have felt a warm connection with particular friends I have not known so well, I have talked about it; at times even to my own surprise: why did I tell him or her? Invariably struck by it, they tell me they "didn't know." How would they; I have infrequently talked about it. Many of my professional colleagues do not know that I am a Child Survivor.

Some, other than my family, have known. I always feel a kinship with other Holocaust Survivors or with their grown children. I feel most protective of my own sons, children of a father Survivor. But I also feel protective of other children of Survivors; I want to put my arm around their shoulders, or hug them, and help them in whatever way I can. I find that they in turn feel a kinship toward me, some want to help me; I see it in their attitude toward me.

As I said, I first went public with my Holocaust story several years ago, in Washington DC; very appropriate, I think; the capital of the country that truly gave me asylum for life. When I read my address to the American College of Psychoanalysts in May 1999, I did my usual, at times tedious, nit-picking, but confident presentation of my understanding of this or that question psychoanalytic, developmental, clinical, or research. On this occasion it was what trauma of this magnitude, specifically the Holocaust, can do to a young human being's emotional development. I wanted to address it especially because it is not as simple I feel as some of my very good colleagues have written. I will present some of my thoughts and conceptualization of this matter briefly in Part III; it is not my point here. I proceeded with my presentation, I think with due trepidation—nobody knows enough about anything pertaining to the human psyche and psychic development—I was, nonetheless, on my usual roll. I like performance; I have experience; I was a professional singer before I went into medicine. All was going smoothly; until I came to the section about how it had affected my development, not that I know all there is to know about that. I said three words, "I was 11 . . ." I choked up. I could not hold back my tears. I stopped. Turned away from the audience. I was totally surprised; I had not anticipated this possibility. I took a few deep breaths, swallowed my tears, pulled myself together, and turned back to face my colleagues. I knew my audience was friendly, many of them were my friends; and Rachel was there in the front row, her eyes glistening as she had welled up with tears. The audience was very patient; they understood; no one left. I later found them, those who spoke to me, touched and warmly appreciative. I was washed out; but I liked that I had talked about it, in public.

It is a paradox, my preoccupation with it and my resistance to tell what happened. But it is not distant from making sense, even though I feel dismay at my delay in getting to my responsibility "to bear witness." Why my avoidance? Because it hurts too much. Everyone, who believes that it happened, understands that. To write about it in the details it warrants, and in the personalizing that would give it reality, it is a self-surgical procedure. You have to be the patient; and you have to be the doctor; at the same time. And you cannot use anesthetics or you will not feel and you will not know what or how to tell.

Maybe, some of our wise minds have thought, without recrimination, our Survivors will not tell what they went through because they bleed when they tell, and besides, who will believe it happened. Yes, it was unbelievable what happened. Civilized human beings would not believe it; after all, we are not depraved.

Wise Primo Levi knew how difficult it is to tell; he felt he had to threaten:

> Repeat them to your children,
> Or may your house fall apart,
> May illness impede you,
> May your children turn their faces from you.

It was not indifference that made us silent so long. It is true that we tend to forget the painful past; that we tend to avoid remembering pain. Especially the dreadful past. It is normal for us to protect ourselves against feeling too much pain. It is a biologically programmed reaction; all living organisms have such a biological self-protective system. Otherwise, we could just die from the pain; this is biological fact. First of all, intense pain is a high stressor; intense pain may just sink our immune system, trigger the production and discharge into our blood stream of powerful emergency triggered hormones that can totally screw up our physiology—and do us in. And pain, if intense enough, of itself can just lead to physiological shock, which also can kill you. In physiological shock your blood pressure drops suddenly and before your body reacts to bring it back up you're dead from insufficient oxygen to all parts of you. It's more complicated than this, but this suffices to make the point that we don't just forget because we are stupid or lazy; we do it to survive. So our wise men are right: we have to argue this self-protectiveness aside; we have to bear witness; the more witnesses, the more the evidence, or it will disappear.

The most obvious factor causing my silence is that it is too miserably painful to think about what happened, to dwell on it in order to be able to sort it all out, to write it down, to enter one's reactions to it, and to go over it and go over it as one writes and rewrites. Even as I write, I itch, and unaware until I catch myself at it, I scratch. It has happened again and again in the course of this writing. So too with re-experiencing ache and rage as I write. Rachel knew this would be so. My sons did; their wives did. I guess I did. It is not just my psyche that speaks of the misery, or my immune system, or my skin; my whole self does. My most personal universe does.

Guilt*

Has guilt played a part in my resistance to tell what I experienced? That odd beast, "survivor guilt," that I am the only one among the four of us—my mother, my father, my brother Emanuel, and I—who got out? Though without definite proof, I assume that I am the only one of us who survived.

I don't consciously feel guilt about this. There is something vaguely close to fate. I don't feel lucky. It is more, "There but for the grace of God go I." That, but without the "God" part. At least not "God" like most people think of. More like Spinoza thought, "God is in everything."

I have thought about this question of survivor guilt. I have looked at it analytically. I did what my mother thought I should do, wanted me to do. Am I trying to quiet guilt by thinking that? I did not know that what happened would happen to her; I expected her to get out.

All true. But why do I need to speak of guilt? I cannot, I do not, dismiss feeling guilty for having survived. I do not know enough to even offer a hypothesis as to why Primo Levi, after so many years of surviving brought an end to his life by throwing himself down the stairwell of his apartment house. Over the course of many years of clinical experience, of the suicidal patients I have treated, I failed with two who committed suicide. It is always tragic; but it sometimes makes sense. Given his sanity—most depression is not insanity—and being the man Levi was, I assume that to him it made sense. Entrained, disciplined by my work, even when I don't try, I am trying to understand what motivated the writer to write what he wrote. Unavoidably, as I

* Guilt and shame are often used interchangeably. We draw a distinction between them in Mental Health. Of the varying definitions used, I hold to Freud's concept of guilt, which is that it arises when one wants to cause harm to someone one loves; to feel hate toward someone one loves. From these origins, with maturation, guilt arises when we want to cause harm to others. Shame is felt when what we feel and what we do are at odds with the ideal standards of conduct, the ideal image we hold up for ourselves, the image of who we want to be.

read, I tried to discern the meaning of Primo Levi's experience. Many readers who are not Psychoanalysts have done the same. But knowing of his suicide, without looking for it, some of the things he said made me think, "Is this a factor that predisposed him to it?" To say it is because he was in Auschwitz is not enough. We all know Auschwitz Survivors who have not and will not commit suicide. To say, yes, but they have *thought* of suicide is saying nothing. We all, at one time or another have found life so painful that then and there we have thought it not worth living. That too is part of "the human condition."

And so is guilt. Mind-boggling; you suffered and then you feel guilty because your mother, father, and brother suffered more! Mind-boggling, but it makes sense. You suffered; but someone you love deeply suffered more and because you have at times been mad at that someone you love, you feel your old hostile feelings magically caused her suffering, even her death. It's your fault; you shouldn't have, once upon a time, been mad at her. We brilliant animals function that simply! Survivor guilt. But often it is not pure guilt. Altruism often comes into the mix; I love her so, I want her life to be spared; I'll die instead. People who love each other are known to have done that; the Nazis exploited that. We can explain such guilt-mixed-with-altruism; but that does not make it reasonable or realistic. Did survivor guilt propel Levi to end his life?

One of a number of reading-moments that gave me pause and raised the question of Levi's eventual suicide was when, in *Survival in Auschwitz*, he speaks of the "selections" to be gassed. He tells us that "Rene, . . . so young and robust, ended on the left [was selected to be gassed]. . . [It was] probably . . . a simple mistake: Rene passed the commission immediately in front of me and there could have been a mistake with our cards. . . . The hypothesis is probable; I do not know what I will think tomorrow and later. . . ." In this, I read that Levi believed he was spared by mistake. Given that Levi was a valuable enough commodity, he was a Chemist who could help them produce their ersatz rubber, his being spared most likely was not a mistake. It may be that his assumption that a mistake had been made was driven by guilt at surviving, at being chosen not to go to the left, to survive.

I too have contemplated that problem, guilt at having survived; it weighs in now and then. Generally, I don't feel guilty that I survived whereas so many of my family including my mother, probably my father and my brother, were "lawfully" murdered. But now and then a most distressing feeling gets hold of me invariably attached to a thought that is difficult to dismiss. I have wondered if my escape from Rivesaltes—and my mother's own subsequent escape and recapture—labeled her as an "undesirable, recalcitrant guest of the Rivesaltes Concentration Camp" and contributed to her being selected for further descent into hell, first of course to the dead-bodies-gas chambers, with their feces and urine remains, and then sanctification by burning in hell. Did my escape contribute to that? Once I was under the roof of the OSE, I was protected against the French Gestapo. Was selecting my mother, revenge? Or simply the whim of some Jew-hater? I have not been able to protect myself against some guilt at surviving.

Reading, again I paused, resonating with Levi's reaction to his inmate Kuhn's prayer to God, thanking him for his not having been selected like Rene was. Levi rages:

"Does Kuhn not understand that what happened today is an abomination, which no propitiating prayer, no expiation by the guilty, which no thing at all in the power of man can ever clean again. If I were God, I would spit at Kuhn's prayer."

What a dilemma to be grateful in such moments, because one is not selected. What words can we use to say well enough what we feel. I know, that's been said many times. But I am trying to bear witness; how do I tell my experience? If I say that Levi is indignant at Kuhn's prayer is that enough? Levi rages at Kuhn's prayer. If Levi could have made it happen, he would have had God spit on it. If we pray, if we believe there is a God, how do we thank God for not having turned the Nazis on those of us who survived? How do we thank God for having been spared, when those who were not were our own family?

Suicide is not usually in the domain of the insane. All good writers and good philosophers are good psychologists. Levi muses. "Strange, how in some way one always has the impression of being fortunate . . . [it] stops us crossing the threshold of despair and allows us to live." And this is one of the puzzling things in all this Holocaust misery. How, with all that happened, how can Levi, and I have felt this often myself, how can we feel fortunate? Where does such positiveness, optimism, come from? I have not yet come to a sufficiently well developed answer to this question. For now, I'll say that finding moments to feel fortunate has much to do with having survived; not with having been lucky to survive; but with having had the mental, psychological and emotional will to survive. Levi writes, "It's raining freezing rain, but it's not windy; it's raining and it's windy but today I get a supplemental ration. . . ." And here is where that will can further operate to decide one's survival: Levi writes, "If you really felt nothing in your heart but suffering and tedium . . . – well, even in that case, at any moment you want you could go out and touch the electric wire-fence, or *throw yourself* under the shunting train, and then it would stop raining." I italicized those words, wondering if this image, coming from Levi's own mind, his own writing, was enacted when he decided to end his life by *throwing himself* down the stairwell, that he "felt nothing in [his] heart but suffering and tedium." I have never felt that kind of unmitigated suffering. But I was not in Auschwitz; I was in Rivesaltes, where the fences were not electrified and there was no gassing and no burning in hell. But my mother was. Is this the voice of guilt at surviving? My guilt pales next to Levi's.

Why did Primo Levi *throw himself* to his death? I don't need to know the answer. Why down the stairwell of his apartment building, from three floors up? Does that matter? A biographer tells us that he was depressed already as a young man, before he was sent to Auschwitz in January 1944. I was in America for twenty months by then. I escaped going to Auschwitz. Had I not escaped I would have been on Convoy #19; I would have made 992 of us. A gift to Hitler's megalomania, courtesy of the illustrious *Gouvernement de la France Libre; Libre? Vichy-France.*

Contemplating his being chosen to work in the Laboratory, out of the winter cold, no beatings, no threats, no insults, Levi reflects guilt-burdened. Guilt-burdened that the others were not shielded as he, he tells us that "the comrade of all my peaceful moments, . . . – the pain of remembering . . . attacks me like a dog the moment my conscience comes out of the gloom." Where does one draw the line? When does one say, "No, I will not be privileged; I will stay and suffer with the others?" When does one do that? Should I have refused to escape from Rivesaltes, should I not have left my mother alone? Should I have refused to leave France for America? Should I have gone with her to Auschwitz?

Shame

Is there shame, that I did not go with her? Some vague misery attaches to this question. Is there shame? About what? I did not know when I agreed to escape from Rivesaltes, and later to come to America, I did not know she would be massacred in Auschwitz. I did not know until years later. Is this the voice of self-criticism; did I expect myself to know what I did not know? Would it have been righteous for me to have argued her wishes and refused to leave? Only my fear argued that I stay. My trust in my mother urged that I go. Then, at that age, I probably did not allow myself to think: if I leave her now, it is for always. Do I feel ashamed that I did not look that awful possibility in the eye? Do I feel that I should not have abandoned my mother. "Abandoned?" That is self-accusative. Shame?

But not one of my Lorenzos said I abandoned her. No one has said I should not have escaped, I should have stayed there with her.

My Lorenzos. Reading Levi, there is this precious moment in his narrative when he tells us about Lorenzo, an Italian civilian worker, hired and paid by the Germans. The Germans were very short of manpower by 1944. Since Lorenzo (Perrone, I later learned) was not a Jew he could not legally be subjected to slave-labor. That privilege was reserved for the "Chosen People." Pausing in the midst of telling us of the miseries the Nazis inflicted on him, Levi tells us that Lorenzo "brought me a piece of bread and the remainder of his ration everyday for six months; he gave me a vest of his . . . ; he wrote a postcard on my behalf to Italy and brought me the reply. For all this he neither asked nor accepted any reward, because he was good . . . ." And Levi goes on, "My case was not the only one. There were others . . . various kinds of civilians . . . [non-Jewish paid laborers who provided *Haeftlinge* (the prisoner underlings, the undesirables)] the means to survive. . . .[They were] their civilian 'protectors' and 'friends.'"

I pause as so many of my Lorenzos pass through my mind. That stranger on the train to Marseille; the OSE's Germaine Masur, Mora, Aranka; those who rescued us from Europe, including The American Quakers, Jewish Social Services, the YMCA, who knows which of the 25 organizations in *Le Comite de Nimes* (the Committee of Nimes). Then, the Wagners, Faye, Harry, Phyllis, Sandy, Evy; the Steinfirsts, Donald, Jane, Dick, John and Susan. They didn't ask for anything from me; they just gave to me, helped me, facilitated my recovery, and made my future possible. They were good. One can only thank; I thank them; I have a million times. I am in great debt; but there is no payment, no direct payment to them. My dedication page tells where most of my indebtedness lies. They, "my Lorenzos" do not feel that I did not live up to the image of a good human being. I too feel that way. But is there a doubt?

How do others look at me? Of those civilians who worked in *Buda*,

Levi wonders how they viewed the *Haeftlinge*, the slave laboring Jews: "they saw us reduced to ignoble slavery, without hair, without honor and without names, beaten everyday, . . . and they never see in our eyes a light of rebellion, or of peace, or of faith." These were as he said, the most ignoble of conditions. The French Nazis too created ignoble conditions for the Jews in Vichy-France. Their view of us is well reflected in how they cooperated, eagerly complied, with the abhorrent demands of the German Nazis. But French Nazi sadism was constrained, probably by those around who had remained civilized; Vichy did not get to the point of shaving our heads, beating us, and of coercing us under threat of extermination to slave for them. When I was there, I don't believe slave labor was implemented in Rivesaltes. But a recent communication from a Holocaust Survivor Organization informed me that I might be eligible to receive compensation for slave labor practices in Rivesaltes. I take it from this that at some point, Vichy-France introduced and instituted slave labor in Rivesaltes. My escape in May 1941 protected me from slave labor—though it might have affected my mother—and who knows, they might have even forced an 11 year-old to share in that misery.

Though my circumstances never got as dire as Levi's did, not by many miles—I don't know how to measure this—I too have felt humiliated. Why us? In Rivesaltes, to a point like where Levi was, goodness was so remote. For Levi, when Lorenzo appeared to him, it reminded Levi of this marvel in human beings. These were conditions when it is possible to forget human goodness. Lorenzo. By his presence, Lorenzo reminded Levi "that there still existed a just world outside our own, . . . a remote possibility of good, . . . for which it was worth surviving." If I had not been with my mother, would I have been able to sustain my hopefulness and optimism? What if I too had been in Auschwitz instead of Rivesaltes? The marvel of Lorenzo's goodness led Levi "not to forget that I myself was a man." I was protected from this sense of self-debasement; I felt loved, valued, approved of by my mother. And when I left her, not one of "my Lorenzos" said "For shame!" But why did I get away, and thousands, millions did not?

And, shifting my focus, do I feel shame at not having been more brave? More brave to talk about my very painful life derailment, to have written my witness report sooner?

And side by side with it, do I feel shame at protecting myself against the agony by forgetting the date when my mother was sent to Auschwitz, by avoiding finding out sooner than I did what happened to her, how, when, where—I know why: she was a Jew. Do I feel shame that I have not made efforts, until now, to find out the whereabouts of my father and my brother, the probable ends they met?

Should I have gone to Auschwitz? I put my head down, and ache.

I have not done these things. I have not done these things that so many others have. I know I have committed myself to doing other things in dealing with my Holocaust experience. I have committed myself to prevention in mental health; to the prevention of emotional problems in children that come from their life experiences, and to the prevention of violence and malignant prejudice. But this commitment cannot serve as an excuse. I have not been able to do many things. They have just been too difficult for me to do. I have as if in compensation directed my efforts and energies to the prevention of violence and malignant prejudice. Is there shame in taking this path to deal with my Holocaust experience?

Also not an excuse, a fact. I have not gone to see Auschwitz not just due to my avoidance. It was enough to ask my wife to come with me to visit Rivesaltes in 1997. If I had suggested I go to Auschwitz alone to spare her suffering it with me, which she does, she would have insisted on going too. Am I asking the reader to let me off the hook? Is it guilt that I think of the reader judging me? Is it Primo Levi's judgment in my ears? And then, what of our sons? They might have pushed to come as well. It is not that I want them to forget about the Holocaust; I do not, and I know they never will. My reasoning on this is not altogether clear to me. Maybe those who read this may have an opinion. That's OK with me. I only know pieces of the answer. It is not due to my wife and sons alone that I have not gone to see the gas and crematoria burial grounds. It's mostly due to my sick feeling, my rage and despair.

I don't know that I could have done differently.

What Was So Awful in What Happened?

I ask myself, and I have so many times: What was, what is, so awful about what happened to me, to so many of us? I lost my first family, my family of origin, and that is awful. It happens to people. But it is especially the reason and the way I lost them, my mother, my father, and my brother, that I rage, we all rage, those of us who were there and those closest to us. I have felt this ache, now quiet rage and despair for years. Can these ever fully dissipate? They lie deeply pressed into my brain, brand-ironed. Fortunately, the years have mitigated the rage and despair; the pain too. Not just the years; it's mostly the family Rachel and I created together that brought about much mitigation of this nasty amalgum of feelings. I have a deeply loving, deeply gratifying—how does one describe it?—family; have had it now for over 40 years. And it enlarged some years ago with daughters-in-law, and then with grandchildren, five of them. My work too has helped to drain my despair, to lessen my pain, and especially the rage I felt in earlier years.

I lost my living past of origin. We were uprooted, like some weeds. Some of us choked on toxins in the air. I cannot fill in so many of the details of where I came from, before my own mother and father, and with my own mother and father and brother. Yes, I can and will commit time to finding out about them. I am setting the way to try to do this by means of genealogies available from a number of sources. But, there are so many details of my mother's family, of my father's family I cannot access, anywhere. I mean the details that only my mother could have given me, and only my father. My two older cousins in Bruxelles, the only known family I have, cannot do so, there is so much they too do not know. I cannot access my own early childhood, those early years we remember so little of without stories, photos, and telling and retelling by parents, uncles, aunts, grandparents. I have very little besides my own memory to inform me. And on many questions, it fails me. Yes, that is awful; it is too much for words. But there is more to cause this ache and rage.

I don't rage, I don't ache because I was dislocated, and had to go with no family at all to an unknown world at 13, learn a language I had not yet thought of—finding it oddly puzzling that I could not understand it then and there, when I landed in New York. Sobering, when, after we both had been in Pittsburgh for some months, my Rivesaltes friend and exodus companion Savic said, "shuddup" to one of our peers, and I, thinking I knew better, said to him, "*Savic, on dit pas 'shuddup', on dit 'shurrup'*" (one does not say 'shuddup', one says 'shurrup'). To which our new friend Laverne said gently, "No, Henri, one can say 'shuddup'"—and was kind enough not to add, one does not say 'shurrup'. She could have said many things to chasen my need to be master of my fate in my New World. An embarrassing but tolerable moment in my trying in our first year in America to speak American English properly! No, it was not that I had to learn a language from the start that filled me with rage and pain. In fact, by my speech, few people pick up the fact that English is not my mother tongue.

I am not sure that I can put what feels so awful about it into words. I come back to what feels, was, and is so awful: the meaning of what happened; that we have been targeted for extermination by other human beings just because we are Jews. So many have said this, many times, Jews and non-Jews. These words just don't say enough. Some have tried to say it in music. Poets have tried to say it better. Some have. I can't compose and I'm not a poet. Maybe if I just break it down and put space around the phrases it will come out clearer, more meaningful.

> How dare anyone,
> whoever,
> decide to exterminate my mother,
> my father, my brother, myself, and many others like us?
> How is that possible?
> What is that?
> That's what enrages me;
> that's what makes me want to exterminate right back.

Just putting this into words makes me scratch my back, overtaken by eczema for the first time in my life!

> Naïve.
> We are human beings; they are human beings;
> That's why they did it to us.
> It's unbearable pain that leads to hopelessness—
> in someone who is not hopeless,
> who has never yet, and never will be hopeless.
> And will never exterminate anyone.

I think this more than the other things, has kept me silent. I cannot tell well-enough, to render it as is due, what is so odious about it. Only poets have the words, like Primo Levi, Paul Celan—Rachel taught me that.

And this too is what has kept me from finding out all there is to know about what happened to my mother, my father and my brother. There is much love between us, much love I feel for them. All evidence points to the fact that the pain they suffered, the odious end they most likely met, is why I have not heard from them, certainly from my mother. Imagining the humiliation and the pain they suffered, what that represents to me, has for years and still does, has been and is sufficiently great that, until now, I have avoided further search for them. I know that this painful research in times past had some part in my choosing to become a psychoanalyst, an explorer into individual human pasts, like an archeologist, Freud said. And why my self-analysis is endless.

But I had to write it—because again, intolerance of another's pain is detrimental to the sufferer. A parent who cannot tolerate her or his child's pain cannot help the child suffer less. My intolerance for my own pain would be detrimental to my people. I would fail to bear witness for the world to get yet further confirmation that it happened. This horror filled history happened. Civilized people perpetrated it. Humans are capable of such self-degradation that can bring such de-humanization of others. We must beware what we can come to.

I am not sure that I have yet answered why it has taken me so long to get to this writing. Be that as it may. I know that in addition to my searches past and present, my ruminations, my rememberings, my private telling and retellings of what happened over there, my sharings with my family, in addition to a lot of things, my work has given me a pathway for expressing what I have experienced and experience still. And in addition, while I have not gone public with my witnessing till now, I have gone public with that of my work that derives, I know, directly from my Holocaust experience.

Of Things I Should Do, I Have Not Done

I have not yet gone to Auschwitz; I have to be there, to breathe the air she breathed before Zyklon B; to ache, to rage there.

I have not yet returned to Lodz, to Poland. I was born there; my family of origin comes from Lodz. But, to date, I have not gone there.

I have and do love to return to Bruxelles; I have done so a number of times. Bruxelles, not Lodz, is the city of my childhood; Bruxelles is my hometown. Memory to the first four years of life is not accessible to most of us; it is not to me; and Lodz is essentially an unknown; it does not have the pull that Bruxelles has. It was not difficult for me to return to St. Raphael-Boulouris, I had done it in 1953 and 1997; these had represented asylum from Rivesaltes. My return to Rivesaltes had taken much longer. It makes sense that I need to be in Auschwitz. And I need to be in Lodz, in Poland. But not yet. When?

I have been preoccupied with the Holocaust since it happened. It has featured prominently in my immediate family, in the life of my wife and of my sons. It has stood out on holidays; it has cast a baseline ambiance in our home, not one of depression, but one of awareness, an omnipresence, even when all is well. And for much of our life as a family, very much has been well. It featured in my two psychoanalyses. It features in my endless self-analysis—a psychoanalyst's way of being. I have read, studied, and underlined some books on the Holocaust. I have watched many movies about the Holocaust, documentary and fiction. But some things integral to it, I have not pushed myself to do.

I Have Not Yet Been Able to Visit Auschwitz

I have often seen it happen,
Only in moments, pieces of time,
The humiliation of being naked
Among naked others.
One second flashes of asphyxiation.
Relief.
She didn't feel anymore.

That I have not yet visited Auschwitz troubles me. I have not yet visited my mother's grave. I have in my mind. The thoughts pass through my mind, "Did she go to the right? To the left? Did she die in a gas chamber?

She was a healthy woman when I left her; she had always been healthy. Did she go to the labor camp next door? Although I know she was sent to Auschwitz, the records that informed Serge Klarsfeld said so. But what happened there? I am not certain. I have all along assumed that, had she survived, I would have known, at least by 1953. She would have returned to Bruxelles, and since she turned to the OSE to help me get out of Europe, she would have turned to the OSE to learn of my whereabouts. My inquiries with the Jewish Social Service in Pittsburgh always came up with no news, which meant, bad news. Savic's mother survived Rivesaltes and got in touch with Savic. My mother could not read or write, but she was very resourceful. I would have heard. But on the question, just exactly what happened to her, I have imagined the details.

Has that been my motive for not going there, that I do not want closure on the question? I have let my doctors know that I want to know; I want to know what illness I have, what vulnerability I have; and if I get cancer, I will want to know then and there. So too if anything life-threatening befalls my wife or any of my sons or anyone in their families, I want to know, now. But on this, on just what ultimately happened to my mother, I shudder. Maybe I am afraid to know. Would I find the answer in Auschwitz?

I have read about Auschwitz; who hasn't? I have seen movies, documentary, fiction. I see so often, in my mind, the train going through the brick building-gates bridged by the arched rod-iron piece, "Arbeit Macht Frei." How many times have I seen the piles of shoes, eye-glasses, bodies strewn in piles and piled in mass pits? These things I have seen, again and again. But I have not gone there. Had she died in the normal course of life, I absolutely would want to know, not just "cancer," what kind of cancer, where did they find metastases, I would want to know. Even if she had been shot by a robber, or by a stray bullet on Broad Street, I would want to know the details. But this was no death what happened to her. It was massacre, evil-in-pure form. Unbearable.

Another factor, a large one though I know it is not the principal one, is that I do not want to further burden my wife with yet more of the Holocaust. She has lived with it for 48 years now; I know that for her too, it is omnipresent. And for her too, it is unbearable. She finds the Holocaust movies unbearable but she sees them with me, I sometimes wonder if it is to make sure that I'll be all right. One time, years ago, while we were seeing the first movie about Anne Frank, we had to leave because Rachel was on the point of fainting. She tells me that I go to these showings readied with defenses to tolerate it. She is fifty percent right; the other fifty percent is that I have to see these things; they help me continue to work it all through. Sometimes, I don't go to a Holocaust movie I would like to see, because I don't want to impose yet another one on Rachel. It is not a matter of my going alone; if I did that, she would feel guilty about not going with me. We both get it from all sides. Some might think that this is evidence that I have not yet "worked it through" sufficiently. The Holocaust, I think one never works it through sufficiently. It can't be done.

I think that as a result my trepidation about absolute knowledge on the fate of my family, my confounded religious dilemma, my incomprehensible mix of living it and staring at it, and my avoidance of so much of it still, my sons are somewhat in limbo about it all. I am grateful that my Holocaust experience is not the only thing I have given them; heh, they got half of their gorgeous genes from me. They know that I am devoted to them; that in my eyes they are themselves, in charge of their own life and fate. And their mother has given them endlessly of the best she has, which is a great deal; of course some of her headaches too. And they have much they have gotten on their own. They are very bright, very well accomplished, self-determined guys. I am not certain whether I do, or I do not want them to visit Auschwitz. Here, as in other matters, I don't know what they should do. And I approve of whatever they want to do on this matter. There's little they have done that I do not approve of.

I Have Not Yet Returned to Lodz

Whether or not to return to where I was born, this too is a morass of feelings. I know too little about Lodz. As a child I am fairly certain I spoke some Polish, though Yiddish was our home language. I have facility in languages so I assume I picked up some Polish. Today, shamefully, I remember nearly none of it. I know that my Bruxelles family, my mother, my aunts, uncles, some of my older cousins, all originally from Lodz, never conveyed to me the greatness, or loveliness, or anything, of Lodz, or of Poland. I heard very little talk about the good old days in Lodz. I got the clear impression that life in Bruxelles was much better than that back home. Given the industrious people they were, it was not poverty that made them leave Lodz. I suspect it was the way Jews were treated in Eastern Europe, the pogroms, the virulent antisemitism, even in cities where Jews were not a burden to society, in fact were contributing to local survival. When from time to time I asked my mother about it, usually questions about my father and my brother, my mother was not her usual smiling, engaging self. It seemed a chore to answer my few questions on the subject. She was not forthcoming. I was not intrigued or enchanted with what she told me of Poland, or of my father for that matter. I estimate that she came to Bruxelles when she was about 30, when I was about 4. Exactly why she left, I never had the chance to learn; I was too young to know to ask more than I did.

Even though my emotional attachments are in Bruxelles, that Lodz is where I was born, makes it a place I want to see, someday. Some may find my saying this amusing. I am now 74, still fully self employed, with a very busy schedule, and the time we have for vacation is distributed between our family getting together during part of August, then briefly visiting Rachel's brother and his wife, and just leisurely doing things that need to get done. Lecture trips mostly or a rare festive occasion as Gregory's wedding takes us to Europe; sometimes I go alone. Though I am not on the point of retiring—I get too much out of my work to do that—time away from work is at a premium. And, Rachel's work, to which she is highly committed, leaves little "free" time at our disposal. This has contributed to our not yet having gone to Poland. But, one may ask why have I not put going to Poland one of the "things that need to get done?" Does what prevented me from going to Israel the first time we scheduled it play a part in my not yet having gone to Poland, to Lodz, to Auschwitz? Like with Israel, a good cause might facilitate my getting there. Resulting from my work, I have standing invitations to several cities in Europe as well as to Jerusalem and in a better day, to Gaza; but none to Warsaw.

I Am Currently Searching the Whereabouts of My Father and My Brother

But our not having gone to Poland is in part at least due to the anxiety I have attached to Lodz, to Poland. Several matters in my life that cause me anxiety have origin in Poland. Among these, one of the most confounding is, "What happened to my father and my brother, and my large family for that matter?" At the urging of our oldest son Erik, I am currently making efforts to find out what happened to my father and my brother. Karl ferreted out our lost family in Bruxelles. Joshua extends his search into our past along much larger historical dimensions, going back to Jewish-Arab relationships centuries back, to Maimonedes and Alforabi, Jewish and Arabic Philosophers respectively, and forward in time to Spinoza, then to Heidegger. Erik's search for lost family members, especially though not exclusively my father and brother, though not a major project of his, seems to bubble up every now and then. Recently, Erik, an Associate at The Hastings Center, a Bio-Ethics think-tank in New York State, in his frequent lectures and travels met a Bennett G. at a meeting in Halifax who, in conversation he found, knew a source that might help me with searching out my father and brother. My read on it is that, once Erik saw that I was getting into the writing of my Holocaust witnessing, it stirred his ever-present interest in helping me find out just what happened to my family, his family. This led to his ferreting out Shirley F., a very knowledgeable Lodz researcher, child of Lodz Holocaust survivor parents, who is dedicated to helping survivors and their children reconstruct their lost families, their lost family tree; she has already been enormously helpful in getting this search started. Again, one of our sons helped me in my at times quiescent efforts, to try to pull my family of origin back together. I know my sons not only want to help me but that they also need to reconstruct as best as they can, as best as we all can, where they came from on the side of their father, me. Again, our sons' efforts may bring success in my emotionally burdened efforts to search out whomever I could of my old family. The search is on.

Why have I not joined local Holocaust survivor groups, or national gatherings of Survivors, of Hidden Children's groups? I'm eligible for all of them; I was given the right to belong to them; I do in spirit, and in other ways, belong to them. This is just as unclear as the other "Whys", "Why has it taken me so long to search out my family's fate?" "Why have I not gone to Auschwitz?" Why?

Is it because it's too much to see others weep, curse and rage, for the same reason as I do? Is there not solace in sharing, even if it is in sharing misery? I feel kinship with Survivors, and with children of Survivors. But I tend to do so more one on one; I don't feel intimately connected in a group, connected, yes, but not in intimacy. It is not that I don't value being in a group; I do; I value being in a group to commemorate, to celebrate, to join voices, on joyful occasions and mournful ones. And I value belonging to a group, to a group of Americans, of Jews, a group of Psychiatrists, Psychoanalysts, Belgians, French-speakers, and when I'm overseas, to a group of English-speakers. All kinds of groups. But these belongings-to do not automatically make me want to tell my story. I note that I am contradicting myself. I value being in a group to commemorate I said, but I don't go to annual or otherwise-timed commemorations. I admit readily that, while I don't like doing so, I can live with contradicting myself, especially on this subject, a subject to which the answers I have are not intended to satisfy me. My answers just move in a direction, but they don't take me to the end of my inquiry. Simply put, other than for my attending meetings of Academic Institutions of which I am a part, and meetings of some of the professional groups to which I belong—a need arising from my work, driven by my participating in one program or another, I don't attend meetings of groups. I am not phobic, I am not antisocial; in fact, I like people in the aggregate. I tend to prefer one on one engagements, family gatherings, small gatherings.

I think that mostly, I don't want to just tell my story to someone with whom I have not in one way or another, by virtue of just everyday happenings, come to feel a place, a moment in intimacy, that makes me want to tell. I need a fertile moment for it; often one that comes after some time together under conditions I have not really identified, but that I know yield intimacy. There is something very private about this sort of telling; it's universally known, but somehow for me, and I think for most Survivors, it's not for the telling anytime, anywhere. Maybe that's why it has taken Survivors so long to talk about what happened to them. Maybe that's why the wise among us needed to emphasize, *you must bear witness!*

Part Three

"Ayeikah"

In his *Memoires 2 . . . Et La Mer N'Est Pas Remplie* (. . . And the Sea is Not Filled), Elie Wiesel tells us that God asked Adam " 'Ayeika?' Where are you, Adam?" Wiesel tells us that, once Rabbi Shneour-Zalmen de Ladi ascertained that the one who asked what God's question to Adam means believes in The Old Testament and believes that it has validity today, the Rabbi explained that by this, God, who since He is God would know where Adam would be, meant, "Adam, where are you in this world?" "What is your place in History?" "What have you done with your life?"

Chapter 11

Where Am I?

How Have I Come to Where I Am?

La condition humaine, not just that we suffer, but that we humans create much of that suffering ourselves, has pre-occupied me from the time of my youth. I have especially searched in my field for ways to explain why we make others suffer and to find ways to get us to stop causing avoidable suffering to others. How did I come to that?

In Mental Health, in Neuroscience, we have learned much about our own brain and psychological inner workings. In Psychoanalysis we have especially looked at and have come to know much about our inner psychic workings and motivations. In a clinical psychoanalysis we come to understand much of who we have become, what we have done, and we come to know much about what we do. But often this knowing of what we do comes after we have done what we have done. Sometimes we know only after we have thrust ourselves into doing. And other times, despite our increasing self-knowledge, understanding what motivated us to action may come quite later, even years later. I am surprised, yet I am not, that so much of what I have done, I have done without being aware until quite later of its major motivations.

I find it striking—yet, so probable—that, looking back, my work has been thrust and directed by my Holocaust experience. I knew from my early teens that I wanted to help children when they are hurt. I knew the pall terrible hurt casts on living. And I later learned how not just each person's terrible pain, but how the destruction of one and one and a half million of ones' children weighs on, burdens those on whom this abomination was perpetrated.

The balm I experienced as time passed, the beneficence of adults so willing to help me, helped so to heal my hurt, and also guided me to a life trajectory. I had models: I had generous help growing up, from a number of "good" human beings. I had my "Lorenzos." I am unashamedly deeply grateful—I recall writing that and saying it when I was an adolescent—to all those who made my life in America possible. It is most natural that I would have followed their example, to pay my "Lorenzos" by doing for others what they have done for me. I don't mind if people think I am a "boy scout;" I have been, in spirit all my life, since my days in Récébédou.

My largest pain having predominantly been of an emotional rather than a physical nature, despite the starvation, the cold, and the threat to life miserable sanitary conditions promised, I turned toward that part of medicine that heals the psyche. It took me some time though, to outright realize that I wanted to help children, adults too, not just to alleviate their psychic pain, but to grow, by coping as best they can with whatever life dishes out to them. This I could do as a psychiatrist, as a psychoanalyst. In time, I came to recognize that I had taken a path toward learning how to cope, to survive even in dire conditions. I learned early the innumerable ways life challenges us, challenges us to make it. I now know that my way was not forged by plan, not by conscious plan. It just followed most naturally.

My primary intention in being a physician has been to help people directly, to be a clinician. But I found that wanting to help kids cope—a direct inheritance of the challenges I faced growing up—I wanted to know what's inside their head; my head too. I am certain that it fueled my interest in research—I had to know things we didn't yet know; I had to find ways to deal with things we did not yet known how to deal with.

My interest in research was there since my first days in Medical School. During my 4 years there I worked in a Neurophysiology Lab with a man and colleagues who taught me a great deal about brain, its anatomy and physiology. I continued research studies through my Residency in Psychiatry and in Child Psychiatry. Out of that training, I followed with training in Psychoanalysis, Adult and Child-Adolescent. It is during that era that, while establishing myself as a clinician and having entered the faculty of a Medical School, I again felt driven to get into some research. I was strongly drawn into child development fully wedded to the principle that experience, starting from very early life, has everything to do with how our inborn makeup gets forged; that experience powerfully determines who we become.

In my clinical work I found myself frequently thinking, this child's or this adult's problem could have been prevented if I had seen this human being earlier in his life. Or, as every doctor thinks, if the problem could have come to attention near its inception, it could have been treated more easily and successfully. Earlier and earlier it went. I became convinced that many of my patients' problems—I have for the most part worked with a non-psychotic population—derived from experiences that went back to early life; not in all of them, but in many. Obviously, people have harshly painful experiences not just in early life, in fact we commonly have painful experiences later as well; but many emotional problems start way back. This is what took me from studying various specific conditions, such as interactions of emotional and physical disease, childhood learning problems, and the like, into the arena of early childhood development research. I was finding my way; the story of many a young doctor.

Studies in Early Childhood Development Open Avenues to Prevention of Social Ills

I was invited to join a Department of Psychiatry—another than where I was then situated—where the Chair and several Senior Faculty wanted me to develop some research of my choice. Unhesitatingly, I selected early child development. We developed the Early Child Development Program at the Medical College of Pennsylvania—Eastern Pennsylvania Psychiatric Institute (MCP—EPPI). With interest in the subject emerging in child psychoanalysis, several colleagues and I developed a well thought out, nicely designed project where we would attempt to correlate qualitative aspects of the mother-child relationship with the development of adaptive functions in the child. Yes, early child development was drawing interest in the field, but I know that I was swayed more by my need to get to the most sweeping way possible to help children cope with life—life can be a bitch. And the question was what can we do to advance ways to help children prepare well enough for their life?

Ready to roll with our project, we called for volunteers for participation in a research project from the community surrounding the Medical School. Many Medical Schools in America are situated in lower socio-economic neighborhoods. Ours was too. 50 mothers volunteered. My new team and I were bowled over. No, it was not my charm or reputation. Our Social Service Section was responsible for this show of trust from the neighborhood. The summer before, our Social Service Section had provided the housing project across the avenue from the Medical Center with

Left to right: Roli Hernit, Sandy Duff, Betty Scattergood, and the author; (Leafy Pollock, Peter Bennett, Estella Harris, Linda Giacomo are not in the picture)

a summer program for the children that the community had appreciated very much. Our Social Workers had won over the community.

Fifty mothers came. We could only accommodate 10, no more. We selected those who were then pregnant. We would start from the birth of their child. To advantage for the purpose of our study, none of the mothers was a first-time mother, a primipara we say. All set, ready to observe and collect data overtime, our protocol in mind, we got started.

While the mothers had all volunteered for the project, our start was not without concern. "So, what are you 'crackers' gonna do for us?" one of the African-American mothers said at our first meeting as a group. She said it with a big smile, winking at another African-American mother. By chance, half of our research subjects were African-American, half were Caucasian. In 1970, the African-American community was well into challenging the social inequities they had long experienced in the land that adopted me. My research colleagues and I were sympathetic with their indignation; we shared in their anti-racism protest, though I did feel they were picking on the wrong people. But I guess it was a class action phenomenon; all Whites were 'crackers.' We were crackers.

My senior Social Worker collaborator, Betty Scattergood, a most gracious Quaker, an admirable human being, smiled at the slight, and asked "Would you like some coffee? With cream?—then we still took cream in our coffee. Sugar?" "Yes, Honey, and stir it with your finger", with a big smile. Betty just smiled and proceeded with her coffee offerings. I took on the task of repeating what we had told the mothers before, namely that we wanted to study their children's development. We could not specify what we were looking for since it might jeopardize the integrity of our data.

This kind of research is not neutral or pure to begin with; we needed to protect our findings from prior knowledge and unconscious accommodation—which as time passed became unavoidable.

Except for vacation during the month of August, we met twice weekly, for two hours sessions, the mothers with their babies and preschool children all in one group. Over the seven years of this project's duration we had a 75% attendance rate, a high attendence rate for such studies. Several mothers had two babies while in the project. For projects like ours—I knew of only 3 other such projects then—we had a good start.

Patiently we met Tuesdays and Fridays. The mothers seemed to be getting to know one another and were quite friendly with each other. Their racial differences did not seem to stand out though a couple subsets did form; two Caucasian women, two African-American women, seemed to seek each other out; more so at the outset than later. The initial racial slurs vanished; we seemed to no longer be 'crackers'; I was "Dr. Parens"; Betty was "Mrs. Scattergood"; Leafy was "Ms. Pollock"; our nurse Estella Harris, a bright-smiling African-American woman, was "Miss Harris", and so forth. We were becoming a working group, the mothers and the researchers, that seemed to like being together, to warm to each other.

I was teaching Child Development in our Child Psychiatry Fellowship Program—seems I have done so since I became a grown-up doctor; that's what you are when you graduate from Medical Specialty Residencies and Fellowships. Strongly believing in teaching beyond book reading, I set it up that the Fellows in Child Psychiatry would rotate through our project, all to observe young children in process of development; several joined us as researchers. The students sat around the periphery of our main observation setting where the mothers sat in couches and living-room type chairs; observers were instructed to not initiate interaction with the subjects, though to respond reasonably, professionally, if addressed by a mother or a child. Now and then I would speak to the Fellows, *sotto voce*, draw their attention to certain behaviors, adding to their own observations.

My collaborators and I learned more than anyone in the project, more than the parents, the children, the students we were training. They learned about child development and how to optimize it—more on that in a moment. We learned about the potential for "prevention in Mental Health". We learned what a wide avenue to prevention it is, to help parents better understand their children and to help them learn ways to optimize their children's development.

Chapter 12

The Many Pitfalls and Opportunities in Child Rearing to Optimize Our Children's Development

Parents as Students

"Whadja say to them?" really got us started. Mothers began to let us know that they wanted to hear what I was telling the Fellows about the children; they too wanted to know. Several inquiries of this kind, "Whadja say to them?" redirected our observational approach. I would now draw attention to certain childhood behaviors openly, speaking to the students and to the mothers, themselves an unexpectedly interested group of students, students in their own parenting. Our research team became entrained in the pleasure that came from this totally unexpected turn of events.

The mothers were students. I was teaching them about child development, of their own children. Soon, the mothers brought in anecdotes from home, about their child's behavior, commonly with questions about them. In conference, after observation sessions, the research team grew increasingly excited by what we were observing. The mothers were interested, they were learning about parenting. Over time, their attitude and behaviors toward their children changed. We later identified and formally studied these changes in them, from growth-disturbing to growth-promoting parenting. An occasional visiting colleague told me that I was doing very good treatment with the mothers; that they and we seemed to have a very good therapeutic relationship. Two of my colleagues, more senior than I told me this. But, I insisted that I was not treating these mothers psychotherapeutically; I was teaching them about their children's development. And, I came to recognize as did my research team, that we were teaching them to optimize their children's development. That's what we were doing; helping the mothers by means of helping them understand better their children's manifest needs and behaviors and how to deal with these in growth-promoting ways.

We were educating them. We were teaching them a course in parenting, a course that would optimize their parenting and therewith their children's development. This was not therapy. That it may have been "therapeutic," made them feel more comfortable with their children, more positive in their parenting, improved their well being—which we later documented to be the case—does not make it psychotherapy. Psychotherapy is a different discipline. A good teacher can be therapeutic, make a child feel good, raise his self esteem, help him grow. A loving aunt or uncle can be therapeutic. Faye Wagner was therapeutic to me. The stranger on the train from Perpignan to Marseille was a balm; he quieted my terror and momentarily cured my hunger. Donald Steinfirst was therapeutic to me. My wife, my children, are therapeutic for me. Good relationships have a therapeutic, a healing, a well being producing effect on us. It is not just what doctors and nurses do to patients that is therapeutic, that stops pain, that heals, that helps us to well being. One may argue what I am saying. We just should not confuse helping people in all kinds of ways as being therapy. Yes, psychotherapy heals, improves well being, fosters growth; it is powerful. But so does being a good teacher, a good mentor, and foremost, being a good parent, a good mother, a good father.

Words are sometimes confusing. Concepts are sometimes unclear. And some things are different and yet they have similar attributes and similar effects. Over several years of the ongoing project, observers told

"The mothers were students"

me that our project was doing these mothers and children a great deal of good. They were right; in a follow-up study 19 years later we documented the effects on both the children and the mothers of this kind of intervention strategy. The children did better than the average population from which they come, in school, with respect to the law, in continuing to advanced education; their aggression profiles were significantly more positive than those around them—more about this shortly. The mothers' lives stabilized better, their self-esteem elevated notably, and they resumed further education. And recently, in a 32-year follow-up study, data collection and analysis now in progress, indications are that these gains have held up over time.

Recently Rachel and I had lunch with Betty. As always, when we meet with Betty, we talk about the project; this time about how the mothers and the now grown children had reacted on seeing us, 13 years after our first 19 years-follow-up reunion, 32 years from the start of our project. The mothers, most now grandmothers, just beamed on seeing us, Betty and I. They hugged us; bubbling; and it was so good to see them. The sad note is that one of the grown children has Lupus Erythematosus (a potentially serious immune system disorder) and another has Multiple Sclerosis. Apart from that serious note, Betty and I were enormously gratified to see how they all had grown; how all of them spoke so appreciatingly of their experience in the project, even the children. Anecdotes abounded.

Betty turned our conversation to my currently writing this book, my memoirs of the Holocaust. Betty knows my story. As we talked, musing appreciatively on our experiences with those mothers, she said, "Those mothers really valued what you taught them."—Betty always makes it my doing, underestimating her enormous contribution to it all. After a pause she said, "Of course, it's obvious, that your interest in helping mothers comes from your relationship with your own mother." I was stunned. I said, I had never thought of that. Betty seemed surprised at my surprise. "Oh, I thought that was obvious." I had known that I want to help children; I had not realized I want to help mothers, parents. Analyze, self-analyze, and after so many years I had not come to see that most likely Betty was right: I wanted to help mothers.

I wanted to help mothers! I wanted to help my mother. My mother, who really was alone (with me) since she had left Lodz. My mother, who worked long hours as a seamstress to give us food and shelter. My mother, who was unable to get our well-to-do cousins to help her (and me) get out of Bruxelles before the advancing Germans. My mother, who told me I must escape from Rivesaltes—and leave her behind.

Was my "interest in helping mothers" driven by my wanting to rescue my mother?

Or was it to atone for, or in some way repair my not having helped her, to be sure, not having helped her enough? Not having prevented her murder?

The determination with which I want to help mothers began to become evident several years into our project. Within 18 months of our start, the mothers began to speak of how much they had learned since in the project, how much they were learning. Several times, one or another of the mothers said, "I wish I had known this before I had children." The mothers listened to us, to what we would say; they learned from us. But I listened to the mothers, we all did; and we learned from them. It is this listening to them that led us, within three years of the start of our work with them, to undertake the challenge of developing parenting education materials.

But, with heart-felt respect for the mothers, another fact powerfully motivated us to develop parenting education materials. The Early Child Development Program staff came to recognize, little by little, that the mothers learning to understand their children' emotional needs and behaviors better, learning to look for what might be driving their children's behaviors, were applying what they were learning toward finding growth-promoting solutions in the handling of their children. We did not need to be astute observers, the mothers told us as much themselves. And they told us that they applied what they were learning about handling their babies to their older children including their adolescents.

We observed and saw that the microscopy of their child rearing was more growth-promoting. Their attachments became more positive because they were more attentive to their young children's turning to them, they listened more to their children's communications, were more emotionally appropriately responsive to them. Their limit-setting turned around. It became progressively more appropriate, discerning, and measured. And the mothers came to understand that what makes setting limits so difficult is that it brings with it disallowing the child's emerging sense of self, some degree of stifling the child's voice at self determination; and that this is what makes a child resist being told what to do, and not that the child is just obnoxious. They came to recognize that when a child experiences separation anxiety it is best to pay attention to it, to help the child tolerate better the fact that Mommie has to go out and will be back (by a specified time); and to not take the child's signs of anxiety as signs of being spoiled rotten. And they learned to tolerate their child's anger with them when they returned home. The mothers came to understand what makes children angry—a critical issue I shall address shortly. We saw such changes little by little. And we saw that by 18 months into the project, they had become "good-enough" mothers, as Donald W. Winnicott said. I hold to, and like telling parents that to be a good parent they have to be prefect 75 to 80 percent of the time. These mothers had gotten there.

To see these changes in parenting, in mothers who themselves have difficult lives and had even more difficult beginnings, was breathtaking. It is breathtaking to consider that one can help parents rear their children in ways that optimize their children's development. By then, I had already been a child psychiatrist for a decade and had never considered this possibility. The finding was unexpected, unpredicted, hope-stirring—an invitation to prevention in mental health.

Another fact we all saw was that the parenting education we were doing, unplanned as it was, was seen by the mothers as helpful to their children, that it gave reason to their childrearing strategies, and that, all in all, their parenting made positive sense to them. Among the many rewards my team got from this project, one mother said to me, "You know, Dr. Parens, you haven't made parenting easy, but you have made it easier." Years later, this mother also rewarded me, immeasurably, with a letter of appreciation for how her four daughters had grown into capable, responsible adults, a letter she wrote at her kitchen table she said, on December 26, 1996, in the very early hours of the night after Christmas, 26 years after the start of our project.

Given what we saw, we drew a major inference from the child rearing of which the mothers had become capable. That by their behaviors toward their children, the mothers were reducing the frequency with which their children experienced conflicts with them, and as a result, these children experienced dramatically less often, the hurts children commonly experience at the hands of their own parents. And important to my thesis, in many homes, Heaven protect the child who becomes angry with his or her parent when the child feels hurt at being shamed, insulted or even beaten by the parent! We have seen parents behave most hurtfully toward their own children. The conviction grew among our team that the mothers of our project had come to see the difference. We knew, by virtue of our concern with pathology, that by their behaviors, these mothers were in effect reducing and in many instances actually preventing the development of experience-derived-emotional disorders in their children.

This is no small matter. As a Child Psychiatrist and Child Psychoanalyst, I am convinced that most mental health disorders, most emotional challenges to healthy adaptation to life come, not from inborn pathological processes as we find in schizophrenia and manic-depressive disease, but from life experiences; and that most of these mental-health-undermining experiences occur in childhood within the child's own home. We became acutely aware that Mental Health clinicians treat patients more for experience-derived emotional disorders than for disorders that have a pure biological origin, predisposition. In this then, optimizing the emotional development and lives of children may well prevent the development of much mental illness in them and the adults they will become. Taking a leap, one more promising than my embarrassing malcalculated leap in Récébédou, I even say that it might reduce the mental illness of society. This thinking, questionable as it may seem to some, thrust us into a major effort toward the prevention of emotional disorders in children, toward the prevention of mental ill-health. A grandiose idea? We saw it happen. Our project mothers were doing it.

Toward the Prevention of Emotional Disorders in Children via Parenting Education: Preparing Children —Preparing Future Parents

When the assignment you take on is to develop parenting educational materials aimed at facilitating and optimizing parenting, these materials must obviously target people before they become parents. That would allow the wish to have "known this before I had children" to be realized. So, what students do you target? There are many "How to" books; in time we would write one of them ourselves. But High School kids who get pregnant, some at 13, 14 years of age, do not read such books. So, how do we get to them before they get pregnant? Parenting education for school age children, we thought. At what grade level do you start, when they get pregnant so young?

We decided to start when school begins, Kindergarten, Grade One,

Elementary School. A teacher told me that, children this age would not be accepting, certainly not drawn to, not excited by such material. She had forgotten her own childhood. In clinical work with young children, and in observing children at play, where there are girls invariably some of the play will be about home life. "Let's play house" is a well known theme for children's play. Observant adults who work with young children know that 5, 6, 7, and more year-olds are interested in playing mother, father, or baby. Besides in clinical work with young children, boys and girls, concerns about home life invariably come up from as early as we see kids clinically, with their parents when very young, or individually at four, at five. All Mental Health colleagues know thar children are preoccupied with their own home life, family life, even as the child progressively widens her or his experience domain to peers, school and the neighborhood.

We were not intimidated by doubting educators or others. Despite their doubts, the educators with whom we were working opened a space for us in a local school to further develop and demonstrate that school age children of all grade levels would engage in learning the types of parenting education materials we were developing. It did not take long to find amply visible evidence in the children's interest in matters pertaining to understanding children's behaviors, taking care of, helping children learn, all in all, in rearing children. We found excitement in students from the earliest grades on through High School. We were pleasantly surprised to learn that many teenage boys have a large degree of interest in babies, in young children, and in child rearing! Some boys got into the materials every bit as much as did some of the girls. By the time we found documentation that school children learn and respond to care-giving challenges in constructive ways, we had already developed substantial parenting materials.

We have now developed a cluster of parenting education materials, *Parenting for Emotional Growth.* The original textbook materials forged our way into first developing *A Curriculum for Students in Grades K Thru 12,* and were later also reworked these into *Workshops for Caregivers* of all varieties, parents, daycare workers, educators. We have presented the rationale for parenting education for "Students in Grades K Thru 12" and for caregivers of all varieties to varied organizations in Mental Health, Child Care and Education, and to Governmental Agencies in many places in the U. S. as well as in Europe and in the Middle East, including Israel and Gaza. We have brought attention to this rationale and these materials to UNICEF. We have taught professionals, in mental health and in education, and some have molded these materials to suit their theaters of operation. Some of these materials or derivatives of them are in schools. This work goes on. Our principal aim is to optimize the rearing of children, to optimize their psychological development, their mental health and adaptation, all children, everywhere—because good mental health is anti-crime, anti-Holocausts, anti-terrorism.

Yes, children everywhere. One of the most critical findings of the 20th Century is that children everywhere have the same basic needs, physical and emotional, in order to thrive in good physical and mental health into adulthood. Universally, when their emotional needs are excessively thwarted, children fail to thrive and to adapt well, physically and emotionally. That children differ culturally, ethnically, in who they are, Moslems, Christians, Jews, Hindus, Chinese, British, French, German, Americans does not bring with it different biological or emotional needs. Recognizing the basic sameness in all the children of Homo sapiens, our parenting materials aim to optimize the development and good emotional and physical health of children—everywhere.

I have become convinced that applying what we learned in our project promises over time to reduce the mental illness in and of society. I know; the kind of thought that cynicism feeds on; cynics smile. Freud envisioned this well before I did, in 1933 and 1939. He held that much good could come from applying what we psychoanalysts have learned in the clinical situation to the rearing of the next generation. In our project we found our way to putting that far-reaching vision to work. But we went further, side by side with our efforts at the prevention of emotional disorders in children and prevention of the mental ill-health of society.

Trying to abate my dislike of immodesty, something else in our work took hold of me even more than my very conscious wish to help children heal their wounds and my up to recently unconscious need to help mothers. Something else derailed me and my forbearing colleagues from our original protocol and our starting hypothesis.

Chapter 13

Aggression–How It Develops and Is Shaped in Each of Us

From the outset of the project, our original protocol and the starting hypothesis we set out to test held sway; the collection of these data was foremost in my mind. What was the status of the three adaptive skills we had selected and what were the characteristics of the relationships the mothers were fostering with their babies? The first year would be predominantly given to establishing beginning attributes of these in the mother-child pairs. The project was setting in; the relationships between the mothers (and their babies) and research staff were increasingly more comfortable. The mothers seemed to feel that we were of good will and we became increasingly reassured both that the mothers would continue in the project and that we were finding our way.

Then about 4 months into the project one of the infants presented us with surprisingly vivid behavior that just gripped me. Before I was certain of what I saw, I began to film it on the 16mm movie camera I personally handled. Our Institution's filming crew was also engaged for special pre-planned filming sessions. But I wanted a mobile camera, not one planted in a corner of the observation setting, since our subjects even from infancy were very mobile creatures. And I wanted it as part of my own record keeping. Comfortably fitting in my left hand, I was able to catch much behavior, sought and predictable, and unpredictable and surprising.

Parenthetically, several years into the project, when one mother or another occasionally teased me, they adored Betty, but they liked being playful with me, one mother quipped that when Jane in her teens is out on a date and I follow her camera in hand, Jane will tell her friend, "Oh, don't mind him. That's just Dr. Parens; he always does that." We all had a good laugh.

Fascinated by 15-week-old Jane's activity, I filmed her surprisingly tireless, pressured intent on exploring an evidently fascinating piece of her New World, a set of plastic rings on a string. She was not just curious, she seemed determined to find out all she could about these little things, to chew on them, stare at them, to pull them, to toss and retrieve them. But what grabbed hold of me was the pressure on her face, in her body as she did this, continuously for 20 minutes; at 15 weeks of age. Putting an equivalent degree of energy she put into it, any of us imitating her would have been exhausted! Others have said this before.

Having studied children with school problems some 6 years before, two of us had found that their being furious within their families was interfering with their ability to concentrate on their school work, to study or pay attention in class. Alexander Weech, my colleague from our Child Psychiatry training days and I, postulated that these kids were unable to sufficiently neutralize their aggression to put it to service into study and learning. We postulated that if we could by means of psychotherapy help these patients neutralize their aggression better they might succeed better in school. We studied four children/adolescents and one young man, a very small sample. But we found that it fact, our efforts paid off; our patients did modulate their fury better, attenuated the level of their rage, and were better able to attend, to concentrate, and to perform in school. We explained that we had therapeutically helped them neutralize their aggression. This is old psychoanalytic theory. Freud proposed that we humans are inherently hostile and driven to destroy by virtue of our in-born death instinct which, by its nature, aims to "return us to our inorganic state." The way we humans cope with this biological gift, our death instinct driven self-destructiveness, is to neutralize what we can of it, and to externalize what we cannot, which turns these untamed self-destructive impulses into murderous impulses toward others. Though increasingly questioned by psychoanalysts over time, this theory still held sway in 1970 when I brought it with me into the project, accepting of it myself. I had had no desire whatsoever to look at this question in the project.

Jane repeated this performance a number of times. So did the other babies, in their own way, within their own universes. Something about it was buzzing in my head. These children are too young to experience such beautifully neutralized aggression. According to Freud's aggression theory such neutralization of aggression could occur only when the infantile ego—in psychoanalysis the ego is one's system of

The author, with camera; Leafy Pollock, with video camera; Peter Bennett, recording. Two mothers (the others and the children are off camera)

Studying aggression, etc. in as naturalistic a setting as our limited funding allowed

adaptive functions—became sufficiently organized, at about 6 months of age. But Jane was not even 4 months old, and already had such accomplished neutralized aggression at her disposal. I was troubled. How could this be possible? Ah, yes: the babies had not read my dear Freud and did not know they were supposed to behave differently! Audiences invariably laugh when, in reporting on this work, I have put forth that light-hearted "explanation."

Totally unaware that a powerful motive was fueling my obsession with this issue, I found myself rather compelled to continue to film such behavioral events. I reported them in our post-observation conferences. My colleagues were well-disposed toward me and my interest. The question stayed with me. It became very clear as I continued to mull it over, that the infants also showed the kind of aggressive behavior we all know them for, such as crying angrily when food is held off too long or when they are colicky. This behavior was not challenging, or at least did not seem so immediately. But how to reconcile what had by now become for me, that other, the Jane-type of aggression? I collected data of both types of aggression. Aggression seemed to gobble up my interest and drain my earlier interest so nicely organized into our original research protocol. Increasingly, rather suddenly I had a problem: What of aggression?

One of my basic theoretical clinical underpinnings was faulty. Aggression is not just what I had understood it to be. I did not know why this caused me such distress since I never was one to operate clinically from theory. In fact, I have been convinced from my earliest clinical years that such an approach to clinical findings, to patients, is seriously wrong. Charcot said something like, "Theory is great, but it does not prevent facts from being what they are." I agree. Clinical facts, the patient, come first, not theory. Being something of a theorist in my field, I say this with full confidence. We can not change facts; theory has to follow from them; we can only change theory.

I came to see that this is what I had to do. But why did I "have to" do this? Our original project hypothesis was still strong; there was nothing wrong with our original protocol. It did not matter. My head was with the problem I had found. What truly is aggression? It was only much later that I came to understand why I was so driven to understand it better, to study it—what drove the Nazis to want to destroy us? Not in all its complexity; in its inherently human psychology. I did not think this then.

At the time, I felt that our theory of aggression is wrong. Not all aggressive behavior is inherently destructive. Aggression cannot in origin be driven by a death instinct. Jane was quite innocently but heftily driven to discover her new world; not to destroy it; it was to learn about it in order to adapt to it, master it and herself in it..

Given what we were doing, I saw an unexpected opportunity to study aggression, as it first becomes evident in the behavior of children; and we could follow it in the course of our young subjects' development. I did not immediately press the idea onto my collaborators. I was not yet certain what course to take. I continued to look, to record in film, to record notes during our conferences and after. To undertake to study aggression, I had to free my head from my best-teacher Freud's theory of aggression. I did not relish doing this even though I knew that Freud had on a number of occasions modified his own views on critical theories he had developed before. Furthermore, he was a good model for making the facts come first, like Charcot. Besides, I seemed to not be in control of this thing in my head.

The facts we found in the children's behaviors just became unequivocal to me. Essentially I had to throw the theory out. Easy to say. But what should I put in its place? Aggression is not just some haphazard thing that willy-nilly drives human beings; it has organization within us. It did not yet, at that time, occur to me to ask: "Why am I so troubled and driven by this finding?" It did not occur to me then, "Don't you think your interest might have had something to do with the Holocaust?" What could have made me suppress this thought then? I felt just driven to solve this problem. It was a problem for me, but I had not recognized that it was a problem I had to try to solve in an effort to further master my own past victimization at the hands of the sadistic, murderous, hate-driven Nazis. This recognition came much later.

Not only did I see aggression that seemed not inherently destructive, but the babies reminded me that in my own three sons, when they were babies, I did not see any signs of their being loaded with wishes to destroy, things or their mother or me. Yes, I did see in our three sons, that there were times when the earlier born one seemed ill-inclined toward the next one born. But this is explained by reasons other than being due to an inborn tendency to destroy. But then I saw, and my colleagues confirmed in conference, that every time one of the babies started to fuss, cry, or become angry, something had happened before that could explain it. "Something" invariably preceeded, seemed to be responsible for a very young child's being angry. That "something" was anything that caused the child distress, whether it was waiting too long to be fed, whether another infant had grabbed the child's pacifier, or mother walked out of the room leaving her 6 month old on a blanket on the floor, etc. We came to be able to predict when an infant might become upset. It would follow the experiencing of any form of "psychic pain," what in psychoanalytic terms we call "unpleasure"—an awkward word but a term that was consistent with the psychoanalytic concept of the "pleasure principle." In the early 1970s that word made much sense.

Furthermore, we found that as the infants developed into toddlers and started to more widely explore their universe many occasions presented themselves when one child would cause another distress which would lead to explicit manifestations of anger and, when more intense even to overt hostility. Adding to the eye-opening observations we were making, I also had occasion, as we all do, to see situations outside our project where, frustrated or otherwise hurt beyond their tolerance, very young children have temper tantrums or outbursts of rage. We saw much behavior within our project that suggested that the more the pain or unpleasure the child experienced, the more intense the reaction of negative feelings from anger, to hostility, and to rage.

And then, it occurred to me that there was evidence of aggression right in front of my nose that also had to be accounted for—and the death instinct did not consider. While it may be less obvious when infants just breast feed or bottle feed, looking at older children and ourselves, the adults, it is easy to see that we all destroy when we eat. We tear down beautifully structured tissues when we eat meat or vegetables; we break down particulate substance to feed ourselves. But this destroying is with no ill intent but simply to eat and survive. We destroy innocently, we take this for granted. Except we did not in Europe during 1940 to 1945. Then, as Primo Levi said, "our old comrade hunger" was always there, waiting for us. He was a very popular fellow in 1940s Europe, at least for the incarcerated.

As the aggression data accumulated, I struggled, including in dreams, to find a way to put together these various aggressive behaviors. I woke up one morning with a solution, with a model. One feature of the model stood out immediately that had a dramatic impact on me. Children are not born feeling hostile and needing to destroy, as the death instinct theory held; we become hostile and want to destroy when the "psychic pain" we experience is sufficiently intense that it somehow generates hostile destructiveness in us; that, is what makes us feel hostile and want to destroy. It became clear to me, this piece of the model that I had found in my dreams.

We do that, we solve problems in dreams.

The Crucial Aggression Equation:

"Excessive Unpleasure → Hostile Destructiveness"

This most striking piece of the aggression theory I was developing holds that anything that causes us emotional pain, "psychic pain," "unpleasure," activates within us a mechanism that leads to the generation of "hostile destructiveness" in us. This mechanism is part of the built-in biological system within us that secures self-preservation. We have known since it was demonstrated near the end of the 19th Century, that when a toxic agent is introduced into a living cell, the protoplasm in that cell will immediately act to detoxify or extrude that agent from the cell to prevent the cell's death. The cell's self-preservative system gets rid of the toxic agent.

This basic biological self-preservative system operates in emotional-mental life as it does in our physical life. When something causes us psychic pain by virtue of our experiencing it as a threat, as toxic, we act to rid ourselves of it. The less the psychic pain we experience, the less vigorous our effort to be rid of it; we may just feel "annoyance." When we feel a little more psychically painful, we may become "angry." As the unpleasure any event causes us is more intense, there comes a point when the pain it causes exceeds our tolerance, we feel "this is too much" or "I can't take it anymore;" it is "excessively unpleasurable." At this point the "*hostile destructiveness*" generated within us reaches the state of feeling what we technically consider to be "*hostility.*" If it gets even more intense, our hostile destructiveness will mount and may reach the maximal level of hostile destructiveness, "*rage.*" There is a spectrum of graduated levels of pain experiencing that has a parallel spectrum of graduated levels of hostile destructiveness. When excessively painful experience is felt repeatedly, frequently, and comes from a specific source, be it a person or a situation, we come to "*hate*" that person or situation.

Thus, when we feel psychic pain (unpleasure) beyond our level of tolerance, whatever that tolerance level may be on a given day, at a given time, this pain activates the biological mechanism in us that generates a force to rid ourselves of the pain. I specify this force as "*hostile destructiveness*" because it stands in contrast to constructive, healthy aggression, that Jane-type aggression that helps us adapt to life, that causes harm to no one, what I have called "*nondestructive aggression.*" By contrast, "hostile destructiveness" makes us want to cause harm, to destroy. I shaped this crucial piece of this emerging aggression theory into the aggression-generation (production) equation: excessive unpleasure →hostile destructiveness.

Yes, it is exciting to develop theory. But my "excitement" was enveloping; I felt a profound feeling of hope when I came to understand the meaning of this equation. The "discovery" of this equation resonated within me with the need to understand why we humans cause one another such enormous pain. I sensed, though not immediately fully, that this equation had a key place in our understanding the Holocaust, and *la condition humaine.* I know, of itself the equation cannot explain the Holocaust; but it belongs somewhere in our effort to understand it. And to prevent another one!

Clinically we have known that the experiences we have mold us, including how our aggression develops. But the explanations in my field for how our experiences mold our aggression have been burdened by the notion that first of all, our experiences have to help us, teach us, how to govern that inherently destructive beast in us. The degree to which we succeed or fail in taming that inherent destructiveness has so much been left to each of us, sinners from the start. The fundamental explanation for wars has been that we are born with a self-killer instinct, and that to protect ourselves, we humans externalize it and hurt others, and kill. Simply put, parents must tame their children's inborn chaotic tendencies in order to tame their obligatory destructiveness. This even in the face of the fact that most babies don't rage, don't look intent on destroying those or the things around them.

The evidence in children under 2 years of age that manifestations of hostile destructiveness seem to invariably follow experiences of psychic pain seemed to me strikingly compelling: we must revise our understanding of aggression and with it the rearing of our children. The thought that how children are treated is where hostile destructiveness starts dissolved the demon death instinct on which so much human destructiveness has been blamed. But much more important than that theoretical riddle, is that if excessive unpleasure à hostile destructiveness, then, staying with the chemical equation in my debt to Primo Levi, the left side of the equation would most seriously determine the right side. This means that in rearing our children, the better children can be protected from "unnecessary" experiences of excessive unpleasure, the less will hostile destructiveness be generated in them.

It was exhilarating to find that excessive pychic pain, whatever the cause, physical or emotional, is what generates hostile destructiveness in us because this means that the weight or intensity of hostile destructiveness that develops in children can be governed.

Young Children's Coping with their Emerging Hostility and Hate

Of course, psychic pain does not automatically stir us to violence. We humans are very clever from early life at dealing with hostility or hate we experience. We can hide it, we can deny it, we can displace it. In fact we found that very young children actively devise ways of coping with the hostile destructiveness that gets generated in them. They do not discharge it freely. Everyday life brings with it excessive unpleasure, be it due to any one of the many bodily pains children experience, or mother's limit-setting, or her having to leave the baby for a while to go to work at the office, or her scolding the young child for some misbehavior. By virtue of the young child's biologically determined infantile dependence, the hostility the child feels toward her or his mother cannot just be discharged freely. The child struggles to control it; the child must; her or his well being depends on it.

Here are a few examples I have reported in the Mental Health literature, to illustrate the large challenge hostile destructiveness presents to the young child.

Twelve-month-old Jane and her mother were developing a very warm, well engaged relationship. Jane's attachment to her mother by then was observably stable, her trust in her mother was evolving soundly; she was securely attached. Both child and mother were in good mental health and each was well endowed with adaptive capabilities.

From the time she was about 5 months of age, Jane would from time to time become quite angry with her mother, especially so when Mother set limits. They would get into rather hefty battles of wills. Battles of wills occur when a child wants her way and mother, often for very reasonable reasons, does not allow the child to have her way. During one such battle of wills, Jane was visibly angry with her mother. In a moment of heat, Jane picked up a 2-inch wood block, raised her arm and flung it, not at her mother but rather at the woman sitting next to her mother. Was her aim poor? I did not think so. Angry with the mother to whom she was already so positively attached, she shifted her aim, and discharged her anger (mild hostile destructiveness) against the woman sitting next to Mother. 12 month old Jane simply displaced the hostility she felt toward her mother onto someone close by.

Thirteen-month-old Mary was absolutely adored by her mother and father, the only daughter and the youngest of several children they had. Mary was a marvelous little girl, in good mental health. She was a quite alert but rather physically calm infant until about 6 months of age when we began to see in her a striking upsurge in her activity level which by ten months evolved into her having become a high activity level child. From 6 months of age on, Mary became a vigorous explorer of her environment, her level of assertiveness was high and qualitatively firm.

From the time of this upsurge of (nondestructive) aggression, Mary's explorations and autonomy-driven activities from time to time came into conflict with Mother's efforts to keep her safe and sound. Battles of wills would now occur and by the time she approached 12 months of age, these battles began to heat up rather sharply. Mother, who was not a high level activity person, occasionally had her hands full. A dramatic battle of wills occurred when Mary was about 13 months of age.

As nearly 13 month old Mary's autonomy strivings—the inner push of experiencing oneself as an individual with a mind of one's own—intensified and organized, she at times wanted to go into the hall, extending her explorations to a cleaning cart that would occasionally be there at a given time during our child-parent observation sessions. Because of her concern about her daughter's interest in that cleaning cart, Mother repeatedly told Mary she was not to explore it and quite reasonably enforced her limit by picking Mary up and bringing her back into the observation setting.

This ignited Mary. At 13 months, Mary's heretofore moderate objections gave way to loudly voiced complaints, her body tensing, shaking, face-reddening. Contorting her body to extricate herself from mother's hold, Mary cried angrily, waved her left arm in a striking movement against her mother several times, kicked her, and twice actually struck her mother with her arm. She once also struck herself.

We saw clear evidence in Mary of intense distress and rage. Mother, still holding Mary, sat down. For the first time since her birth, we saw that Mother could not calm Mary as she had easily done so many times. Now, whether Mother continued to hold Mary or tried to put her down, Mary's crying and manifest hostility continued. Mother tried to explain, comfort, and distract, Mother could not calm Mary. Once her crying stopped, Mary looked sober and serious. She sat on Mother's lap, erect, as if frozen at the edge of her knees, resisting Mother's gentle efforts to bring her close and sharply complaining when Mother tried to offer her a toy. After about 15 minutes in this state of immobilization, Mary's body tone gradually softened, she relaxed passively into her mother's body, thumb in mouth, and stayed there, awake, pensive and downcast for twenty to thirty minutes more.

Thirty-Eight-month-old David was born with low threshold of irritability, a too short reactivity lag period—some infants react to stimuli very quickly, some more casually—, difficulty in organizing intense emotional states, in calming, and more. He was an intelligent, lovable kid. But his inborn tendency to experience distress and pain more easily, due to low thresholds of sensitivity and of irritability, led him to have quickly activated outbursts of hostile destructiveness, which in turn, cause much distress to him and his parents. From about one year of age on, his outbursts of hostile destructiveness began to organize into temper tantrums. David had his hands full; so did his mother. Here is how I have described one of his tantrums.

This particular morning David seemed on edge when his mother rolled him and his eleven-month-old sister in a stroller into the observation setting. Mother, who was weary but because she now understood her son's inborn vulnerability could also be very sympathetic toward him, did not immediately respond to his pressured need to get out of the stroller. He squirmed vigorously, made efforts to get out himself, conveying intolerance of the restraint and the inability to get on his feet and do what he seemed just driven to do! Once able to, Mother helped him out of the stroller, while trying to calm him as she helped him in his distressed eruptive efforts to get out.

Phew! He could now move where he wished. He darted to the fruit on the table; smiling, he signaled to his mother that he had noticed it there. He went to the toys, briefly interacted with two peers there, and busily manipulated toys, making them move. During this time Mother had gotten to his sister, a much calmer and easier child, and helped her out of the stroller. Ten minutes had passed when David brought an apple to his mother; it was not clear if he wanted her permission to eat it or simply to inform her that he was doing so. Mother did not want him to have it because he had complained of stomach pain, and she feared, she told him, it might upset his stomach more.

He erupted! Virtually at once his face evidenced intense pain and rage, with crying and blustering nonverbal vocalizations, and he dropped to the floor, kicking and pushing away, all the while flailing at his mother who had just taken the apple from him. Mother looked pale, embarrassed, and moderately bewildered—she, and we, had been through this with David before—as she tried sympathetically to calm him, telling him why she had prohibited the apple for now. His kicking and flailing made her pull away some, but as he calmed a bit, she came closer and continued her effort to explain and calm him further. Within thirty seconds he let her hold him, and she, now seated in a soft chair, continued her efforts. Both child and mother looked pale, drained, and tensely in pain still—both, it seemed, trying to contain David's still palpable potential for eruption.

About one minute into the calming phase, as another child picked up the wooden car with which David had been playing before the tantrum, he erupted again, though not as harshly. As David raged, complained and demanded the return of the toy, he picked up a block and threw it toward and nearly hit, not the child who was playing with the car, but another group mother, a person totally uninvolved in the event. David, further frustrated by the second child's resistance in returning the toy, in quick sequence grabbed his sister's bottle, which was at hand, threw it at her, picked up another block, and threw it at me (the project principal investigator), nearly falling off the chair in doing so. He looked at me anxiously, more surprised than enraged as I told him I was sorry he was feeling so bad but that I did not want him to throw things at me or to fall off the chair. I wished he could talk to his mommy or me, I said, about the things that were making him so upset. Simultaneously, his mother, scolding softly, was telling him not to hit his sister, that Dr. Parens had not done anything to him, and made good efforts again to calm him, telling him he could not throw things at people. With his mother's help, the second child returned the car to David, and David became calm as his mother continued to talk to him. Both David and his mother now looked exhausted and pained.

As he recovered gradually, David began to annoy his sister by taking the toy with which she was playing, looking at his mother as he did so, smiling provocatively. The teasing continued and intensified into taunting; Mother now became angry with him. At the moment when he was on the verge of going too far, David abruptly changed his activity, asking his mother to take out his letter cards and play with him at identifying the letters of the alphabet. As she did so, David and his mother continued to look emotionally drained.

Fourteen-month-old Richie—a severely traumatized infant, a child nearly destroyed by what was done to him and by the rage within him.

When we first saw Richie he was 14 months and 11 days old. He was depressed, hypervigilant, with a distrustful look and very sad eyes, eyes that cast unbearable pain. He was subdued, his movements were sluggish. Physically he looked no more than 8 months of age. Although he probably experienced some stranger responsiveness in our setting, his initial response to us was one of withdrawal and mistrust. Richie was brought to our group by one of the original research mothers. She brought him to us because she was deeply shocked by what had happened to Richie, by what had become of him, and by how difficult he now was to care for.

Richie, his 17 year-old mother and teenage father, all lived with Richie's maternal grandmother. Richie was well developed and healthy at birth. By history and by a series of elegant photographs of him, we could ascertain that he had been in very good physical health and mental health until 6½ months of age. At this time, Richie's teenage father gave his young mother the alternative of moving away from her mother's with him or that he would leave her. Bewildered, she moved with him into a rented room. Within two weeks, father abandoned mother and his child.

Probably acutely depressed and immobilized, perhaps hoping her boyfriend would return, rather than returning to her mother's, Richie's mother stayed in that room with her baby. Becoming more and more depressed, she could not tolerate his complaining, whining and not eating. Increasingly bewildered and finding her baby's crying and refusal to eat unbearable, she would put him in the hall when she could not get him to stop crying. According to the referring mother who had known Richie before, at 9 months of age Richie had changed painfully, dramati-

* Reported in Parens, 1987, pp. 332-333.

cally and became withdrawn. We assumed from her descriptions that he became severely depressed—yes, infants can become depressed, some severely so. At 9½ months of age, Richie was brought to the Emergency Room at our hospital due to a burn on his back. Mother said that during a fight with Richie's father, her clothe-pressing iron fell and burnt Richie. Seeing mother and child in their respective emotional states, Emergency Room staff assumed child abuse and Richie was placed in custody in a City Shelter. He remained there until just before he was 14 months at which time, maternal grandmother took him into her custody. Now very difficult to care for, Richie's grandmother brought him to get some help in our observation-educational setting. Here are a few abbreviated and paraphrased excerpts from our data recordings.*

At 1 (year)-2 (months)-25 (days), Richie continued to be depressed and emotionally and physically sluggish. Exploratory activity was minimal except for his visual hyper-vigilance. He occasionally smiles, bounces on his knees; several times seemingly spontaneously, he threw toys harshly, the pressure of his aggressiveness eliciting immediate limit setting.

At 1-3-1 of age, emotional state was unstable, depression dominated. But he also beamed, for the first time, when 2½ year-old Doris engaged him to play ball with her. She rolled a 3-inch ball to him, and he brusquely rolled it back to her. She rolled it to him again, and again he returned it her. In the spirit of play, Doris hid the ball between her legs. Richie appeared confused, suddenly unbearably frustrated, cried and banged his head on the floor to the dismay of Doris. Mrs. V intervened. Soon thereafter he went into a rage when he could not have a toy he wanted.

A week later his depression was softer, he seemed less morose, smiled more at people. Physical activity expanded and he reached out to several project children. Explored more and used toys more constructively. Nonetheless, in exploring the toy cart he threw toys out harshly one by one, which elicited the need to contain him. We hypothesized that the load of rage he was experiencing flooded his physical activity, which made it too harsh and destructive. Relatedness with others was improving. We were told that he now began to waken during the night screaming. Grandmother could comfort him within minutes. This suggested to us that he was now having nightmares. Yes, infants can have nightmares!

Twelve weeks later, at 1-6-7 of age, he was walking without support, wobbly but upright. He had sudden bursts of explosiveness, suddenly throws toys sometimes in a wide trajectory that would alarm the mothers and bring immediate intervention.

At 1-7-23 of age, his mood was much improved. Sudden, too aggressive outbursts with toys continue; but we have not seen him lash out at people nor at babies whom he now approaches with interest. After outbursts seems emotionally low-keyed. Relatedness with others is enriching.

At 1-8-23, enormous strides in development; improved emotional stabilizing, control of aggression, functioning physically and emotionally at more advanced level, relatedness more positive. At this time we saw no explosive toy throwing. He now folds his hands on his chest as if to control himself and at times shakes his head "No" at such moments. He continued to have about 3 nightmares per night. He is now saying things that make people laugh. Grandmother and Mrs. V said that it brought back memories of how he was responsive and entertaining at 4-5 months of age—which one could easily infer from his engaging, smiling photographs taken at about 5 months.

Defenses Set up to Cope with Hostile Destructiveness towards Primary Caregivers

What made Jane miss the target of her anger? What made Mary freeze sitting on her mother's knees? What made David's rage spread to overreact to a child who took the toy he had been playing with before, as well as to his sister and to me? What made him tease his sister? What made Richie externalize his rage all around him, on things and on others?

In all four children, their respective behaviors were set in motion by hostile destructiveness they experienced toward their own mothers then and there. Clearly the level of hostility generated by the given incident and of the accumulated hostility in each child was very different. But even when mild, actively felt hostile destructiveness in young children is experienced as threatening, to themselves and to those to whom they are attached. By its inherent tendency to rid oneself of the hurt-inflicting source ("the noxious agent"), like a limit-setting mother (Jane and Mary), or a slow to act unbearably frustrating mother (David), or a neglecting and physically abusing mother (Richie), these hostile destructive feelings of themselves become frightening to the child.

How could a young child just get rid of, just aim to destroy his or her own mother? The child "knows" he or she needs the mother. But even more powerful, the child is attaching or attached to the mother, which means the mother is invested with positive emotional feelings that by 18 months will evolve and organize into what we all call love—human young develop those feelings that we call love and hate only by about 18 months of age; the feelings children experience before we might call proto-love and proto-hate. The child's own hostile feelings are experienced as dangerous, creating an intolerable inner conflict of feelings. To not psychically disorganize, the child uses self-protective means of dealing with that hostility that are ingenious, they use "defense mechanisms." Remarkably, all young children seem to use the same types of defense mechanisms—that brilliant discovery, one among many, we owe to Freud.

As the four children I described showed, defense mechanisms commonly set in motion in and by the young child to deal with his or her own anxiety-producing hostile destructiveness are amply visible or readily inferable in children's behaviors from very early on. They include:

Displacement: as when 12 month-old Jane was acutely angry with her mother and, in a moment of peak, picked up a block, raised her arm, and threw the block, but struck the mother sitting right next to her own mother. This 12 month-old adroitly displaced her hostility onto Mother's neighbor.

Inhibition: as when 11 month-old Mary, angry with her mother, raised her arm ready to strike her, but arrested her arm in mid-air. She inhibited the discharge already set on the trajectory to strike her mother.

Externalization: via splitting off the bad self and the bad mother representations. We have found much evidence in our field in support of the idea that we have mental representations of much that happens in our life. This includes representations of oneself and of those to whom we become attached. Early in life, we tend to catalogue what we experience as good and as bad. From clinical experience colleagues have proposed that when our bad feelings are intense, we may "split them off" in our mind from the good feelings, in order to protect these good feelings from being destroyed by the bad ones. With this we set in our mind representations of oneself as bad and as good. Thus we have a mental concept of a "bad self" and a "good self;" of a "bad mother" and a "good mother." The defense of splitting mental representations can become a serious disturber of mental health. It does so when the inner conviction of bad self and bad other are too firmly kept apart in our mind from the good self and good other. There is good and bad in each of us, in all those we know. No one is all good or all bad. At times, the child may cope with the distress caused by intense hostile feelings by externalizing them outwardly, onto anything or person who can contain them. Commonly what is externalized is the "bad mother" representation. But we found that this is not always the case. Complex an operation as this seems to be, we see evidence of it quite early.

Turning again to 12 month-old Jane, she was again annoyed with her mother. Jane of late occasionally got into the "play" of stepping and hopping on her mother's foot. Mother had already told Jane she did not like this "play" and told Jane again not to do this, that it hurt Mommy. Mother did so again, now. Jane left her mother's side, crossed the observation area and sat down next to a visiting Social Work student whom she may have seen only once or twice before, looking at her very sweetly. While thus sweetly engaged, at intervals she glared across the room at her mother. In essence for a few minutes there, Jane found a "good mother-substitute," a stranger in effect, and *externalized* "good" *split-off* feelings to her, while she glared at her "bad mother" there, across the room. As I said, this is a remarkably ingenious but also potentially serious-problem-causing defense.

A more direct manifestation of *externalization* occurred in 14 month-old Richie who had been severely traumatized since he was 7 months old. At the slightest irritation he would explosively throw toys, anywhere.

Projection: When he was 17 month-old, severely traumatized Richie had ascribed hostile intent—where we inferred none existed—to lovely 2 year-old Denise when she momentarily hid the ball they were playfully rolling to each other. I inferred that projecting his own hostility into her action led him to experience Denise's act as hostile. Of course, we know that projection is the basic mechanism that underlies paranoia.

Rationalization: When Jane and Mary could not consciously face the hostility they felt toward their mothers, like most children, they would rationalize why they did what they did. Jane looked puzzled when the block she threw hit her mother's neighbor. Children need explanations for what happens to them and much clinical and observational evidence tells us they are often quite adept at developing their own explanations; children are truly generators of theory. It is then not too far a stretch to assume that explanations for their actions congenial to their needs would be generated by these bright little girls. And, indeed as they learned to talk, rationalization usually linked with denial were not uncommon, e.g., "No, I didn't do that, it was an accident!"

Somewhat later in development, a significant cluster of what I consider to be *defenses specifically intended to distort reality* are added to cope with accumulated loads of hostility and hate. These defenses include *reductionism, caricaturing, depreciation*, and *vilification*, defenses that facilitate delusion. These then often lead to *generalization*. These latter distorting defenses are well known to facilitate and activate malignant prejudice. We saw much of these reality-distorting defenses grossly used by the Nazi propaganda wizards during World War II. The Nazis were not the inventors of such strategies to attain their miserable end; humans all over the world abuse these defenses; the Nazis were just highly dedicated to them.

The operation of psychic defense mechanisms that have their start in very early childhood played a crucial role in the most unseemly place. Like many of us, Primo Levi needed to explain, to himself and us, the incomprehensible behavior of "the Jewish Prominents." "The Jewish Prominents," those in the camps who became selected to serve as lieutenants of the Nazi camp administrators, added a dimension of bewilderment to the experience of being criminally abused by the Nazis. "But they are Jews! How can they do this to us?" was no doubt in the mind of every victim still able to complain.

We have all heard that some of these "Jewish Prominents" were notably brutal to their own Jewish charges. The Nazis knew how to select candidates for these positions from among the deportees that arrived at the camps in prodigious numbers. Levi explained the "Prominents" behaviors on the basis of their "displacing" their own pain-generated-rage and hate, away from their own torturers, onto their Jewish brethren, now their victims. Levi was right. In our own research on the development of aggression, we found in very young children the basic hostility discharging strategy Levi observed among the "Prominents." Experiencing hostility toward their own parents as threatening to their relationship, young children "displace" it onto a less meaningful other. Side by side with this, the same strategy is used when one is abused by someone much bigger and more powerful than we are. It is just too anxiety producing to discharge the hostility instigated in us by abusers more powerful than oneself, and one displaces it on the next possible or otherwise chosen victim. In the case of the Prominents, the danger of directly letting out the rage they felt against their Nazi torturers made them displace it onto non-threatening others, their own devalued brethren. In addition to displacement, they also used the other defenses I listed before.

But the "Jewish Prominents" used yet another rather too common, regrettable defense that has early life origins which, we saw in our research population and we see in the clinical consultation room and in Mental Health clinics. In addition to various defenses listed before, in children we soon also saw evidence of "doing to another something that was done to you," an adaptive strategy that borrows the well-known developmental phenomenon, "*identification.*" Identification with those to whom we become attached makes a major contribution to children developing into persons who "fit" in their own families, in their own communities. This major developmental phenomenon is also crucial to another related part of my work, which I shall later bring into this account of my "Ayeika."

This basic developmental phenomenon identification, when linked to experiencing maltreatment by a parent, gives shape to an identification that is set to function only in specific circumstances; it becomes an identification with the hostile-hurtful parent, thus an "*identification with the aggressor.*" Anna Freud who proposed this mechanism in the early 1930s pointed out that this crucial defense mechanism is born out of the experience of feeling helpless in the face of dread. A little girl told her that she is no longer afraid of ghosts. Impressed, Anna Freud asked her how she came to achieve this. The little girl said something like, "Simple, I pretend to be a ghost, then I'm not afraid of ghosts!" Creativity in children is awesome; to see it evolve—which sadly passes unobserved by too many parents—is to witness the miraculous development of intelligence, of adaptation. The child identifies with the frightening threatening ghost in order to withstand the fear and pain this ghost, figment of her imagination, causes her. But the child pays the price of not actually constructively reducing and resolving the rage that abusive hurt has generated within her or him. Such rage and hate accumulates in the child's psyche. Later, finding an accommodating occasion, the child discharges the rage and hate stored in her or him by such an *identification with the aggressor enactment*, by being the one who abuses and terrifies someone else. By doing this the child temporarily frees herself or himself of presently activated fear and rage or of past-experienced, repressed rage and fear. The "Jewish Prominents" did this. They identified with their Nazi torturers, and they themselves became torturers. To be sure, the biologically programmed need to survive plays its part; it does so even when it's doing is so ugly; better to beat others than to be beaten oneself.

But we all know well, that not every Jew incarcerated and criminally abused by the Nazis would have chosen this path to survival. Like with the child's use of identification with the aggressor, this defense is used generally by those who have been subjected to abuses at the hands of others, the more the emotional investment in the abuser, the greater the pain, and the more likely that identification with the aggressor will be used to survive.

And we should consider the probability that this troubling factor may have played a part in the Prominents' brutality, that their behaviors were, in part, fueled by the sadism accumulated in them by their own pre-existing traumas. Some traumas generate hostility, hate and even cruelty in humans. So far as the accumulation of sadism in these "Prominents" reactive to traumatic experiences they suffered antedating their own camp incarceration, their patterned sadistic behaviors may have given evidence—the Nazis were miserable human beings but many among them were not dumb—that they would be good candidates to bully their own brethren into submission. We might assume that from early on in life they were reared by emotionally troubled, probably harsh and hurtful parents. Emotionally disturbed Jewish parents unwittingly hurt their own children just as badly as non-Jewish emotionally disturbed parents do. Many Jews, having suffered substantial hurt in the course of development at the hands of their own troubled parents, came to the Holocaust with pre-existing internalized loads of hostility and rage. There is a good possibility that some of the "Jewish Prominents" brought some of this old baggage with them and found their camp "job" a fitting vehicle for the discharge of their past, repressed hate and rage.

Hurt is part of life; but it is a highly variable experience. In Jane and Mary, the hostility generated in them was of everyday vintage. Life makes such hurts unavoidable. Responsible, loving parents have to set limits for the sake of protecting their children and to help them socialize reasonably. Many a mother needs to work outside the home and thereby causes separation pain and challenges for her young child. Or it is that the young child is gifted—not at his or her request!—with the birth of a new sibling. Loving parents cause their beloved children pain. Jane and Mary were well loved, valued and their other childhood rights were also well recognized—rights for food, shelter, protection, to be a self, to require education, and more—and the love they got and felt far outweighed the distress they experienced and the hostility it generated in them. Their load of accumulating hostility was modest. That their hostility was modest was discerned in observation as the children grew into 4 and 5 year-olds and as was later documented in our 19-year follow up study on our project children.

The other two children mentioned here, David and Richie, were symptom-burdened children who were brought into the project setting by very concerned project participants who knew them from their communities.

David was burdened from birth on, so were his parents, by developmental immaturity of his central nervous system, in consequence of which he had low thresholds for irritability, frustration, and pain, had a short fuse (was a quick reactor), had difficulty regulating his wide ranging emotional reactions, all of which made for his too easily experiencing excessive unpleasure. This led to his accumulating greater than average loads of hostile destructiveness. At 3 years of age, he could rage toward a peer who in truth had done nothing to warrant his rage; the other child had every right to the toy David laid claim to. The toys belonged to the project and David had stopped playing with it. And David too easily teased his little sister in an overflow of his temper tantrum. Children like David tend to have greater than average painful experiences and tend to accumulate more than average levels of hostility and rage.

The tragedy that we see in Richie is that unlike the adaptive dysfuntions David's brain burdened him with, what happened to Richie did not need to happen. It was not destined by Richie's biology to happen. It happened by virtue of the experiences he had. Some experiences hurt us immeasurably. The Holocaust did.

Richie was well endowed physically and emotionally at birth; being nicely cared for, he was thriving. The photographs we saw of him at about 5 months of age could have easily been selected for an advertisement "The little prince is entertaining his court" or "OK now, where's my lunch!" He was a poster-child of good health and well being.

When he was 7 months his world was turned upside-down. His very young mother became depressed when Richie's father abruptly left them. Hanging in mid-air waiting for her boyfriend to come back, mother's depression increased, she was neglecting her baby who reacted by complaining, he was suffering and no doubt lost his sense of well being and may well have become depressed himself. In a child his age one could expect a clinical infantile depression, what we call an "anaclitic depression."

The behavioral and emotional evidence we saw strongly suggested that much of his suffering had come from losing the experience of being well cared for, of being comforted, loved, in short, from losing his "good mother." The excessive pain he thus suffered generated much hostility and rage in him. Mother-child interaction deteriorated progressively, becoming flooded with pain and hostility. Then, to be sure, the physical abuse to which he was subjected made its large contribution as well. We saw the spilling out of the rage that flooded his being, flooding those around him.

This tragedy makes the powerful point that injury like this can be made to occur and, on the other hand, can be prevented. There was no evidence of rage in Richie during the first six months of his life. All evidence points to the likelihood that it got generated in him as his hurts increased; and with each occurrence of hurt, his accumulating hostile destructiveness, hostility, rage, increased. When we came to know him, at moments he was explosive; in repose, he was a little time bomb. With no intervention, with no positive reparatory change in his life, he would become a big time bomb.

The conviction that this tragedy could have been prevented got further documented and was progressively born out in our day in and day out research observations, evidenced in the microscopy of parent child interaction, in the contrast between the mothers' handling of their children at the start of our project and the way they did so by about 18 to 24 months later. Over time we saw their action-moment changes going increasingly from growth-disturbing to growth-promoting handling. We live in an era when we can make such determinations. We can do so by virtue of the piece our work contributed to the large volume of information we have accumulated during the 20th Century about what is growth-promoting and what is growth-disturbing in rearing children.

Because I am convinced that whatever the child's inborn vulnerabilities and endowment and that most mental health disorders come from life experiences, we developed our variably applicable parenting education materials. Our aim: the prevention of experience-derived emotional disorders in children. The prevention of mental ill-health. My team and I labored to get these prevention materials and strategies into the public domain in many places. Inroads have been made; but much more needs to get done.

We want to see a parenting education curriculum as part of the obligatory education of children everywhere. The summary statement of our *Parenting for Emotional Growth: A Curriculum for Students in Grades K thru 12,* starts with the paragraph:

"It is the role of Education to prepare our youth so as to make them able to live as socially responsible individuals; to make them able to work, love, and play responsibly. We prepare them for work at all levels and in all fields. Yet, most of us do a critical job for which no formal education or training is required! The work of parenting, of rearing what many believe to be our most prized asset: our children. More people work at parenting than at any other kind of work. Yet, for this difficult and complex work, no training is required. More and more people are becoming aware that this is a mistake! We want to remedy this serious lack in the education of our young, the consequences of which to society are known to be large."

We became convinced that if Richie's mother had had a parenting education curriculum as we envision it—not one 4 or 8-month course, but a progressively graduated set of courses over the school years—embedded in her education, Richie's tragedy probably would have been prevented.

It verges on the tragic too, that rearing our children is so taken for granted and assumed to be self-evident knowledge. If you are born, you can be a parent. Yes, biologically that is so. But child rearing goes well beyond our biology. It is not true that by virtue of our once having been a child and having had parents we know all we need to know to be growth-promoting parents. Of course, many have succeeded without formal education of parenting. The fact is though that parenting has come to be seen as being full of challenges. We have learned more during the 20th Century about the complexities of child development and about the measures required to *optimize* that development. We now know that understanding child development is insufficient; that it is essential to know how to optimize that development.

Society has still not sufficiently seen this now highly evident fact: that to be a garage mechanic, to be a teacher, to be a doctor requires all kinds of education, yet, to rear ones children in an informed and qualified manner requires no education. And this, in the face of the fact that more people work at parenting than at teaching, doctoring, or auto repairing. And, the object of our parenting is our "most prized possession"! Not requiring formal preparation for parenting competently is seriously short-sighted.

During this era of my work, the crucial aggression equation, that excessive *unpleasure* → *hostile destructiveness*, and children's ways of coping with it, especially children like Richie, reverberated "prevention" in my head, not just of experience-derived emotional disorders, but now specifically of the generation of excessive hostility and hate in them. With this then, we might achieve the prevention, or at least the reduction, of violence and malignant prejudice.

Toward the Prevention of Violence and Malignant Prejudice

The assumption I make is simple, self-evident. If what we do, we parents and other child tenders, daycare workers, educators, school and camp counselors causes children excessive pain, there is a good chance that we will generate hostility, hate, and even rage in them. What we generate anew will add to that already internalized in the course of prior experiences. Harsh handling of the child, such as by rigid and punitive home or school discipline and standards of conduct, shaming and humiliating, belittling, ridiculing, physical abuses, etc. all are experienced as too painful and generate hostility.

The more that hostility is generated, the more the defenses troublesome hostility self-protectively engenders in the child, the more likely that hostility, hate, and rage will be on hand to be displaced onto others when an opportune moment presents.

The more the child handling is reasonable, thoughtful, done with respect and consideration, the less likely that hostility will be generated, and the better the child's well being. I do not hold that children ought to be coddled or overindulged, be it with kindness or sweets. Reasonableness, thoughtfulness, respect, and consideration do not translate into coddling or overindulging. We can demand that our children become reasonable, thoughtful, respectful, and considerate of others and of our world.

It is that straightforward. It is this feasible to reduce hostility in children, tomorrow's adults. The pitfalls and the opportunities for generating excessive hostility and hate in the rearing and education of our children are many and real.

Child Rearing and the Development of Hate and Violence

We learned during the 20th Century that how children are treated at home contributes to the child's personality formation and aggression development. But side by side with this learning, we have assumed that in large part this contribution lies in the parents' taming the child's inborn hate and destructiveness. This thinking left us with explanations for the Holocaust as failures to tame human beings' inborn destructiveness, hate, and violence. Our only failure as parents and society was that we failed to tame beasts. If only God had not made us so violent and full of hate to begin with, sinners from the outset, no Holocaust would ever have happened!

I find it totally incomprehensible that educated, skilled, and even brilliant as many are in my field and in others, that we have held to such a key assumption in the face of what we see in and we can infer from newborns' and very young children's behaviors. And also, in the face of what some of our psychoanalytic pioneers showed, like August Aichorn and John Bowlby, that delinquents, thieves, criminals, all have histories of serious abuse, maltreatment, humiliations experienced the length of their childhood and adolescence, within their own homes.

Our study of the development of aggression in children observed twice weekly from birth through their (on average) first four years of life, showed that *Homo sapiens* infants come into the world equipped with aggression to help them master themselves and the world into which they are born. And that, part of their biological self-preservative systems include the reaction of wanting to rid themselves of any agent that can threaten their survival, their well being. Hostility is not there to begin with. It's all the little and large experiences of distress, discomfort, physical pain, anxieties, depression in reaction to losses of all kinds, the pains caused us by mother or father being angry with us, and even with each other whereby they create a threatening environment, in short, any experience that causes us to have bad feelings, brings with it "psychic pain." If I insult you I cause you no physical pain, but I do cause you emotional pain, psychic pain.

I want to look a bit more closely at our finding that the intensity of psychic pain experienced determines the degree to which hostile destructiveness is generated in us. Just as not all psychic pain we experience is the same, not all the hostile destructiveness we experience is equivalent. The range of hostile destructiveness generated at any given time is discernible in how it is expressed; it can be spelled out in the words we use to express to what degree we feel hostile destructiveness.

Least psychic pain experienced will lead to a young child's showing that he is *irritated, annoyed.* If the pain is somewhat more intense, the child will manifest anger. To this point the psychic pain experienced is moderate, it is bearable. A critical point is reached when the pain experienced crosses a line of tolerance, "it's too much!" This line of tolerance, or threshold of tolerance, is subjectively experienced. All pain we experience is subjective. Pain cannot be measured like electricity or weighed like a loaf of bread. The same actual pain may feel differently at 8 in the morning than at 8 at night, from one day to another. How we experience it at a given moment is what gets registered in us. The foremost factor that makes pain subjective is the meaning we give to the experience. I'll return to this point shortly.

For now the critical matter is that once that threshold of pain tolerance is crossed, the pain is subjectively felt as "this is more than I can take," "this is too much" or the like. This state of "*excessive unpleasure,*" not only intensifies the degree of aggression it generates, but it gives to aggression the quality we feel when we feel *hostility*. We might think of it as: pain changes the quality of aggression in its "pure" or "original" form, which serves adaptation to life, to mastering ourselves within our universe. Aggression now takes the form of hostile destructiveness, first of "hostility." Then, if the pain reaches yet a higher level of intolerability, we experience "*rage.*"

Each of the hostile destructive levels, from irritability to rage is episodic; it tends to be precipitated by a hurtful event, and it lasts as long as the psychic pain is felt. If irritability can be expressed then and there, it will be discharged. If anger or hostility or rage is experienced and permitted expression (in reasonable ways), the anger, hostility and even the rage, will be discharged, if not in full, at least in part. When these experiences of hostile destructiveness are not discharged, they may either be metabolized psychically or they will accumulate in the psyche. Note that in these comments I have not included *hate*.

When a particular person or thing causes us frequent or intense enough hostility, the feelings of aggression they will engender will take the form of *hate*. In contrast to the other levels of hostile destructive feelings, when the hostile destructiveness experienced organizes into *hate*, it is not disposable like the other aggressive reactions. *Hate* sticks. Hate lasts. To diminish *hate*, it must be metabolized psychically by the child or the person toward whom the hate is felt must "repair," must work to undo the hate the child harbors. Repairing with gifts and chocolates works very feebly; it only patches *hate* over, like a band-aid. Interpersonal, interactional repair works most effectively. The parent who harms the child too frequently, too harshly, must find a way to personally undo, apologize, work at repairing the emotional damage caused. When no effort is made to repair emotional damage, hate tends to be further fanned by new hurtful events and accumulates in our psyche to greater levels. Often, while to a degree it may be repressed internally, *hate* tends to pervade the personality and manifest in a variety of ways. As a source of destructive energy, it lies in wait for displacement, externalization, and discharge. Unconsciously, it seeks a target. In both Europe and America, the 1929 economic crisis, the enormous psychic pain it caused people generated *hate* in them that with compulsion sought discharge. In both parts of the world, the target of choice seemed to be, the Jews

Excessive unpleasure → hostile destructiveness. Child rearing is replete with moments when parents are challenged by their children. Throughout the extent of childhood, children challenge their parents mercilessly. As a result, the opportunities for unduly hurting our own children are numerous and stretch over nearly 20 years. Either a lot of hostility in the form of hate is avoided or is generated. As parents, our hands are full. It is to help parents avoid the unnecessary generation of hostility and hate in their own children that they must know what causes children psychic pain. It is remarkable how many parents forget what it was like when they were children. Of course, many remember only too well.

But as with so many fine explanations, it is never so simple. A number of factors determine whether and to what degree a hurtful experience leads us to feel psychic pain. Two sets of factors play their part. There are factors that pertain to the *hurtful experience itself*. And there are factors that pertain to the state of the self when we experience the pain.

What event or conditions cause the hurtful experience? Who is causing us this experience? Is it *accidental or intentional*?

The *state of the self* has everything to do with how we experience the hurtful event.

The mix of these factors is always at play.

What event or conditions cause the hurtful experience? As a clinician of children I find that more than we like to think, events and conditions that cause children psychic pain occur in their home. Certainly many also come from outside the home, from the neighborhood in which one lives, from the community in which we live—where malignant prejudice is cultivated—, from wars, crimes against others, individual and collective. While we need to put our vast energies to tend to these causes of psychic traumatization coming from "outside the home" to prevent socially experienced atrocities, we must also consider the condtions that shape each individual who eventually becomes a perpetrator of psychic pain "from outside the home." Those who do so come to it as individuals themselves shaped by large pschic pain at home.

Types of home-bound events that cause immense psychic pain range from a parent not being sufficiently "emotionally available" to the child (Margaret Mahler said), to parents' intolerance for their children's complaints, for even mild reactions of anger and hostility, to being abused, emotionally, physically and sexually. Child abuses abound in too many home; emotionally, such as by being shamed and humiliated, to being often physically beaten, or sexually taken advantage of and traumatized. Any one of these may be enough to load any biologically-well-endowed-child with volumes of hostility and hate. It is not uncommon that a mix of these types of hurt is combined to victimize the child. Also many children are severely neglected, rejected, as well as harshly beaten and humiliated to the point of one-day lashing out in crimes against others, as August Aichorn, John Bowlby, and Jim Gilligan have shown. Criminality does not just arise in children heavily loaded with hostile destructive genes—there is no such thing.

We saw the range of hurt such home-bound events cause, from mild and very tolerable in Jane and Mary, compared to traumatizing and highly destructive as we saw in Richie. We could envision the fates of Jane and Mary as compared to Richie. While there are many Janes and Marys in Philadelphia; there are far too many Richie's here too. Multiply that number by the x factor that would cover the United States; America; Europe; Asia; Africa; Australia. There are many Richies in the world.

Neighborhood hurtful events abound in childhood. School is a large crucible for being hurt as well. Shaming children for weak performances is still too common a strategy employed by sadistic teachers who regale in crushing a child's self-esteem publicly, most painful of publics, the child's own peers. And there is the torture visited on kids by peer bullies, bullies themselves being kids who are maltreated at home to a pitch sufficiently high that they are compelled to externalize and displace their hostility and hate on lesser threatening peers—identifying with their own aggressor(s).

From the community in which they are reared comes that foulest of human malfeasance and injury, malignant prejudice. I want to take up this issue later.

Who is causing the child pain? Who causes the child harm is cricial. Pain is experienced as much greater when it is caused us by someone we love, someone from whom we expect love, protection, and care. It hurts harshly when it comes from someone we thought we could trust. It hurts far less if it comes from someone who does not know us, or knows us little, like a teacher or a neighbor. It hurts least, though another factor heightens the hurt and consequent hostility we feel, if it comes from a rival, or someone with whom one is in conflict, from an enemy. It hurts less, but it is large because of the hate we already feel for that rival or enemy. What happened to us in the Holocaust goes to the heart of the matter. It may seem an exercise of little merit to say that barring extremes, to be overly neglected or harshly rejected or abused by one's own mother or one's father, one's mother especially, may cause a greater degree of life-lasting psychological harm than having been subjected to the Holocaust. Yes, it may seem outrageous to say this, but clinically, we find strong evidence for it.

I am a Holocaust Survivor. I capitalize Survivor out of respect for them, for us, for having suffered so at the hands of degenerated humans.

And I say that it is psychically more harmful to be rejected, neglected, abused by one's own mother or father, or both, during the length of one's growing years. The reasons for making this assertion are that to be hurt by one's mother or father hurts more than if anyone else causes us pain, and that one's home is the crucible in which our genetic make-up is forged into who we become over time. The foundation of our personality, from the development of our intelligence to the development of our self-esteem and our abilities to cope, all require "good-enough" care-giving for their optimal, even for their adequate development. If that care-giving is excessively hurtful over years, it may not only generate blaring volumes of rage and hate that produce delinquents and criminals, but it will at the same time produce crippling of the psyche, the personality, and with it rob the individual of the ability to cope in life and in society in ways acceptable to all of us. Who causes us immeasurable hurt is highly determining of the psychic pain it causes us. More on this in a moment.

Is the pain caused us *accidental* or *intentional*? It is remarkable how large a factor this is. It rivals "the Who caused the hurt" in harm potential. If my arm is broken in an automobile accident it hurts far less than if it is broken in the course of my father physically abusing me. This is reflected in how Society acts. If what happened to Richie had been thought to be accidental Richie would not have been taken from his teenage mother. It was assumed that the iron burn was intentional—albeit in a momentary explosion of rage. But it is not just Society that reflects this condition, accidental or intentional, the afflicted individual suffers far more when it is intentional.

To be hurt *intentionally* has a powerful bearing on the degree of "psychic pain" we experience. *Psychic pain* is that pain we feel when our sense of self, our self-esteem, our "narcissism" is threatened or attacked. When the hurt is unintentional our narcissism may be threatened. When the hurt is intentional our narcissism is attacked. We are speaking of "healthy narcissism," that self-regard essential for our sense of well being. It is not vanity; that is troubled narcissism; vanity is usually a self-protective strategy aimed at healing severe injury to one's self-regard, to one's sense of self. It is just in this that the saying "Sticks and stones may bread my bones but words will never harm me" is false. I have seen many a child feel demolished by his or her mother's devastating "Look at all the trouble you cause me! I wish you had never been born." Or by a father's "You'll never amount to anything, you good for nothing little . . . ." These are direct attacks against our self-regard, our sense of self. Coming *with intention* to lash out at us, to hurt us, from those from whom we yearn for love and protection, words as these generate much hostility and hate in us.

Hitler's, the Nazis' declared *intention* to rid the world of us in the 1930s was a cardinal abomination that causes enormous injury and rage just at the remembering of it to this day. The German Nazis' putting it into official action on January 20, 1942, less than one year after actual massacres through gassing began in Poland and Russia, compounded the abomination into crime. That it was *intentional*, not only pre-meditated but in fact *pre-planned* is one of the most odious and unbearable of facts about the Holocaust. That the "final solution" was *intentional* multiplies its criminality.

All these factors, *what, who, intention,* give meaning to the hurtful event. We interpret, we assign meaning to our experiences. Meaning, how we interpret what we experience, is a crucial dimension in determining how much we are hurt by the given event.

The *state of the self* too has everything to do with how we experience the hurtful event. Engaging in the clinical treatment of traumatized children and adults, clinicians of my type, psychoanalysts, "dynamic psychiatrists," come to learn how critical to our efforts to understand and help a matter it is, that we know where the patient's state of self was at the time of the trauma. Consider just the question of a father striking his child in the face with his fist. What *state of self* factors make a difference?

Where is the child in terms of his or her psychological development? If he is 3 years old when this occurs, its impact will be far more devastating than if he is 8, or 18. In fact if the adolescent is 18, his reaction would no doubt be far different than if he were 3. The same event has vastly different implications depending on the child's age.

Then, there is fact that not every 3 year old holds up to pain equally, nor does every 8 year-old or 18 year-old. Some children and adults are better genetically endowed than others to withstand pain. Thresholds of pain tolerance vary from person to person. Furthermore, that pain threshold will vary according to many factors such as those I mentioned earlier, what, who, intention. In addition, our pain threshold varies during the day, commonly we feel less resistant to pain in the evening and night than during the day. In children and adults who have been traumatized before, their threshold of pain may be very low and lesser pain will be experienced more intensely than might be expected.

The child or adult's adaptive capabilities matter enormously, such as the ability to problem-solve and cope with stress and will play a part in our experiencing pain. The better able to cope and problem solve, the more likely the sense that one can do something about the pain one is feeling. Even if the pain cannot be prevented, the individual is more likely to feel he or she will find psychological strategies to cope with it.

A very large factor in experiencing and coping with pain is the child's, and the adult's too, awareness of those around him or her to whom he or she is attached, who mean much to the child, and by whom the child knows he or she is loved and valued. Having a network of relationships as we say, even if that network is small, is enormously supportive in the face of excessive pain.

The role of relationships is well recognized in Mental Health. Much work, research and clinical, has documented the fact that the child's entire development, physical and psychological, is profoundly enhanced where relationships are good, are loving, respecting. The better the child's relationships to the parents, the better the chance of healthy psychological development, including personality formation, intelligence, capability to adapt constructively to life—and the less the chance that the child will develop large volumes of hostility and hate.

A substantial factor that helps the child, adolescent and the adult as well, face enormous pain and survive comes from the inner sustainment the child derives from internalizing good, loving, respecting relationships. That which we experience in relationships becomes internalized, and we draw on it, we feel sustained by it, in the face of excessive pain and adversity.

Several years ago, I agreed to speak at a professional meeting, my assignment being "What were some of the effects of the Holocaust on the development of those who suffered it?" At my host's request, I personalized my remarks. I presented the effects of the Holocaust on development framed along the line that multiple factors combined to determine its effects on children. I did so especially because I have felt, and I am not the only Survivor in my field who feels this, that the early pronouncements on the effects of the Holocaust on Survivors were too uniform and too pathologized. I pointed out, and some Survivor colleagues are in accord with me, that too many factors were operative to ascertain that all Survivors suffered similar outcomes. I was intent on spelling out some of the variables involved that called into question some of the generalizations that have been made.

I spoke on

1. The nature of the varying holocaust traumas that happened to us;
2. The state of the self at the time of traumatization and the status of our relationships.

The Holocaust—What We Experienced

It is well established that what we experienced in the Holocaust varied widely. Since I was speaking of development, I focused on children. Different conditions were experienced by children when (1) they were in concentrations camps, (2) when they were given over by their parents to be hidden in individual generally benevolent Christian families, or (3) when they were separated at the wishes of their parents from families and sent to protected children group homes. In addition, many children were subjected to a combination of these.

Those in concentrations camps were either in enforced detention, or forced to labor, or they daily faced extermination. These were all life-threatening camps; but the extermination camps were outright programmed death camps. They all were governed by malignant-prejudice-determined forced incarceration, abusive treatment, family fragmentation, starvation, miserable unhygienic living conditions, separation from home communities and from the outside world. Unequivocally the extermination camps were the most dreadful of these. Their impact on those who survived them was the most extreme. They included not only all the conditions I listed, but also actual mass murder of one's own and the imminent possibility, daily, of being murdered oneself. Much has been documented about these latter conditions by a number of those who suffered them, including Rudolph Vrba, Abraham Biderman, mental health colleagues Anna and Paul Ornstein, Henry Krystal, Yehuda Nir, much better writers than anyone like Elie Wiesel and Primo Levi, and still others.

Those children who were given over by their parents for asylum into benevolent Christian families were subjected to a very mixed experience. On the one hand, they suffered separation from their parents and families though many had the good fortune of being given asylum by generally well meaning people. But, as Kestenberg and Brenner who studied child Survivors reported, quite a number of these generally well meaning families were not well equipped psychologically and emotionally for caring for their assumed to-be-temporary charges.

Many of the children who were given asylum in group homes may have fared better than those hidden in individual homes because (1) being in the group homes did not require the at times harshly imposed cover up of their Jewish identity unavoidably required of children hidden in individual families. (2) Because the group homes were often run by Social Workers, Mental Health professionals trained to some extent in child development, under the auspices of the International organization OSE, *Oeuvre de Secours aux Enfants*. In her review of Vivette Samuel's *Sauver les Enfants*, Marion Oliner, a Child Survivor herself, thinks that in Vichy France between "8,000 to 10,000 children were saved by "Jewish organizations" with the help of the French Resistance, the U.S., Britain, Switzerland, Protestant and Catholic groups, the American Quakers, the YMCA, the Red Cross, and others.

There is the further complication that some of us who ended up in group homes did so after an unforgettable period of time in an Auschwitz-destined detention camp such as Rivesaltes or Gurs in Southern France. Kestenberg and Brenner knew that the experiences of the children were not uniform and they tried to address the impact of the Holocaust on children based on these varying types of experiences. But equally determining of the impact on development as the type of experience, again, is the status of the self at the time the traumatizing experience occurred.

For Each of Us: One's State of Self and of One's Relationships When It Happened

The State of One's Psychological Development: In assessing the impact of severe traumatization on development, we need to consider the developmental status of the child's adaptive functions as these are set in motion to deal with the many unique events that for each child constituted the Holocaust. It was not just one massive traumatic event. It was a period of one's life, a period for most of us that lasted 18 months to 50 months duration or more. It was a period of myriad events, in fact, not all toxic to our psyches.

In addition to the status of the development of the child's adaptive functioning, psychoanalysts and others are likely to also wonder about the status of conscience formation in the child, as well as the degree of inner-sustainment versus torment, internal conflict, accumulating ambivalence, love versus hate, and shame and guilt. A crucial question I asked my colleagues to consider was, "How much pathological character formation was already, or was in process of becoming organized when the traumatic period began?" A massive cumulative trauma does not ignore these pre-existing conditions; nor does it obliterate them. Anna Ornstein agrees that "we have to consider the significance of pre-existing conflicts and character traits in the assessment of the Holocaust survivor, and we cannot dismiss these because of the massive nature of the trauma." The trauma is experienced by and impacts on the more or less already burdened or indeed resiliently adaptive individual. Even in the face of uniform traumatization, differences in our experiencing the trauma may be as wide-ranging as day and night. Well, maybe night and darkest night, or the second circle of hell and the pit of hell.

The State of One's Relationships: Psychoanalytic and attachment theorists of varied persuasions agree on the fundamental importance to the developing self of one's relationships. All agree that the quality of relationships is a major determiner of self development, of how we feel about ourselves and about what is happening to us. Our relationships co-determine our hopefulness or hopelessness, our self-trust and trust in those we perceive we can trust, and mistrust of those we are right to dread. They also co-determine our realistic or distorted appraisal of what is happening to us and why it is happening.

Like Kestenberg and Brenner and Ornstein, I hold that our experiences in relationships were central to our adaptations to the traumas we experienced. One of the seriously flawed generalizations that have been made of Holocaust Survivors is that they all suffer from problems in forming sustainable relationships and of creating heavily troubled lives for their children. We hold that post-Holocaust troubled relationships were invariably associated with pre-Holocaust troubled relationships. In fact, Kestenberg and Brenner summarize that "Children from nurturing families had more trust, and thus a greater hope that they would survive, than those who came from dysfunctional or motherless families." Anna Ornstein reports poignantly, how in Auschwitz, the formation of nuclear groups co-existing as if in families or miniature communities sustained each other by interactive experiencing meaningfully supportive for those involved. In Rivesaltes, 3 of us 11-year-old boys, in addition to having capable and affectionate mothers, became a rather constant trio. Often by day we would be together, just loitering about or pretending we were "The Three Musketeers"; by evening we would occasionally meet with two girls our age and we would even dance to my singing in a small vestibule at the entry of our miserable, incarcerating barrack.

In her *Journal Rivesaltes, 1941-1942*, (rendered in a narrated video sent to me by my dear friend Lotte Koehler from Munich), Friedel Bohny-Reiter tells us that "It didn't take much to give joy to these unfortunate children" (my translation). Friedel Bohny-Reiter was amazed to see how readily, under conditions of horror children can try to make themselves feel as if conditions were normal. While internees were being shipped by horse-wagon—the French do not seem to transfer cattle, but they do horses—from Rivesaltes to Auschwitz, via Drancy, children sang songs. Friedel says that "in the face of starvation, their appetite lost, but they sang." While it may seem incomprehensible that this might be so, I did that in Rivesaltes. I was 11. Children find creative ways of making impossible life livable.

While in quite different environmental circumstances than Anna and Paul Ornstein who were in Auschwitz whereas I was in Rivesaltes, a detention, not an extermination camp, like Anna Ornstein observed in Auschwitz, the behaviors I experienced between in-mates in Rivesaltes was quite civil, even mutually supportive and caring. Unlike Primo Levi's experiences in the "Buna" labor camp, I saw no violations of others' starvation diet food portions, or their few clothing or straw mattresses or space; and I saw no displacement on one another of the rage we felt. But then, "Kapos" in Rivesaltes did not directly abuse us one on one; our transport took us just to the second level of hell.

It was our Vichy France camp guards we despised. And those French Government Nazi authorities responsible for our incarceration! And this point pertains to one of the most critical determiners of how we experienced this traumatization. It is that the trauma was perpetrated on us *by an enemy.* Unlike home-based child neglect and abuses, all of which effect a degree of "soul murder" as Len Shengold said, the Holocaust experience, however enormous the traumas, was perpetrated on us children by a source outside our families, from outside our ethnic family, from *outside* our immediate social communities, in fact from some that actively demonstrated hate for us. Although the Holocaust did ravage our lives, that the ravaging did not come from those we love, just this gave the trauma a lesser degree of destructive potential. Anna Ornstein weaves her thoughts about this question side by side with another important aspect of the trauma. She notes that "traumas that have been suffered by whole communities, such as . . . war or the Holocaust, create memories that can be shared with those who participated in it. Rape, incest, or child abuse, on the other hand, [tend to be] endured in silence and emotional isolation. [And she adds,] Most importantly, child abuse is most frequently perpetrated by people who are supposed to love and protect the child. Hitler, on the other hand, never promised the Jews of Europe anything other than persecution and extermination" (1994).

In *Survival in Auschwitz,* Primo Levi looks at the issue of survival, as *The Drowned and the Saved,* the title of his last book. He looks at survival in the face of dreadful abuses driven by malignant prejudice, the discharge of collective hate and sadism. He, like others, makes efforts at understanding how and why some survived the atrocities that happened to us, and some did not. Is it an unanswerable question? Whether it is or not, some of us do not know how to not try to understand, how to not try to answer.

As I read Levi I wondered if he was commenting on the survival of the fittest in Auschwitz. In *Survival in Auschwitz* (a commercially-driven retitling of his *If This is a Man*—carefully dissected out of his shattering poem, the one I use on entry into my story—Levi was not dissecting the question to its bare bones. Nor can I. But I want to amplify on what he said of it, on what made for surviving or not surviving there, because it has a bearing on how we withstand excesses of hostility and hate. I take his cryptic phrase, "the drowned and the saved," to be a cynical reduction of what he probably thought of it all. Nonetheless, Levi touches on matters that made for having been exterminated by or having survived those 1940-1945 atrocities. Though some have given much thought to the issue, we Mental Health professionals have not yet addressed the issue sufficiently. Although I have said a few things on the question in my field, I bring this issue into this narrative because it is, and it should be, of great concern not just for any one professional field, but because we need to talk to one another about it across fields.

What made for our surviving or not surviving in the camps? Most of us accept what Darwin proposed about the survival of the fittest. But we all know that there is more. It is not just genes, not just what we inherit. I should note that Darwin, as best as I understand, did not specify that the survival of the fittest derived only from our genes or just what we inherited. I leave this for those more scholarly than I on just what Darwin said, to affirm or reject this statement. Of course, it is genes and what we inherit, but as I have emphasized, it is also what we experienced before we got to the concentration camps. I expect that no one will protest that what we experienced before we got there enters into what made for survival in the death camps.

This question became important to me too years ago, when those sweeping generalizations about the traumatizing effects of being a Holocaust survivor. I have ruminated on this question. A bit more of it now. The blanket assumption that surviving the Holocaust left one seriously emotionally crippled proved inapplicable to Survivors I have known. I have heard the explanation though, that the reason some respected colleagues put forward so harsh a pathologizing thesis was in the service of insuring that the German government would be compelled to pay reparations to Holocaust Survivors. Though I have not been able to confirm this, perhaps it was. If it was, I have no comment.

Survivors suffered serious ill-effects of their traumatizing experiences. No Survivor escaped suffering. Some suffered much more than others. From the loss of family, home, the dislocation from one's universe, immoral and sadistic abuses driven by malignant prejudice, starvation, inhumane and disease-producing living conditions, slave labor, the constant threat of extermination, and the ultimate, outright sadistic murder. Everyone, child and adult experienced at least 3 or more of these enormous insults, as we physicians sort out in diagnostic appraisal. The permutation of these factors, the "*what*" was experienced, of itself, makes generalization of their effects difficult. Just as any assumption that "the survival of the fittest" is simply the by-product of inheritance is flawed, to assume that being traumatized by the Holocaust yielded the same, even a similar result in all Survivors is also seriously flawed.

Then there is the crucial factor, how each one of us interpreted the experiences we had. I agree with Anna Ornstein and others that "trauma is not defined [nor can it be measured only] by its immediate descriptive characteristics, but by its uniquely *individual meaning* and

---

* "'Yes' is one of those little words, the other is 'No', the two little words contain the whole world for me."

long-term consequences to the individual" (a quotation Anna credits to Marcus and Rosenberg, 1989). We interpret experience from very early on in life; children need to interpret life as they live it, to make sense of what happens to them and around them. We do not usually put it into words, but each of us gives a specific meaning to what happens to us. I would not put aside the probability that while some of us felt enraged at being so sadistically maltreated, that others felt their prediction come true, that someday, they knew they would get punished for having done something in the past they deemed totally unacceptable. And this, our need to interpret what happened to us as we experienced it (and after) made its enormous contribution to whether we survived or did not, and whether in survival, we became emotionally crippled.

A very large additional factor to those I detailed before, has to be taken into consideration when trying to explain what contributed to surviving in the camps,

"circumstantial chance." To be there or not be there, at just the wrong moment. Primo Levi defined it well: you survived by a "Yes" or a "No." Poets have written about that, though they have a very different context in mind than did the Nazis. Franz Schubert put such a poem by Wilhelm Mueller, one that speaks of unrequited love, into one of his over 700 *lieder*:

"Ja' heisst das eine Woertchen,
Das and're heisset 'Nein',
Die beiden Woertchen schliesen
*Die ganze Welt mir ein."**

The Germans knew that. In Auschwitz whether you got a 'Yes' or a 'No' depended on circumstances. The first had to do with how you appeared health-wise and how labor-capable you seemed at the time; and the second was on the one hand, how rushed the Nazis were to get that "final solution" executed, versus, to what extent they needed free, slave labor. Levi took note of his good fortune as he put it, at having been incarcerated in January 1944, when the German war machine was in serious need of no-cost slave labor, and in need of war materials of all kinds. Two years before, healthy, though starved as my mother was, she passed under "Arbeit macht Frei" in August 1942, six months after the Nazis unleashed their "final solution"; it had to be expedited. The first set backs the Germans experienced in the war, set the "final solution" into high gear. The atrocities peaked in 1942. Contributions to the German

Nazi call for Jews to be exterminated was swift on the part of a number of European governments. The Poles and the Russians, well known for their vicious antisemitism contributed to the "final solution" even before the January 1942 Wannsee Conference that thrust the program into high gear. The Swedes and the Italians were the only contribution resistors, the Italians delayed compliance substantially, the Swedes contributed none. French Nazis in Vichy made a strong showing, though not as vigorous as the Poles and Russians, but these French malignant bigots were quite dedicated to the "final solution" and contributed some 77,000 Jews. My mother was on the 19th of the many convoys of human beings sacrificed by the Vichy Government. Two years after they murdered her, in 1944, Levi was incarcerated. It seems quite later that Levi postulated, that as a chemist he probably was deemed usefully employable; "Let him help us develop chemicals and ersatz rubber needed for our war machine." Circumstances made him a valuable commodity.

Thus, to the factors "*what?*," "*who?*," "*intentional?*" "*the state of self*" and all these encompass, add "*circumstantial chance.*" Circumstances contributed to the destruction of my mother, (probably) my father and my brother, and they contributed to the survival of Primo Levi, of Anna and Paul Ornstein, Henry Krystal, Marion Oliner, Robert Krell, Savic and I, and others.

And finally, I should not leave out the frivolous play of "*non-circumstantial chance,*" just *plain luck*. Since each factor has a wide range of possibilities, it is extremely difficult to generalize to what degree we were terribly hurt, and what outcome it effected. Who drowned and who was saved, too has multiple possibilities, but that question is heavily determined by *what* the victims suffered, and to that consideration, being in an extermination camp, Chelmno, Auschwitz-Birkenau, Dachau, Bergen-Belsen, heightened infinitely more the possibility of being among the drowned.

Looking at it in the aggregate, at the numerous variables, I cannot measure, how we interpreted what was happening to us as it was happening. In the decades that have followed, one foremost interpretation is clear: because we were Jews, abhorrent crimes were committed against us. One communal interpretation of it is, this was the greatest crime against humanity ever committed. One can hold to this on the basis of its distinctive feature: it was sanctioned, premeditated in print, written into law, and executed by a country viewed by the entire world as civilized, a premier law-governed country in the Western World. This interpretation holds for all surviving victims, their families, their children and grandchildren especially, their friends, their communities, and many other civilized people.

One might believe that perhaps the young, who had not yet come to know the venom of malignant prejudice, or at least not its fullest virulence, did not interpret what was happening to them as did our elders. I, then an 11 year old did not know what my mother knew in early 1941. She knew Polish antisemitism, one of the most virulent strains, and she probably had learned of the massacres of Jews already going on in early 1941, in Poland and Russia. Her knowing saved me; but it must have terrified her. Why did I not see that she was terrified? How could she not have been terrified? I did see her on the threshold of terror when we rushed out of Bruxelles. But I did not in Rivesaltes. Was she able to mask her dread so well? I was a good behavior observer already then. Was she denying it all? No, or she would not have proposed, encouraged, and prepared me to escape. Was I too frightened to see it? I probably could not tolerate to see her terrified. I have tried to envision her as she walked into the showers. The thought closes my eyes. Some things I cannot let myself see; I could not yet go to Israel that first time I scheduled to go; my photophobia warned me. As I already said, some things I still have not seen, or done. Then, I could not let myself see my mother terrified. We both had to survive.

While I had not known in May 1940 the dreadful lash of malignant prejudice, I gradually came to have an idea of it as the Holocaust unfolded, though I did not at the time let myself fully know the potential consequences of what was happening to me and what I was doing, even as I escaped from Rivesaltes, even as I said goodbye to my mother. I had to go on; I could not falter then. Over the years I have come to know the virulence of malignant prejudice. As I grew, like so many around me, I came to know, and let myself feel, the terrible crime that happened to us.

On Rosh Hashanah (the New Year) and Yom Kippur (the Day of Atonement), though I don't go to Shul (synagogue), over the years I have ritualized thinking, reading, listening to Yiddish songs and Hebraic cantorial music. The past two Jewish New Years, I also read some of the thoughts Primo Levi left us. I have not tried to sort out why Primo

Levi's thoughts draw me to them more than other remarkable survivors' writings. For me the High Holidays are always times for contemplation, to a point maybe, rumination. I have plodded through Primo Levi; I don't rush to get out of there fast. I plod, and I pause to indulge some of my own relatively parallel remembrances, associating to what Levi says, comparing his experiences in the Buna, the slave labor camp part of Auschwitz—where he spent a year, 1944, until the end of January 1945—to my experiences in Rivesaltes.

In *Survival in Auschwitz*, Levi touched many consonant chords in me. I know he has similarly affected others. I smile even now at his detailing the food we ate at these for-Jews-only asylums. The odor, he writes, no doubt emanated from them; not from the food, from us. "The odor of turnips and cabbage, raw, cooked, and digested." I smile because it is long past. From readings of interned victims telling of the food we got, I get the impression that whether it was turnips, cabbage, artichokes, corn, whatever delicacy-featured menu we got, it seemed to be the same things for months. The camps' commandants must have gotten trainloads of whichever of these delicacies it was; so that once introduced you could count on getting it for the duration. We did not have cabbage in Rivesaltes, not when I was there. Nor artichokes or corn. According to Paul Niederman who told Vivette Samuel (in *Sauver Les Enfants*, pages 188-193), of his incarceration in Rivesaltes, where he came from Gurs perhaps a little after I had escaped on 1 May 1941, during Niederman's stay, Rivesaltes served a constant diet of artichokes and then of corn. Niederman tells that he and his brother supplemented their diet by pilfering the garbage bins behind the camp kitchen. On reading of Niederman's brilliant diet supplementation, I regretted not having known about the garbage bins, and shake my head in mild dismay, the kind that comes with smiling, why didn't I think of that! Niederman, by the way, proposes on the basis of their garbage bin expeditions and findings that while we were starving in the barracks, the French camp administrators, guards, etc. ate plenty. Self-righteously, though not without risk, the Niederman brothers helped themselves to a supplementation of their barrack rations of artichokes and corn.

But Primo Levi's delectable telling of the odor of the food we ate, led me to think, and I often have long before I read Levi, of the turnips and rutabagas, the hell food that constituted our diet. To this day I never want to see a turnip, and even more so, a rutabaga. Just the thought of rutabagas brings with it not only its musty odor but a physiological reaction on the way to regurgitation. I don't know why Nature ever made turnip and rutabaga; they are no more than slightly disgusting waterlogged cellulose pulp. I give it to turnips, they have a sliver of taste; but I never want to see the things again. I guess even Mother Nature doesn't always succeed.

I smile now, but it was no smiling then, being in the constant company, as Levi speaks of it, of "our old comrade hunger," a very popular comrade among the incarcerated.

Levi tells us that Clauser, his *Buna* co-inhabitant, had carved "*Ne pas chercher a comprendre*" in his eating bowl. "Do not try to understand." "No point trying to understand." Passively tolerate the intolerable, otherwise you'll wrench your gut, shake your head to exhaustion, cry yourself dry, rage to despair. Just keep going, day by day. Many of us did. Even young men, quite older than I, tried to glide senselessly through time, avoiding trying to really understand what was happening to us. Unbelievable; it at times feels impossible that it happened the way we all know it did.

Levi wrote, "Today, at this very moment as I sit writing at a table, I myself am not convined that these things really happened." I know what he means. I have belabored the question, "How could they do this to us?" Maybe I have never doubted as poignantly as he did that it happened because what I experienced was not as terrible as what he went through. Excessive trauma will do that. We speak of it as "dissociation"; by which we mean that one psychologically disengages from whatever self-threatening experience is happening to us. My friend Lotte tells me that I do not remember our goodbyes, between my mother and me, because I dissociated at the time, to not decompensate psychically or retreat from my mother-given assignment to go! Whether like Levi some of us at times have also felt "not convinced that these things really happened," we all remember it only too much. I think Rachel feels that way sometimes, that I remember it too much. I know that she feels at times that she just can't deal with it now; she can't as I always seem to. Why should she always think about it? In truth, I don't want her to always think about it; nor do I want my sons to. I take it that there were moments when Levi remembered and felt so bewildered, the memory reviving the traumatic experience so harshly, that he momentarily "dissociated" and could not tolerate its realness. The Germans, a civilized people; the French, the Italians, the Hungarians, civilized people! I remember it, all of it, even if I can't remember many details.

It happened. I just caught a glimpse of a photo of our two youngest grandsons, then 5 year-olds, Ben and Arthur. Cousins, they are the best of friends. When our family gets together, they seek one another out before they look at the rest of us. I have walked behind them, musing as I watch them. I see that unforgettable moment when they were 5, colleagues in some deep discussion about something of large interest; they are not smiling, they philosophize, at 5! They are now 7 year-old friends. I never tire of looking at this photo, they each have one arm around the other's shoulders. How can kids like these, maybe not exactly like these, but in essence like these, grow into doing to others what the Nazis did to us. Of course it's not just shrinks who ask this. Many who are not Mental Health professionals wonder this too. Primo Levi the Chemist, Novelist, Poet wondered this, and wrote about it better than nearly everyone. Those Nazis once were little kids.

How did they come to be capable of such crimes? How did they come to be capable of such ignominious acts of malignant prejudice? In Mental Health, but also in Sociology, we know that delinquents, criminals, for the most part were children who experienced serious maltreatment, abuses, at the hands of their own parents, within their own homes. For the most part, these parents had been reared by parents who themselves were very troubled persons, and who in turn, became troubled in their growing years by being reared by very troubled parents. It passes from generation to generation—unless one stops it. One can. Other factors too may play a part, such as traumas that are not perpetrated by their own parents; but these traumas are much less likely to produce criminality. The alternative genetic assumption of a "bad seed," a child as a bad seed, leaves me very skeptical. Speaking as a mental health child developmentalist, I have never seen such a child. Nor so far as I know, have any of the Child Psychiatry, Psychology or Social Work colleagues in my community.

Not lyrical, not poetry: "maltreatment begets maltreatment"; it is fact. Is this not a piece that should be taken into consideration when we ask, "Could this have been prevented?"

I know, factors other than home played their part in making those children eventually capable of such crimes, economics, political philosophies, education, ethnic lore, well-dosed distortions of religious dogma, each of which facilitated the organization of malignant prejucide in them.

But what drives malignant prejudice? I have some idea of what drives me. What has driven me even without my being fully aware of it: my need to understand and find at least part of the true answer to this question! What factors are required to turn malignant prejudice to criminality? Our studies in aggression point distinctly to what anyone looking at it would find in any act of malignant prejudice: that in largest part, it is driven by excesses of hate. I know, that is obvious. My sons' reaction to my saying something obvious has never stopped me from putting into words ideas that I think need to be said. That it may be obvious should not deter me from saying that high levels of hate drive malignant prejudice; often this hate takes the form of revenge, behavior motivated by wedding together *hate* and *rationalization* (self-serving reasoning). I would not object to a smiling, "Of course, dummy, where have you been?" But if I say on the basis of my own experiences and that of many others like me, that hate drives malignant prejudice, how far am I from being overtaken by the idea that we are inherently sinners or that we are driven by a death instinct?

No; another hypothesis came together in my head. Given my commitment to the prevention of the consequence that follow from the fact that *excessive unpleasure → hostile destructiveness*, looking at prejudice, certain development facts organized in my brain. What within us might predispose us to develop prejudice in the first place?

Chapter 14

The Development of Prejudice—Benign and Malignant

How Do We Come to Be Prejudiced?

So often many among us find in ourselves a bias toward someone and feel uncomfortable about it. Of course we don't always feel uncomfortable about it; we sometimes feel quite justified in feeling so. But when we do feel uncomfortable, we search and ask—ourselves, of course; we are not happy that we feel this—"Is it because he speaks with a heavy German accent?" Or, "Is it because he's Black?" Or. . . Those among us who are committed to equality, justice, and consideration for others, all know these uncomfortable moments. Some of us have struggled to feel no bias toward anyone! Others, more knowing than I take comfort in saying "We all have prejudices; that's just the way we are." I don't like it. Why is it "just the way we are?"

Serious thought brought to this question opens to view the fact that prejudice is not simply one thing. Our English dictionaries give several definitions of "prejudice." They essentially propose prejudice to mean "suspicion, intolerance, or irrational hatred of other races, creeds, etc." (Webster). And they also propose a broader definition "a judgment or opinion formed before the facts are known; preconceived idea, favorable, or, more usually, unfavorable" (Webster). There is justification for defining it so complexly. Having researched this question through the lens of Mental Health, I have come to see that there is benign prejudice and there is malignant prejudice.

Certain factors known to all psychological development microscopists give reason and support for the proposition that we experience differing forms of prejudice, one benign, the other malignant. It also makes clear why those who say, "We all have prejudices" are right. But which is it that we all have, benign or malignant prejudices? Do we experience both?

Normal Psychological Developments Make Each of us Prejudiced

Obsessing on the question, "What made them behave so treacherously toward us?" I came to recognize that several major normal psychological developmental factors facilitate the organization of prejudice in all of us, in children like my grandchildren, in children in Germany, in France, everywhere. These universal factors include, how the child's own identity and love relationships get formed; and that the child's unavoidably experiencing feelings of hostility and hating toward those the child loves creates in the child a large dilemma. The first of these developmental factors sets up the tendency in us to develop prejudice; but this prejudice is benign. The second is the largest factor that converts our benign prejudice into malignant prejudice. I explain.

How the Child's Own Identity and Love Relationships Get Formed?

Psychological theories of development converge on the fact that the child's own psychological development, the child's developing into a self, into an individual, and the development of his love relationships occur simultaneously, reciprocally. Homo sapiens newborn come into the world "pre-wired," as some say, to attach to his most intimate caregivers, those who most invest emotionally in him. In fact, this happens in all mammals and birds, and probably in other species. It even happens across species. Konrad Lorenz, the renown Ethologist planted this line of thought into Biology when he found that the geese he had observed and tended to since their birth, when of age began to enact their mating rituals with him as the object. He explained this seeming bizarre behavior by telling us, and it is now well documented, that the geese had become attached to him and this is why they reacted instinctively, ritualistically with him as they did. The geese were fine; they just did what comes naturally with the organism that had been so attentive to them from birth. It did not take long for this finding to be applied to *Homo sapiens.*

Coming from clinical work, even well before Lorenz made this brilliant ethological discovery, Freud had amply described, and a number of psychoanalysts following him documented much evidence that the child's relationship to his parents has everything to do with his psychological, mental development. Freud's theories, those of Erik Erikson, Rene Spitz, John Bowlby, Margaret Mahler, Louis Sander, Daniel Stern, and others, all hold that the development of the child, of his sense of who he is, evolves hand in hand with the development and establishment of his love relationships. This is now basic Developmental Psychology.

In that reciprocal bilateral development several factors active from the beginning of life have a direct bearing on our tendency to have prejudices. These include

The obligatory biological nature of forging one's identity and of forming stable, enduring relationships;

The experiential factor Freud pointed to that gives rise to our becoming specifically who we become, what he called *identification*; and

Factors that progressively specify those we love as unique, distinguishable from all others. Let us look more closely.

The obligatory nature of forging one's identity and enduring relationships. Several key factors combine to compel the child's developing his or her own specific identity. We all know only too well how important it is for each of us to have our own, unique voice. This was left out of the Communism program and, I believe, was one of the major factors in its collapse—that individuality, uniqueness was discouraged, denied. Communist philosophy forgot that Homo sapiens must have self-identity, must be able to be a self.

This is made obligatory by biological factors that serve every living organism's task of self-preservation, which in turn, secures that other primary biological task, the preservation of the species. For this latter task it is essential that every offspring, of every species, attach to an organism of the same species. Konrad Lorenz taught us, however, that instinctive attachment responses occur that may not serve the preservation of the species at all. The studies following on his discovery of "imprinting," confirmed that attachment is not restrained by species boundaries. Everyone who has a pet knows this. It was lovely of the geese to so favor Lorenz, but in doing so they forfeited their privilege and responsibility of preserving the species. This tells us as has long been known, that for the sake of preserving the species "species-specific attachment" is obligatory. It informs us well to also know that the earliest attachments have a long-range effect, as Lorenz showed, so that even across species, sexual behaviors are compellingly directed to the object of earliest attachment. Species preservative: sexual feelings follow the path forged by love feelings that are laid down in attachment. This forms the basic model in us for the preservation of the species.

Of course in humans, this basic model of sexual behavior being channeled to those objects of our earliest attachment cannot be permitted to materialize; were it to do so it would constitute an enactment of the "Oedipus complex" (and its counterpart in girls). This basic model though, while undergoing progressive developmental modification, becomes the template for our eventually forming love relationships that aim at and serve the reproduction of the species. In addition, this model opens the possibility of sexual behavior in the number of variable ways known to humans. For now, it is enough to say that the development of self and of love-relationships occur in reciprocity, and that thereby they secure the potential of preserving the self and of the species. But there is more.

The role of identification in forming one's identity. It is critical that, although the human neonate is biologically "pre-wired" and driven to attach to another organism and to become socialized, the actualization, the specificity of attaching and being socialized are profoundly determined by the experiences the child has over time. In the course of these experiences, the "pre-wired" neonate will be programmed to develop in such a way as to eventually, so to speak, bear the stamps "Made in Germany" Freud said in 1939, and more specifically, "Made in the [put in your last name] Family."

Two major factors bring about this *self-specifying* stamping. First, our genes, which make their enormous biological contributions to our looking like, sounding like, even aspects of our personality being like our parents'. And second, it is especially those *identifications* with our primary caregivers Freud talked about, which become visible in behavior already during the second year of life, that give us our specific experience-based stamp "Made in the [X, Y, or Z] Family." These powerful genetic factors and specific identifications complementarily create our individual self-identity; it is specific, distinctive, and variable.

And it is essential in order to be a member of and to maintain the specific distinctiveness of a family that children identify with those in their family who care for them. This in turn leads to their becoming members of a specific community and society because, again as Freud said in 1939, these parents are the representatives of their respective community and society to their own children.

With regard to the development of prejudice, this unique identity formation factor, *identification*, plays a powerful role. I think of identification as a *"self-specifying"* factor. In addition to the distinctive contributions it makes to the specification of self, to specifying "I belong to my family," identification also brings with it the internalization of familial and therewith societal-cultural mores. These will include familial and societal-cultural prejudices. These prejudices, on the one hand, may be in favor of accepting all people as equally valuable including those different than we are. On the other hand, these prejudices may bring with them a negative bias, a hostile bias against people different than we. The multiple ways of interacting by which parents and later neighbors convey such biases are compelling and make such positive and negative biases toward "others" an unavoidable part of identifying with our parents, the representatives to us of society.

This aspect of identification, specifically the negative, hostile bias toward others, challenges the biological tenet that mixing gene pools gives rise to more vigorous species. Is it a stretch to wonder if the mixing of specific, distinctive, and variable identities may be of benefit to humanity, to all of us? No doubt the dread of the loss of one's self and cultural identity, a positive identity factor, is invoked by such a line of thought. Yet, even in our time, it seems that nowhere today is evidence of the vitality and generativity of the aggregation of different healthy identities more demonstrable and acknowledged than it is in the USA. Have we not found richness in healthy identity distinctions, in healthy individual differences? Perhaps; but no doubt heads are shaking. It is an encumbered proposition.

Crucial developmental factors progressively specify those we love as unique, distinguishable from all others. My proposition is encumbered because attachment, and the identifications that come from it, makes not only for the specificity of our identities and our relationships, but also for the differences among us, differences we each come to value. Among the elegant theories about the development of self and of our relationships in our psychoanalytic repertoire, Rene Spitz and John Bowlby were notably generative. A little more detail opens to view the third of the factors that side by side with identification is part and parcel of normal development that sets up in each of us our tendency toward having prejudices.

Part of this reciprocal process of developing one's "sense of self" and one's relationships, requires the distinction not only of "self" from others, but also of those to whom we become attached, our primary caregivers, from all others. Earlier I said that "the human neonate is biologically pre-wired . . . to attach to another organism." To whom we become attached is critical to who we become. Lorenz taught us the eye-opening lesson that specifically to whom we attach cannot be assumed to be programmed in our brain. The geeselings he studied so enthusiastically had become attached to him and made him the object of their sexual interest! Mother Nature smiled.

Lorenz's lesson taught us clearly that we have to attach to members of our own species. But we individually need to specify those other members of the species to whom each of us becomes attached. Responsive to our experiencing, we sort out from among members of our species those who emotionally care for us; we select them out from persons more or less indifferent to us as infants. Thus we need "specifying" processes for each of this dual, reciprocal process of self-identity and relationship formation. This is why I have suggested that identification is a major "*self-specification*" factor. In a complementary manner, *attachment* also brings with it a set of "other-specification" factors. Both are central to our concern with prejudice.

In his studies, Spitz found that at about midpoint in the first year of life, infants seem to rather suddenly experience a set of polarizing anxieties. Spitz noted that these two reactions of anxiety, separation anxiety and stranger anxiety, seem to emerge at the same time during the process of the child's attaching to her or his specific caregivers.

The first, *separation anxiety* is triggered by the prime caregiver's even momentarily separating from the six-month-old child; this separation may be experienced when mother just walks into another room. The reason for this bewildering reaction is simply due to the fact that the infant does not yet have the ability to retain a mental image of the mother to whom he is attaching, so that when the mother "disappears" from the child's visual field, she has magically vanished from the infant's perceivable world. The infant is in an insecure stage of forming these critical attachments to others, an attachment to mother, to father, to siblings; to those that seem to always be in the child's immediate world.

These specific attachments will form the basic models for the child's subsequent attachments. Spitz and Bowlby detailed well what Freud had said in 1926; the child experiences *separation anxiety*, the first dread of losing someone of vital importance to child's organizing emotional life, the fear of losing that special person or set of persons in whose hands his or her psychological development is fully dependent. This set of persons becomes emotionally valued over all others; by virtue of who they are in the child's life, they are specific, preferred, chosen. But even though it stamps the to-be-loved-ones as preferred over all others, separation anxiety, is not the weighty culprit when it comes to our developing prejudice.

That regrettable privilege falls to the second of these twin "*other-specification*" factors, "*stranger anxiety*." This *other-specification* factor, *stranger anxiety*, carries with it the potential for generalization that may lead to the rejection of others who are different than the others-to-whom-we-attach, those we depend on and with whom we identify.

Stranger anxiety and the roots of xenophobia. "*Stranger anxiety*" weighs in heavily in our normal tendency to develop prejudices. But it is important to emphasize that it is not generated by some inborn destructiveness or hate within us. *Stranger anxiety plays a crucial role in the formation of love-relationship.* Our observations documented well that infants are not born with already well developed attachments; their mothers are well attached—more or less—to their babies, so are fathers; but the babies are new to all this. Close observation of them, infants look like they feel very vulnerable when they experience separation anxiety. So too, one sees that vulnerability when someone the infant has not seen before picks up a 6-month-old. I have seen such intense anxiety reactions in young children 5 to 20 months-old. True, the young child has not seen this person before. Why does this cause a problem? Why should the young child be afraid of this person? This happens when a grandparent who has not seen her or his grandchild for several months joyfully picks up the now 6-month old who just bursts out screaming, disappointing everyone. Grandfathers seem to have perfected this practice. Welcome, grandfather! But the child is innocent; truly no ill intent. Just *stranger anxiety*.

The psychologically organizing process of attaching to primary-caregivers progresses slowly, complexly, during the first three years of life. As it evolves it progressively stabilizes. During the period of instability until attachment is set and stable, the infant self-protectively takes steps to mentally and emotionally hold on to the mental representation of the caregiver to whom the six-month-old is in process-of-attaching. The twin anxieties play their prescribed role well. Speaking teleologically, we might say that while "separation anxiety" secures the infant's holding onto the caregiver, that is, to not want to let go of mother, "stranger anxiety" is activated to orient the infant away from any newcomer, toward the primary-caregiver. Stranger anxiety compels the infant to turn away from whoever does not seem to be "my mother," "my father." Thus, biologically compelled, *stranger anxiety* serves to contain and direct the infant's inborn attachment tendency away from any unknown other and toward the caregiving other(s). We infer that the infant seems to experience this unknown other as a threat to the establishment within his mind of attachment to the needed, valued, preferred other.

It is in the nature of human thought that no matter what one proposes critics are likely to rise up against it. In this spirit in 1954, Szekely argued that contrary to Spitz's explanation, an instinctively programmed "inborn xenophobia" is what leads the child to experience stranger anxiety. Szekely proposed that "already during the first weeks and months of life the infant reacts to the mother's face with anxiety or fear." Szekely must have been looking at traumatized infants! In maltreated infants, yes, anxiety and fear appear from very early on when the infant sees the caregiver. But it is not so in average-expectable conditions of caring for infants. Spitz argued his position well, and my observations add to the collective documentation of a number of "child watchers," that it is stranger anxiety that predisposes the child to xenophobia, and not the other way around. From decades of observation, we infer that it is due to the fact that in early life attachment formation, the infant experiences a transient period of insecurity during which any perceived interference with the consolidation of that attachment induces anxiety in the infant.

These factors then,

The obligatory nature of forging one's identity and enduring relationships;

The role of identification in becoming a "self," in forming one's identity; and,

The twin attachment anxieties that progressively specify those we come to value as unique and distinguishable from all others, and *especially stranger anxiety (the roots of xenophobia,)* all combine to create in us a tendency toward prejudice. It creates a preference for one's own.

But what kind of prejudice do these normal developmental factors lead to?

Do any of these factors carry with them a need to, or even foster in us a wish to destroy or hate others?

Does the need to develop a self-identity? Does the need to develop human relationships? Neither does.

Does identification? It may; but only if that identification brings with it a hostile bias toward others, commonly a bias that has to be re-enforced with cultural education. Or if the identification is of the defensive type, "identification with the aggressor"; but this is a special case of identification that usually occurs in emotionally abusive families, in "dysfunctional" families as we say, like happened with Richie.

Do separation anxiety and stranger anxiety lead to the wish to destroy others? While separation anxiety makes the child angry with mother, unless it intensifies to a panic state, it does not lead to the wish to destroy the mother. To the contrary; the need is to secure mother to one self. And all that is required for stranger anxiety to stop is for the stranger to leave the child's visual field or for someone to whom the child is attaching to appear. In and of themselves, these normal developmental factors do not lead to hate and to the wish to destroy. They lead to the development of *benign prejudice.* This is why those who say that we all have prejudices are right! But of itself, this type of prejudice does not cause Holocausts.

These prejudice-facilitation factors cannot account for the development of *malignant prejudice* in people—even where identification with familial and cultural mores bring intense negative prejudice against "others." Understanding the nature of malignant prejudice requires that we take hate and the wish to destroy into account. It is hostile destructiveness in the form of hate that forges out of our developing identity and preference for one's own, prejudice of a quite different kind against those who are different. Without hate, the distinction of others from the self, does not lead to the driven pressure to harm or destroy that distinctive other.

What hate, what wishes to destroy are we talking about? An inborn hate of others as early psychoanalysts proposed based on Freud's death-instinct-based theory of aggression? Melanie Klein for instance proposed this. Or, an inborn xenophobia as Szekely proposed? Our developmental research and clinical observations have led me to another explanation: it is that ambivalence—to hate someone one loves—in primary relationships is the most powerful, common contributor to the generation within us of wishes to harm or destroy "others." Let me clarify.

Our Potential for Becoming Carriers of Malignant Prejudice

What is the Child to Do when He Rages or Hates His Own Mother or Father?

One of the cardinal difficulties in human relationships is the often unavoidable mix of feelings we have for one another. Even those we love most, at times make us very angry with them. When that anger is intense, often provoked and persistent it is likely to convert into hate. Ambivalence, speaking as we psychoanalysts do, means to experience coexisting feelings of love and hate (as well as hostility and rage) toward the same valued, loved person. Even as adults we cannot escape guilt when we are angry with our mother or father. It is not difficult to envision the difficulty this mix of feelings creates for each of us. Consider then how much more difficult it is for the young child, whose adaptive functions, whose ability to tolerate intense feelings, and conflicted feelings at that, are only in their early phase of development; their adaptation system is only in the process of becoming.

In direct observational research and in the clinical situation again and again, one can readily see how the *child's experiencing hostile destructive feelings toward his own mother or father, toward whom the child is developing love feelings, creates in the child a large dilemma.* In 1979 I wrote that, because of the unavoidable pains of everyday life, the frustrations and constraints, the disappointments and the hurts, all of which occur within the crucible in which we rear our children, we found that the first person the child comes to be angry with, and eventually may come to hate, is his own mother. We can extend this as well to the father who engages early in the care of his infant. In direct observation we have seen ample evidence from which we can infer with confidence that these feelings create in the young child a very problematic emotional conflict, to use Freud's phrase, "a conflict due to ambivalence." Our observational findings confirmed the clinically gained impression that ambivalence in early love relationships creates enormous anxiety in the child.

Earlier I described the troubling dilemma visibly experienced by lovely 13 month-old Mary. For good reasons Mary's mother prohibited Mary from doing what Mary wanted to do. As mother held the line to protect her baby, Mary became enraged with her mother. I could not escape the perception that at this time, 13 month-old Mary's behaviors made clear that she felt pushed from within to "harm" the mother she so positively valued. This mix of feelings, of rage toward, and of needing and valuing her mother, created such a dilemma in her that she sat erect at the edge of her mother's knees for 20 minutes, paralyzed. I inferred that Mary's coping system, her ego we say, was overwhelmed with anxiety and consequently was transiently paralyzed. She could not act, nor could she let her mother act in any way. She needed time to stop everything while she calmed the conflict within her and could decide what to do. We all know those moments when we feel, "Stop everything; I need to stop anything else from happening. Stop time!" Mary was not the only child who taught me that; yes, children so young can try to solve problems, and need to cope with internal crises.

It is basic psychoanalytic clinical experience and theory that when the child experiences anxiety of such dimensions, the child, overwhelmed, may be unable to function at all; like Mary. This is not the adaptive freezing one postulates occurs in animals that try to deceive a predator who searches only for live prey. This is freezing due to unwelcome psychic paralysis. One of the major strategies for coping then with wishes to harm or destroy one's mother is to employ some self-and-mother-protective defense mechanisms. I assume that it surprises no one that the anxiety the wish to harm or destroy the highly valued mother or father, would lead to the erection of defenses specifically tailored to dispose of these hostile destructive feelings. Earlier, I pointed to a number of the defenses commonly used in early childhood in the face of feeling hostile destructive feelings toward their mother, defenses that of themselves, then play a key role in the organization of *malignant prejudice.*

Our studies of aggression made clear to me the many ways in which, just everyday life leads those who care for the child to be held accountable, whether guilty or not, for the pains the child experiences, and become the one to whom the hostile destructive feelings experienced then become attached. It sounds deplorable that we get angry most readily with those who most love us and who nurture and take care of us. But we choose well, when as infants the first person, or persons, with whom we get angry or even enraged is one who really cares for us. If this person did not love the baby, there is a good chance that at his first infantile rage, the baby would get thrown out. It is most safe to be angry with those who love us; they are least likely to walk away from us.

And it is in fact highly opportune that the child first experiences anger, hostility, and hate toward those who love the child. Because the child is pre-wired to attach to those who care for him, as he attaches to his mother and father, he himself soon comes to be very troubled when his own hostile destructive feelings are directed to such emotionally valued others. The young child becomes very conflicted by these hostile feelings—it is not simply because the parents shame the child for being angry. Feeling conflicted is compelled from within the young child: "How can I want to harm the Mommy I love?" Mary made it clear. So did Jane and David. Being angry with the mother or father we love is the central workshop in which the young child learns to deal with the anger, hostility, hate and even rage he experiences toward those he is progressively coming to not only know he needs, but also loves. It is a remarkable, highly beneficent workshop, that hostile-destructiveness-managing space between self and a loved one.

We saw how when 12 month-old Jane *displaced* her hostility on the mother sitting right next to her own mother. Eleven-month-old Mary, angry with her mother, raised her arm ready to strike her, but she *inhibited* he action and seemed to freeze the discharge of hostility mid-trajectory. We inferred from 12 month-old Jane's behavior that she was *splitting bad and good self and care-giver representations* when she looked very sweetly at a stranger while at times she glared across the room at her much valued mother. And, we inferred from much of severely traumatized 17-month-old Richie's behavior that he was *projecting* his rage onto the world around him, including into toys and persons. And most sad, most serious, we found that he ascribed hostile intent where none was evident, as was the case when 2 year-old Denise hid the ball playfully which led to his raging outburst. We have learned how we project our own hostility when we feel it intolerable, ascribing its origins to lie outside one self, "I don't hate him; he is the one who hates me."

Headshaking, I look again at the tragedy contained in Richie's reaction to 2 year-old Denise. She was so lovely to him; she was the child who more than the others made efforts to bring him out of his isolation.

Empathically, with tender sympathy, Denise seemed to feel that he felt awfully pained. Richie's experiencing was tragic because it was so pointedly evident that Denise had tried to help Richie feel better! But Richie's inner torture and projection blinded him to the goodness Denise was bringing to him. If we insult, crush, traumatize our adversaries, our "enemies" soundly, will they ever be able to see, to trust, our goodness? Perhaps. But what a risk we take.

Trauma and the Predisposition to Malignant Prejudice

So far, other than speaking of Richie, I have talked of levels of accumulating hostility, internal emotional conflict, and the psychic defensive strategies we see in normal, Jane and Mary, and moderately biologically troubled David, all three quite well cared for children. Consider then the challenge and the struggle the child faces, like did Richie, when he or she experiences highly intense excessive unpleasure at the hands of his or her primary categiver. Consider the noxious influence of trauma, and the hostile destructiveness it unavoidably generates, consider how it bears on the ambivalence dilemma I described.

Considering the occurrence of trauma in childhood, with an eye on helping parents reduce its occurrence where possible or diminish its harmful effects where unavoidable, my collaborator Cecily Rose-Itkoff and I were confronted with the wide range of traumas children may be subjected to from within their home and from outside their home.

The most egregious of traumas that occur within the family include emotional neglect, harsh, rigid, growth-disturbing child rearing, especially that laden with physical abuse, sexual abuse, and the less well recognized but equally injurious many ways in which parents abuse their children emotionally, as by shaming, insulting, depreciating. Then, there are parental separations and divorces which children experience as directly caused by their parents. Children assign intention on the part of their parents, which multiplies their degree of emotional injury. And there are the shockingly sudden or painfully slow losses of a parent or other loved one, whether through tragic illness or accident.

Then there are traumas from outside the family, neighborhood violence and crime, home hazards like fires, robberies, idiosynchratic or pre-meditated assault of one or more family members. And there are the wider-ranging disasters as societal violence far too evident everywhere, hate crimes driven by malignant prejudice, and wars.

In consequence, all things considered, the child's inborn givens, adaptive development, the quality of relationships and prior history of traumas, the more children are traumatized, the heavier their burden of hostile destructiveness, the less likely it is that the child will be able to deal constructively with it. The hostile destructiveness that cannot be resolved and metabolized will accumulate and be an internal constant, pressing for discharge. The more increased the inner pressure to discharge accumulating hostile destructiveness, the more the need to erect variable clusters of the defense mechanisms noted before. The more the defenses set up to cope with intense ambivalence persist, the more they become patterned in us. Neurobiological findings of the past two decades help us understand that these patterns of coping become structured in brain neural pathways and thus become part of the individual's character. The greater the accumulated hostile destructiveness and hate in an individual, the greater the chance that malignant prejudice will organize in him or her.

****

Pause: August 14, 2003–

Today, in Wellfleet, one year after the start of my writing these Memoires.

On this day sixty-one years ago, 61, six decades ago, my mother, along with 990 other Jews were locked into train horse-wagons in Drancy and sent to Auschwitz. The horror of that day still blankets me. It's a familiar weight. It's become part of me.

Josh, that wonderfully sensitive man now, gently touched my shoulder and said quietly, "I'm with you, Dad." Rachel too is always with me. Erik and Karl have not yet arrived. Erik and his crew will this afternoon; Karl and his two days from now.

Some have said that many Survivors have resisted mourning the losses caused them by the Holocaust. Resisted mourning, or avoided, or delayed, or waylaid mourning. I don't feel that is what it is. Losing a loved one can be, should be mourned, in order to go on living on a healthy plane, able to form good love relationships, enjoy work and play—the signs of good mental health, Freud said.

No, this mourning is different; it cannot end. This mourning is not just for losses of those we loved, of home, and the past it shattered, it cut off.

It goes beyond the admonitions of our elders, beyond Primo Levi's pained threat.

Beyond, "Sh'ma Israel, . . . You have been slashed into!"

It has to do with the tortured wonder, "How could they have done this to us?" It is the injury to our psyche, each of us, all of us together. We say "narcissistic injury"; but it is not strictly our actual body self, but the essence of our self, our psychic self—we Jews. It wounded our soul.

Of all things, I think of *Amfortas*' unhealing wound. Wagner (Richard, the Jew hater) thought he could bring Jesus in to heal *Amfortas*' unhealing wound on the eve of Easter. Parsifal, Jesus, healed *Amfortas*' wound.

Where was God? Where was God!

One cannot fully mourn a wound that cannot heal.

One can only continue to mourn privately, slowly, patiently, quietly raging, trying all one can to not burden with it those we love and who love us.

One can only continue to put ointment on it, like on my still, one year later, raging skin.

One can try to heal those around us who suffer, especially kids, whose suffering leads them to all kinds of ways of dampening or numbing or denying their pain, like by playing games in hell, like "*Les Trois Mousquetaires.*" Helping others suffer less, even turn their lives around, they have said; that heals well too. As we say in my field, it is so rewarding to see a child whose development has gone off track, get back onto a promising path.

And for me, doing what I can to contribute to those among us who want to prevents Holocausts, that too heals. Let cynics laugh.

And my mother, from within my psyche, from somewhere in our Universe, said to me, "Ar'n, Ayekah?" And I said to her. . .

****

Continuing . . .

Given the normal difficulties of everyday life, the generation and accumulation of hostility and hate within us is just unavoidable. These are multiplied many times by parent-induced traumatization. Considering the crimes against humans that plague Society merits my noting again that starting from the early 1900s into the present, a number of analysts have found that delinquency and criminality become organized in individuals with long histories of high-degree physical and emotional abuses often accompanied by neglect in childhood and adolescence. I am a clinician of individuals, not a student of biography. But I know enough to know that both Hitler and Stalin were intolerably humiliated during their growing years. In a personal communication, the authoritative biographer Robert Tucker told several of us that Stalin, the adolescent, warned his father that if he struck his mother ever again, he would kill him. Stalin did not kill his father; he killed near 50 million Russians instead. And Dr. Theo Dorpat has just come out with a book detailing Hitler's profound childhood, adolescence, and even young adulthood humiliations.

I do not want to misrepresent the complexity we encounter in both our understanding of and explanations of the behaviors of humans so traumatized. To be sure not all humans subjected to abusive childhood experiences become delinquents and criminals. Beethoven was much humiliated by having to repeatedly go to the local tavern to fetch his alcohoic father. He turned his misery to creativity, producing the best music ever written. Many others too have turned their terrible hurts into creativity of all kinds.

Many factors contribute to the fact that humans do not uniformly turn malingnant prejudice to antisocial and criminal behaviors. Many individuals so traumatized turn to other pathologic formations, including depressive and masochistic character formations, what we call "borderline" and "narcissistic" illnesses.

In addition, though many heavily traumatized individuals will erect the cluster of defenses we have taken note of, these may not lead them to develop malignant prejudice. Their acts of criminality will not organize in this manner. They may not target a given group of "others" toward whom their hate and rage is discharged. Their acts of criminality are less directed and specified. Nor do many such individuals share their outrage with others; they act in solitude, sometimes with unspecified target victims. I do not want to simplify the many ways in which excessive accumulation of hostile destructiveness governs humans. I simply want to give an explanation as to how trauma at the hands of our own mothers and fathers, facilitates the predisposition to malignant prejudice.

And unfortunate spin-off of the emotional dynamics that come with being heavily traumatized and heavily loaded with hostility and hate, is the unyielding need for retribution, for revenge. Jim Gilligan said, There is then a more or less constant pressure to seek one or more others for this retribution, for this revenge. This may give rise to what Vamik Volkan has explained in his book, *The Need to Have Enemies*.

In line with this I want to also note the tendency commonly found in humans that may contribute to the organization of malignant prejudice: it is the all too well known *need to blame*. The origin of this dynamic most likely lies in the tendency in childhood, so readily inferable in observation, to idealize our parents. This leads young children to believe their parents can prevent all hurts and evil. the child has a built-in need to feel they should do so. When five-year-old Jane fell down the stairs and her distressed mother came to help her, Jane's immediate complaint was "Why did you let me fall?" She unquestioningly assumed her mother could have prevented this event from occurring and she, most outlandishly, blamed her mother for its happening. This tendency to blame mother or father facilitates the tendency to blame what we fantasy to be malevolent others. We know that many among us who believe in GOd accusingly blame God for their intense pain and suffering. For so many Holocaust survivors, "Where was God!" has been an irrepressible complaint.

Chapter 15

I Insist, We Can Act to Reduce Malignant Prejudice and Violence

As we have labored to get parenting education into school systems, into the hands of child caregivers, parents, teachers, daycare work ers, aiming to lessen the development of experience-derived emotional disorders in children, we also saw and learned from the equation, excessive unplesure à hostile destructiveness, that by their handling, child caregivers can lessen the accumulation of hostile destructiveness in their children. There is little room for doubt that given the basic factors that go into the development hostility, hate, and of malignant prejudice, we can see ways whereby their generation can be reduced. No one is born loaded with hate or malignant prejudice. These get generated in us by experience; we may become that way.

That means that we can be less that way. Our work for the past 3 decades has led my colleagues and me to insist that prevention, or at least significant reduction of these destructive forces can be put into effect. All things being equal, if parents can prevent their children unnecessary psychic pain, can stop all forms of child abuse, not only the physical and sexual, but especially too, emotional abuse and neglect, their children will be less hostile, less full of hate. Richie is a prime example of the tragedy that happens to too many children, born beautiful, tragedies that can be avoided. I wonder to what extent, a less traumatizing childhood might have prevented the development of Hitler and Stalin into the tyrannic killers we came to know.

In coming to these assumptions, we have not only trusted our clinical sense in the observations we made over time, we have also relied on long-term findings of our studies. While other studies are ongoing, here are some findings from the 19-year follow-up of the study we started in 1970. This and other studies have been presented and published in professional domains. While our original study involved only 16 socially disasvantaged children, our findings firmly support preventive intervention.

Over the 19 years period from the outset of our study, none of the youngsters in our project had any encounters with legal authorities. By contrast, in the population from which they come, during that era, over 10 percent of adolescents in the United States got into trouble with the law. The incidence of drug abuse for the study group was less tran 7 percent. With regard to the population at large, among U.S. high school seniors, illicit drug use was reported greater than 50 percent; alcohol use was over 90 percent. Less than 7 percent of our small population dropped out of school. None of these children failed to achieve grade level work. In the population from which these youngsters come, about 40 percent drop out of high school. Among our subjects who were of age, 50 percent went on to college as compared to 20 percent in their peer population.

While the number of children is small, the findings are not. Furthermore, we want to emphasize that our study team believed the study group was not predestined by life conditions to do well. They did.

Our interest in the study of aggression led us, 19 years later, to look at our subjects' aggression profiles. We were not surprised by the statistical analyses of these children's aggression profiles; they not only confirmed what we had seen over the time of our study, but the development we saw continued and was sustained at 19 years. Getting ahead of my 19 year follow up study lay out, at our recent study reunion, 32 years after our 1970 start, these aggression profiles have held up.

In overall anger, violence potential, and in passive aggression, our project subjects fared better than their control peers, falling into the mildest of the three categories proposed by the Fitzgibbons Anger Inventory. The average comparison adolescent populations tested fell in the moderate category.

We also found that our parenting education materials were significantly benefial to the mothers themselves.

Hand in hand with these studies documenting the effects of optimizing child rearing in an educational group setting, we were looking at the effects of our Parenting Curriculum for school-age children. We found that the formalizing the preparation of children for the hard job of parenting is also showing to be feasible and beneficial. Teachers who formerly worked with us have developed parenting education materials that have been in schools for about 20 years. Comparative study of those students who took such classes and those who did not, showed that they understood themselves psychologically better, and that they settled interpersonal conflicts with peers better. In another study, those students who had these instruction modules proposed more growth-promoting solutions to problems in rearing a child than those students who did not. Important in these studies is that, good parenting education materials show positive effects on the students soon after they have taken these classes.

While these short-term effects are attractive, most important I believe are the potential long-term effects of parenting education. Our team has seen evidence that they are likely to lead to a reduction of (1) excessive hostility, violence and malignant prejudice; (2) school dropout and lower school performance; (3) child abuse; (4) drug abuse and alcoholism. And, overall I believe these may (5) reduce experience-derived emotional disorders in children, and will (6) increase the child's ability to adapt constructively to life and society. Again, even though the sample is small our 19-year follow-up study findings showed support for these long-term predictions.

The application of these materials in the form of Workshops for parents, day care workers, nannies, teachers, too has shown beneficial, in terms of the challenge of rearing and of caring constructively for children. Some of these materials are organized into Workshops; others into Classes for Parents and Parent Educators. A more recent set of materials on "Helping Parents Help their Children Cope with Trauma" is gaining interest as well.

In our studies we have found that when parents feel equipped with better understanding of their children and more options with which to parent constructively, this increases their confidence, reduces their anxiety, and generates more adaptive responses in them and in their children. The value of these *Parenting for Emotional Growth Workshop*s replicates the positive findings such parenting educational materials have shown using the various settings in which they have been implemented. These findings support the key assumption that mental-health-informed parenting facilitating programs as these may have a significant prevention potential.

I join those among my colleagues who assert that the prevention of tomorrow's violence and malignant prejudice must be undertaken today. Society has fallen victim to the promotion of fast foods, to the advocacy of short, quick, and low cost solutions that, many of us know have no chance of resolving these problems. Long term strategies and more money are needed to deal with violence and malignant prejudice, and to lessen their perpetuation in the next generation. Whatever the cost, the cost of preventing tomorrow's violence and malignant prejudice is far less than would be required to handle next generation's violence if it continues on its present course.

Reaching Out – Joining Interdisciplinary Efforts

Of course, Mental Health types like we psychoanalysts and others, cannot account for all that goes into the generation of malignant prejudice. That accounting is a multi-disciplinary challenge. It is clear that experiential factors, quite different and additional to those I have talked about, combine with them to generate malignant prejudice. Factors outside our individual familial universe commonly contribute to its actualization. For instance, the terrible pains that followed on the heels of unemployment in Germany of the 1930s, the overcrowding and the scarcity of food in France in the early 1940s, no doubt contributed to the eventual persecution of Jews respectively in Germany and in France. The pains of joblessness and of starvation generate excesses of hostile destructiveness in those subjected to them. These stresses, pains, are not of familial origin; but the pain they cause facilitates the activation of malignant prejudice in those psychologically primed for it by past experience.

Side by side with these social, economic, political woes, stand the centuries' old ethnic and religious conflicts, reciprocal assaults of ethnic or religious groups upon one another that seem to have been with us from the beginnings of time. By means of *education* and *propaganda* strategies, ethnic folklore and religious liturgies have and continue to be exploited, rationalized and justified by historical pains, and are compelled forward in time from generation to generation. They are ultimately held up in communities as banners to fuel disasters that are viewed as honorable and heroic. The Third Reich—the fanatically advertised Millennium Reich that lasted just, but nonetheless dreadful, twelve years—was particularly effective and virulent in its ethnic educational and blatantly distorting propaganda strategies. That magnificent instrument of evolution, Education, that has so richly served civilization, was so shamefully used by the Third Reich in the service of achieving the ultimate narcissistic aggrandizement of its megalomanic leader.

Education has been dishonored by ethnocentrism and religious fundamentalism in every corner of the globe. It matters that we emphasize this fact in that, malignant prejudice cannot be maintained in the absence of the distortions wrought by the reality distorting defenses used by groups in the name of ethnic righteousness. The Third Reich was masterful in establishing, by means of formal education and heretofore never-equaled propaganda strategies, the distortions of Jews, distortions essential to Hitler's demonic intentions. Without such malignant distortion, assiduously programmed to become a sustainable *malignant distortion*, Hitler could never have achieved the level of *malignant prejudice* he and his henchmen achieved that made the Holocaust what it was.

Education never reached a steeper degradation. It was not the first time in the history of civilization that this type of degradation of what we all hold so meaningful for civilization took place. Nor will it be the last—as we currently hear rumblings that such *sustainable malignant distortion* education-propaganda strategies are employed in terrorism training and in our own reactions to acts of terror against us. But it is doubtful, and we must work in the larger community of humans to see to it that no country, or ethnic or religious group, will ever match the degradation of education suffered by the German people, and acquiescing Europeans, under the Third Reich.

Among other extra-familial factors that add to the potential for malignant prejudice among us, is that immoral economic rationalization, that it is to "our" advantage to enslave "others," "lesser people than we" in order to serve us gratuitously, an abuse of "others" that also goes back for thousands of years. This too was greedily exploited in the Nazi concentration camps, not just by the German Nazis. In a different universe, we in America, have made a shameful contribution to that history.

And there are yet other experiential, social factors of this order that engender and stir up malignant prejudice. How well we know that these contributors facilitate the group phenomenon Freud talked about in 1921, how the individual loses himself, his morality and humanness in the sweep of the mass will and whim. Aware of these extra-familial factors, some of us, have exerted much effort to bring psychoanalytic knowledge and expertise into service, in the hope of reducing the effects of these societal factors and with it reduce inter-ethnic conflict and acts of malignant prejudice.

Vamik Volkan has started to make meaningful inroads into helping leaders of communities embattled in ethnic conflict to achieve conflict resolutions that do not depend on malignant distortions, malignant prejudice, and murder. Afaf Mahfouz, has wrestled with time and polemical resistance to open an entry way for the International Psychoanalytic Association into the United Nations' Non-Governmental Organizations, where we have already taken a few, child-like steps, to bring Mental Health knowledge to bear on the U. N.'s concern for the world community. This entry into the U. N. community, gave us a chance in May 2001, to see to it that the United Nations General Assembly's Declaration: "A World Fit for Children," include due attention to and concern for the *mental health* and well being of children throughout the globe, as well as for their *physical health*.

None of us has all the answers or explanations for what causes prejudice. I have emphasized the large role trauma, suffering terrible emotional hurts at the hands of our parents has in facilitating the organization in us of malignant prejudice. I share Munich psychoanalyst Lotte Koehler's view that each of us brings to social events and to social conditions what we have internalized. This, in the face of the group's imposing conduct antagonistic to our sense of morality and humanity, this determines whether we comply or refuse to comply with the group's morality or lack thereof, with the group's prejudice-weighted ideals and goals.

We Have to Find Ways to Live Together—With Our Differences

I do not tire of asking, how could so civilized a people as the Germans, a people with such illustrious scientists, writers, poets, composers of music and everything else, degrade to such a level of decivilization? There have been other mass murders; Stalin killed more

Russians than Hitler killed Jews, Gypsies, Homosexuals, political enemies all put together; and there have been massacres by Chiang Kai Chek's Nationalist Chinese of Communist Chinese and then vice-versa; and there has been Cambodia, Rwanda, Bosnia, Sudan, and others. Humans massacre humans. It reaches back to before the Crusades. Though there have been numerous massacres, the one perpetrated by the German Nazis during World War II is the only of these ordered by laws decreed by government to be executed against a non-combative mass of human beings. This more than any of the massacres was driven by *malignant prejudice*, that malignant human ailment that results from a massive flooding of *malignant distortions* of who, and what, "undesirable" human beings are.

Some say, this is human nature; *Homo sapiens* murders. My clinical and research work do not support these indictments. We are not born murderers. But we can become that way.

Not aware of its motivating force, my work led me to the question: "How do humans come to hate and become so viciously destructive of others?" I know that the direction my work took was not accidental; pretty clever of my unconscious mind to lead me there. I wasn't smart enough to do it when fully awake.

At times I have avoided looking directly into the gullet of my past. It is not a pastime or a sport. Though I have too long delayed getting to my bearing witness, I am here now. I remember my past; I want to remember it, and I want to join those who inform others of it, hoping they will not let it happen again. Nor wish to perpetrate it again. Idealism?

In his last book, *The Drowned and The Saved*, Primo Levi asks: "What can each of us do so that in this world pregnant with threats at least this threat . . . [of a return] of the concentration camp world . . . will be nullified?" I believe we can nullify it. But we have much to do to get there. I am among those committed to that end.

After 60 years, I come out of my Holocaust misery with the strong conviction that we will not eliminate our differences; that we have to learn to live tolerantly enough with them. My solution, no doubt one among other efforts toward that end, is to try to prevent or at least reduce the development of malignant prejudice. I have talked and written about this within the Mental Health Community. What I have said in that community I know feel I must say everywhere. I recently had occasion to do so on a wide stage. The International Psychoanalytic Association's Committee to the United Nations, of which I am a member, presented yet another Panel by Psychoanalysts to an audience of individual members of the many Non-Governmental Organizations (NGOs) that make up that part of the U. N. that is not governmental. For instance, UNICEF is such an NGO. The effort was to bring some of our psychoanalytic thinking to these NGOs on what the U.N. might consider with regard to the question of the Israeli-Palestinian conflict. Here is what I said, in the 10 minutes each of us four panel members was allocated:

"*Sales Juifs*. Dirty Jews! I saw it everyday. I passed that wall going and coming from school. Brussels, my hometown, was not free from malignant graffiti: Sales Juifs. On 10 May 1940, the German army invaded my country. I was 11. We had to flee our home. Why? Because my family had heard Hitler's ranting to destroy all Jews and then came *Kristallnacht*. We did not escape his megalomanic arm. We ended up in a French concentration camp. At my mother's urging, I escaped; I was 12. My family was sent to Auschwitz. Why? Because we were Jews.

Prejudice is universal. Many factors go into what causes prejudice, political, racial, religious, ethnic. But the prejudice that kills our children and families requires the input of individual psychology. Normal development makes us all have prejudices. Here's what I mean.

Psychological development makes it necessary for the infant to attach to human beings, but to do so with one or more specific human beings. The newborn does not come into the world with ready-made relationships. He has to develop them. The process whereby specific relationships are developed brings with it two conditions that make us prejudiced. The first is "stranger anxiety," the second is "identification." "Stranger anxiety" is a major factor that secures the infant's attaching to his particular mother, father, siblings. Simply said, "stranger anxiety" makes the infant reject strangers, and sends him clinging to the person who cares for him, to his mother. In this, "stranger anxiety" is an early life factor that predisposes the child to reject others.

In addition to attaching to us, our children become who they are, "our" children, by the process of "identification." All children want to be like those who care for them. This is what makes Palestinian children Palestinian, Israeli children Israeli. Freud said it is as if the child bears the stamp, "Made in the Wallerstein Family," "Made in the Awad Family." [Wallerstein and Awad are two of my colleagues who were on the panel.]

The need for *specific attachments, stranger anxiety, and identification, make us all prejudiced.* They lead to our feeling: I prefer to be with members of my own community. I don't hate my neighbors, in fact I like them; but I feel more comfortable with my own. This is benign prejudice. But this benign prejudice makes us vulnerable to developing "malignant prejudice." Life, with its hurts and hardships unavoidably generates hostility and hate in us. The more we feel hurt, the more we accumulate hostility and hate that is ready to attach itself to anyone, whether they invite it or not. It is the "*hostilification*" of our benign prejudice that makes it "malignant prejudice." But to justify my hate toward that neighbor I must distort and vilify who he or she really is; I must create a sustainable "*malignant distortion.*" I will now fabricate a sustainable theory as to why I dehumanize him and how righteous I am to want to rid the world of his kind. This "*malignant distortion*" is needed to sustain "*malignant prejudice.*"

We authority figures have the perfect vehicle for perpetuating our malignant prejudices, *education*, that magnificent tool of civilization. Children hunger for education. *We educate our children to hate* Palestinians, to hate Israelis, to hate Hindus, to hate Muslims, to hate Blacks. We praise them when they learn well, when they comply with our teachings. And we shame them, we even punish them, when they do not comply with our teachings to hate others. Palestinian and Israeli children are expected to comply with teachings of hate. They must accept "*malignant distortions.*" But study of Israeli and Palestinian children, who spent some time with one another, has revealed that before they met, both Palestinian and Israeli children thought the other to be bad, vile, evil. They were surprised to find themselves so alike and liking each other. While "malignant distortion" is required to sustain "malignant prejudice" it is also its Achilles heel. This study of Palestinian and Israeli children suggests that when we expose our "*malignant distortions*" to the *light of reality, malignant prejudice weakens.*

On behalf of our children's health, physical and mental, we must act to counter "malignant prejudice." When, as we need for good mental health, the defusing of the hate we feel is disallowed, we become hate bombs ready to explode. While we intend hate to be directed toward our enemy, such explosive hate can be triggered by others too, including those we love. Hate can be programmed and aimed at specific targets, but its discharge is often target-blind.

Not only is hate a psychic burden, but it also brings fear, the fear of loss of self-control and the constant fear of attack by the hated other. Hate and fear create internal stress. Stress interferes with children's ability to learn in school. This is no doubt occurring in Palestinian and Israeli children. Also, stress is a major cause of physical and emotional disorders. Stress not only causes these children anxiety and depression, it also lowers their immune system's ability to fight infection, it increases the frequency of asthmatic, allergic, and diabetic episodes, and it causes still other illnesses. "Malignant prejudice" kills; where it does not, it causes disease, physical and mental.

I weep the loss of the social progress being made in the Middle East just three years ago. For example, Yolanda Gampel, an Israeli Psychoanalyst, was training Gaza Mental Health Community Professionals. Through her, at the invitation of our Palestinian colleagues, in 1999, our team went to Gaza and to Israel to help colleagues there develop programs to optimize the lives of parents and children in both populations. Also, Vamik Volkan and I were about to initiate a project for Israeli and Palestinian High School kids to get to know each other, test their "malignant distortions," and solve co-existence problems together. Since the eruption of the Israeli-Palestinian conflict, children on both sides have lost the fruits of collaborative co-existence.

All of us at the U.N. must put our energies into exposing "malignant distortions" and teach tolerance for differences. We must get the children of our small world to know each other."

****

We just turned into a new century.
What did we learn from the one we just left?
What should we bring into this new one?
What should we not bring into it?

We must not let it happen to us again.
We must not make it happen to others.
We must not be victims, and
We must not be perpetrators.

We must learn
To live together
With our differences.

A good friend, a good healer, who is striving tirelessly to bring to the public a method of medical treatment which he believes—and sounds eminently biologically plausible to me—, and has been shown to be, capable of destroying all kinds of disease-causing bacteria, viruses, and fungi, is painfully oppressed by the constant flow of news that brings one or another massacre in our world to our attention. He is tortured during sleepless hours when he listens to the BBC detailing the brutal, wretched loss of life in this or that part of the world. The flow of news is so constant that I sometimes do not record the events reported in memory.

Why do we labor, he and I, he asks, to try to find ways that may improve the lives of people when in the end we will all destroy each other?

I tell him I can see his dread. Maybe he is right. He smiles.

I think he hopes I will prove him wrong; and perhaps not. I can't do either.

He is right that crimes against others, often innocent others, occur every day, every night, somewhere in the world. These days we have heard what goes on on the other side of our world, in overt conflict areas, Bosnia, Rwanda-Burundi, the Sudan, Israel and the Palestinian territories, and elsewhere, in more remote places not inscribed in our awareness. We see the crimes that have just taken place irrefutably, visually, on video, on film, in news photos. How many trimes have we seen the crime perpetrated against us, the unbreachable fortress, America, the destruction of our magnificent "Twin Towers," that ended the life of over 3,000 unsuspecting, innocent individuals and brought trauma and grief to over 3,000 families? Yes, my friend is right. Our world's man-made destruction breeds despair.

We just left the century of the two Great World Wars, the Holocaust, Hiroshima and Nagasaki. What have we learned?

But I say to my friend he is wrong. Our technological advances in all the sciences have made us all more accessible to knowing one another. Our imagination is constrained by what we see on TV, in film, on the Internet, hear on the radio. No, the Chinese do not have tails; Africans are not savages who eat their enemies, the only "human" who has horns is Michelangelo's Moses who sits, pensive, in an old church in Rome, turned away from the Colloseum. No living humans have horns. Jews and Arabs do not have hooks for noses. We can no longer bedevil anyone—except in blatant distortion and vile caricature.

The world is accessible to us all. We know each other better than ever, not just in the present but also in the past. We have different skin color, facial details, but we are physically, biologically, and psychologically so alike, it is difficult to refute God. Yes, we have slightly different mores, we have different manners, but even these are really more similar than they are different. We have ways of greeting we all recognize, ways of saying goodbye we all recognize; ways of praying, of causing injury, of insulting that we all understand. We react similarly to pain, to insult, to love, to respect, to everything we experience. We have learned that children all over the world have the same basic physical and emotional needs to develop into human beings sound of body and mind. This is why the United Nations can speak to the rights of children, all of them, everywhere.

It is in our interpretations of each other and of life around us that we slide away from the truth. My youngest son, Joshua, a Philosophy Professor, is now working on a thesis put forward by the 10th Century Arab Philosopher Alfarabi, who held that religions are imitations of the truth, and that some religions are virtuous. Alfarabi, a Muslim, argued that Islam cannot be "the" true religion; that there cannot be just one. We may be convinced that we have the true religion. But determination of what that is leads these philosophers to the finding that no one religion is truer than another. What we are taught, what is inculcated in us by our parents and our community is not always truth; it is our beliefs, that powerful but most subjective and often distorting of human experience, our beliefs.

No need to belabor my point I say to my friend; I can't argue well enough either against your thesis or for mine. I think that civilization is growing, not just in size, in maturity. Civilization is learning. And some among us in our civilization are coming to see that we cannot win for long if we continue to try to destroy one another. We see again and again that the destruction of others compels the counter-destruction of us, perhaps not immediately, but in time. Much of what we have learned in psychology this past century is learning that can be brought to bear on all of us to lessen our reciprocal destructiveness. For instance, we have learned about rearing children in ways that may make them less hostile and less hurtful to others; we also know the consequences of programmed atrocities, of collective humiliation of others, of bullying, of provoking crime in others. A number of colleagues in Mental Health are engaged in bringing this knowledge in ways that can be implemented in all communites, in preventive strategies we only started last century.

One thing seems amply clear. The purpose of the Holocaust, "the final solution" was not achieved because it is not achievable. The aim was not just to cause suffering; that it did only too well. The aim was to destroy, to make disappear, a people. And that, no group can achieve, no coalition of peoples can do.

We must act to change *la condition humaine.*

We must not let the Holocaust happen again,

To anyone.

Rachel in 2001

The author in 2003

Henri Parens was born in Lodz, Poland in 1928. Escaping the German occupation, his mother took him to France and was able to send him to America before she was transported to Auschwitz, where she perished. He was taken in by an American family, received his medical degree from Tulane University, and became a world-renowned child psychiatrist and psychoanalyst. He wrote extensively on the development of aggression in early childhood, on the prevention of violence and malignant prejudice, and the prevention of emotional disorders in children. In recent years he has worked for promoting understanding between Israelis and Palestinian Arabs, and other peace causes.

High praise for *Renewal of Life*

What a wonderful book and so moving! It is both an autobiography which attests to an extraordinary story and a message of the struggle against violence and malignant prejudice. With the author we relive the flight from Bruxelles in May 1940, the tragic journey on the roads in France, the concentration camps in Vichy France which became a trap for transfers by Germany to extermination. Then, escape. . . and his eventual welcome in Pittsburgh by a totally unknown family. Years later, the psychoanalyst asks: how do we fight malignant prejudice and racist hatred? Today when hatred is everywhere, society must fight its generation from childhood onwards.

—Prof. Daniel Widlocher, Paris, President, International Psychoanalytic Association

A truly compelling story of a childhood devastated by the Holocaust experience in a concentration camp, followed by the account of the searing torment lived and relived in the six decades that followed, with, at the same time, the hopeful note of a life transformed into dedication to care and help for suffering humanity, and to the enlightened upbringing of children, that can play their part in helping insure that the horrors of malignant genocide never happen again

—Robert S. Wallerstein, M.D., Former Chair, Dept. of Psychiatry, Univ. of California in San Francisco; Former President, American Psychoanalytic Assn. & of Internal Psychoanalytic Assn.

Disarming in the simplicity of its narrative, no reader can fail to empathize with the pain Henri Parens sustains, a Holocaust survivor; but even more, to marvel at his tenderness of spirit. Such a human story, including a young man's coming of age, suggests there are ways out from the pernicious cycle of victimization so widespread today.

With the perspective of his life in Poland, Belgium and France and then the United States, one cannot but admire the authors lifelong interest in children, education of parents, and his transcending generations and cultures.

—Afaf Mahfouz, Former President, UN Non-Governmental Organizations; Chair, International Psychoanalytic Association's Committee on the United Nations

Henri Parens' book *Renewal of Life—Healing from the Holocaust* is a welcome addition to the Holocaust literature. With merciless honesty Parens provides insight into the life of a man who at age 12 was separated from the most important person in his life, his mother. Young Henri entered the life of a homeless refugee with remarkable confidence as he adapted to the many strange and unexpected situations in his wanderings. Based on the early experience with his devoted and resourceful mother, Henri retained a remarkable vitality and creativity throughout his life. The book gives evidence not only to the cruelty of man and the psychic pain that had to be endured but it is also a beautiful account of accomplishment and renewal.

—Anna and Paul Ornstein, Survivors of Auschwitz, renowned psychoanalysts

This is a book of remarkable courage, deep insight, and hope. Parens is brutally honest about the pain his experience caused his family, yet it was a uniting process for them all. His lifelong coping efforts are reflected in his professional interest in growth-promoting parenting and in prevention, as both part of that coping and as an antidote to the destructiveness of the Holocaust. Readers will emerge from this book changed; horrified anew, deeply sad and ashamed, and yet paradoxically hopeful. Parens notes, "a parent who cannot tolerate her or his child's pain cannot help the child suffer less." This book will help us bear the pain and learn from it—for the well-being and future of our children.

—Stuart W. Twemlow, M.D.,Professor of Psychiatry, Baylor College of Medicine, Med. Director, HOPE Unit, The Menninger Clinic

Henri Parens, in this most personal and searing account of his life, provides us with an unparalleled opportunity to understand the evolution of a great man, from his flight from Poland as a child to his escape from a concentration camp at age 12, to his becoming a leading expert in the fields of child analysis, the development of aggression, and the prevention of mental illness. In his lifelong pursuit to come to terms with the murder of his family, especially his mother who planned his escape, Parens epitomizes resilience, sublimation, and generativity. His account is truly a unique contribution, which must be read by everyone interested in the human condition.

—Ira Brenner, M.D., Co-author with Judith Kesternberg,
The Last Witness—The Child Survivor of the Holocaust,
and editor, *Reverberations of the Holocaust*

Powerful. . . emotional. . . Parens has confronted his Holocaust past, examining the thorny complex of feelings and moral issues connected to it. Out of this courageous journey, which includes the working through of personal and historical mourning, stems a rare opportunity for hope—the deep belief that improved rearing of children can mitigate destructive forces and moderate such malignancies as prejudice, violence and genocide.

—Ilany Kogan, Psychoanalyst, Rehovot, Israel, author,
***The Cry of Mute Children*—A Psychoanalytic Perspective**

Dr. Parens combines his experience as a Holocaust survivor with his work as a child psychiatrist. His deep understanding of children and their difficulties in growing up under extreme conditions has given him insight which very few authors have.

—Leon Tec, M.D., Child Psychiatrist, author of *Adventure and Destiny*

Dr. Henri Parens offers a Holocaust memoir told with a unique view of childhood memories through the lens of psychoanalysis.

—Leora Kahn, author, *When They Came to Get*
My Father—Voices from the Holocaust

(continued on back cover)